BECOMING
REAL

ABOUT THE AUTHOR

STEVEN JAMES

Steven James is an award-winning author, popular conference speaker, and creative solo performer. As one of the nation's more innovative storytellers, Steven James appears weekly at conferences, churches, and special events around the country sharing his unique blend of drama, comedy, and inspirational speaking. Steven is the author of more than fifteen books and has spoken more than a thousand times all across North America in the past five years.

When Steven completed his master's degree in storytelling in 1997, there were fewer than one hundred people in the world with the same degree. Since then, he has been in demand throughout the country as a conference presenter, family entertainer, youth speaker, and performance storyteller.

Steven lives with his wife and three daughters in eastern Tennessee.

STEVEN JAMES

BECOMING REAL

Christ's Call to Authentic Living

HOWARD
PUBLISHING CO.

OUR PURPOSE AT HOWARD PUBLISHING IS TO:

- *Increase faith* in the hearts of growing Christians
- *Inspire holiness* in the lives of believers
- *Instill hope* in the hearts of struggling people everywhere

BECAUSE HE'S COMING AGAIN!

Becoming Real © 2005 by Steven James
All rights reserved. Printed in the United States of America
Published by Howard Publishing Co., Inc.
3117 North 7th Street, West Monroe, Louisiana 71291-2227
www.howardpublishing.com

05 06 07 08 09 10 11 12 13 14   10 9 8 7 6 5 4 3 2 1

Edited by Between the Lines
Interior design by John Mark Luke Designs
Cover design by Smartt Guys Design

Library of Congress Cataloging-in-Publication Data

James, Steven, 1969–
    Becoming real : Christ's call to authentic living / Steven James.
        p. cm.
    Includes bibliographical references (p.).
    ISBN 1-58229-429-1
    1. Christian life. I. Title

    BV4501.3.J36 2005
    248.4—dc22

                                                                    2004060871

for
Randy and Becky Cox

CONTENTS

Acknowledgments ix

The Day You Became Real 1

PART 1: EMBARKING 3

Chapter 1: **MIRROR, MIRROR ON THE WALL** 7
Coming to Terms with Who You Are

Chapter 2: **THE GAME YOU CANNOT WIN** 21
Walking the Road to Humility

Chapter 3: **THE JOURNEY OF NO RETURN** 33
Being Honest about Life and Death

Chapter 4: **NO CARICATURES IN HEAVEN** 45
Understanding What Christianity Is All About

Chapter 5: **PSST . . . I'VE GOT A SECRET** 59
Getting Real with God

Chapter 6: **LETTING GO OF THE BOAT** 71
Learning to Live by Faith

PART 2: AWAKENING 81

Chapter 7: **WORSHIPING GOD BY DOING THE DISHES** 83
Discovering an Authentic Spiritual Life

Chapter 8: IN SYNC WITH THE SPIRIT 95
Walking Intimately with God

Chapter 9: TOO BUSY FOR YOUR OWN GOD? 107
Pursuing Peace amid Busyness

Chapter 10: AT THE FEET OF JESUS 119
Rediscovering Yourself and Esteem

Chapter 11: FLIRTING WITH THE FORBIDDEN 133
Confronting Temptation

Chapter 12: SLAYING THE MONSTER 145
Experiencing and Extending True Forgiveness

PART 3 : EMERGING 155

Chapter 13: THE MILLION-DOLLAR MAN 159
Exploring True Wealth and Poverty

Chapter 14: THE VISIBILITY SYNDROME 169
Redefining Success

Chapter 15: ANSWERING THE CALL 181
Beginning to Live for God

Chapter 16: WELCOME SIGNS 193
Reprioritizing Family Relationships

Chapter 17: THE ROAD TO REAL 201
Becoming Transparent with Others

Chapter 18: WHAT ARE THE CHRISTIANS GONNA DO? 213
Showing Genuine Compassion

Questions 225
For Discussion and Life Application

Notes 239

ACKNOWLEDGMENTS

Special thanks to my faithful research assistants, Dana Standridge and Marian Green, for deciphering my scribbles and offering such useful ideas; to the editors at Howard Publishing and Between the Lines, for believing in this project; to Pamela Harty, for her optimism and continual encouragement; to Dr. White, Jeff Keeling, and Sonya Haskins, for their manuscript suggestions; to the guys in my small-group Bible study (Mark C., Wayne, Mark K., Grant, and Jerry), for challenging me to wrestle with authenticity; and to my wife and daughters, for showing me what real love looks like.

THE DAY YOU BECAME REAL

All the world's a stage, and all the men and women merely players; they have their exits and their entrances; and one man in his time plays many parts.
—WILLIAM SHAKESPEARE, "ALL THE WORLD'S A STAGE"

Imagine what life would be like if we could stop stepping onstage all the time. If we could simply be real with God and honest with others and up front about the things that are really important to us. If we could just be *ourselves*. Simply me. Simply you. Honest about our shortcomings. Genuine with our love. Transparent about our motives.

Imagine a life where we could peel away all the pretenses and let the world see us for who we really are—vulnerable, valuable, hurting, hoping, dreaming, believing, wondering, wandering people who just want to be known and loved and accepted "as is" . . . both by God and by others.

Imagine not worrying about what people think of our wardrobes or our job titles or our cars or our houses or our haircuts or our abs.

Imagine that kind of world.

Imagine a world where religion isn't a show. Where it's *real*. And God walks with us through our days and isn't impressed by anyone's spirituality, nor is he ashamed to call us his friends.

I don't know about you, but that kind of life sounds pretty good to me.

And that's the kind of life God offers.

Yet most of the time, we're too busy playing our parts to find it. We're masters of disguise. We have a whole set of identities that we slip on and off for different occasions. We wear one face at work to impress the boss, another at home to control the kids, another at church to keep up appearances.

One role after another.

The Super-Mom . . . The Successful Businessman . . . The Perfect Little Churchgoer Who Never Does Anything Wrong . . . The Career Woman . . . The Family Man . . . The Guy Who's Got It All Together . . . The Caring Hostess . . . The Invulnerable Athlete . . . The Peppy and Supportive Soccer Mom . . . The All-Around Nice Guy . . .

And we get used to our roles. They begin to define us as we grow more and more comfortable wearing disguises and burying the truth of who we really are.

Yet all the while God is waiting and watching and whispering, "Stop all this nonsense. Be real with me. Don't hide or run or pretend or fake it any longer."

Because God already knows the truth about us. And he already accepts the parts of our lives we're too ashamed to let anyone else see. He says, "Come as you are. That's the only way anyone ever really gets to know me. I can't stand it when people try to impress me all the time."

That sounds refreshing to me—the kind of spiritual life I'd be interested in.

And it's the kind of life we were meant to have all along.

Paul wrote in Colossians 3:3, "Your real life is hidden with Christ in God." Becoming real is the process of discovering our true identities within the love of God. It means opening up to God, being honest with ourselves, and then living authentically with others.

There are no hoops to jump through. No games to play. No requirements to meet. No religious rituals we need to perform so God will finally accept us. He already has. We can stop playing the games of religion and sincerity and perfection. We can meet him in the quietness of our hearts, where there is no more pretending. And we can tell him about our hurts and our questions and our wounds and our dreams and our deepest and most intimate secrets. He will listen. He will care. He will come to where we are.

He's waiting for us to be that honest with him, because that's the day we'll begin to grow closest to him—the day we step off the stage of appearances and start to finally become ourselves.

A day just like today.

PART 1
EMBARKING

My wife and I set down our backpacks and gazed along the Hawaiian shoreline. No one else was in sight. The lava-strewn coast disappeared out of sight in both directions, and I pointed. "There!"

About thirty yards away, water crashed into a tide pool, then eased back into the ocean.

She looked at the foaming water as it sprayed into the air and slammed into the rocky shore.

"Is it safe?" she whispered.

I wasn't sure. The water was deep and the currents were swift. We walked together to the edge of the ocean.

"Of course," I said, busying myself with the backpacks, pulling out face masks, snorkels, and fins and laying them on the lava. I was hoping she'd go first.

My wife stared at the crashing, coursing waters as I pulled on the snorkeling gear.

"You go first," she said.

"OK," I replied, trying to sound confident. "No problem."

I eased over to the tide pool and timed the waves.

In and out . . . in and out . . .

The water looked about twenty feet deep. It swirled and churned in a nest of boulders as big as my car, pulsating with the tide.

Oh boy.

In and out . . . in and out . . .

I closed my eyes and plunged in.

The ocean closed over my head as I tried to avoid getting sucked up against the boulders or into the coral reef below. Foam swirled around me until I reached about seven feet below the surface, and then, all at once, the waters were calm. I rode a slow wave out toward open water and then back toward shore. Ten feet below me, the reef burst into life with all its crazily colored fish and bristling activity and blooming coral.

I surfaced. "C'mon in!" I yelled.

My wife watched the sweep of the waves in and out . . . in and out . . . and then leapt from shore to join me.

We dove and swam and marveled together at the colors of this hidden coastline, venturing farther and farther into the deeper waters, where the sharks were said to live.

THERE ARE **TREASURES** FOR THOSE WHO ARE WILLING TO DIVE IN.

The water here is clear.

Is it safe?

Well, no. Not really. There are deep currents and dangerous fish and sharp reefs.

Then again, it's never safe to dive in deep. It's always safer to skim along the surface—or not even get wet at all. Maybe that's why we were the only ones on that deserted stretch of beach that day. Because it's safer to view the ocean from our cars.

But there are treasures for those who are willing to dive in. To go deep. To risk the sharks. To submerse themselves in life.

Danger kisses freedom in that place. And the currents flow more freely with every passing moment.

> God,
> part of me wants to hold back,
> to stay on shore,
> to keep getting by with the status quo.
> but i feel you tugging at the chords of my soul;

i feel you drawing me deeper
toward freedom.
toward you.

help me take the next step toward becoming real,
wherever it leads.
it may not be easy;
it may not be safe.
but here i am.

lead me deeper into the waters of this moment
and the freedom that lies beyond.

Chapter 1

MIRROR, MIRROR ON THE WALL

Coming to Terms with Who You Are

Whoever wants to see the form of his naked soul should make wisdom his mirror.

—ARISTOTLE

"Mirror, Mirror, on the wall, who's the fairest of them all?"

Who wouldn't like to be called the fairest or the bravest or the strongest or the kindest or the wisest of them all? Who wouldn't want to wake up every morning and have the mirror give compliments?

Too bad that only happens in fairy tales.

In real life, mirrors don't praise us, they reveal the truth about us. They don't flatter us, they unveil us. There's nothing like looking into a mirror to shock us back to reality. Because mirrors don't lie. They show the warts and the wrinkles, the gray hair and the varicose veins, the bags under our eyes and the extra baggage around our waists, the scars and the pimples and the receding hairlines.

Mirrors remind us we're not as flawless as we like to think we are. Plato once said, "Truth is removal of the veil."[1] That's what mirrors do for our bodies: they remove the veil and show us the truth. And that's what God's Word does for our hearts. It removes the veil of excuses and illusions and lies and rationalizations and shows us what we really are: "For the word of God is full of living power. It is sharper than the sharpest knife, cutting deep into our innermost thoughts and desires. It exposes us for what we really are" (Hebrews 4:12).

The pathway to becoming real begins in God's operating room, where we lie down before him, bare our souls to him, and let him wield his scalpel of truth.

And believe me, it hurts. (I know. I've been through his surgery more than once.)

It hurts to feel God's Word pierce our lives. It hurts to have our dishonesty and duplicity sliced away. It hurts to expose our hearts to God and to see ourselves for what we really are.

That's why most of us don't do it. We don't look into God's mirror, because it's too painful. Too much is at stake for our egos. As the saying goes, "The truth hurts."

Yet it's a healing hurt and a helpful pain. For when God's Word has pierced us, when his truth has operated on our souls, we emerge from surgery free from the cancer of our own self-love. Only then are we able to live honestly and humbly and transparently—when we come to terms with who we really are.

WE DON'T LOOK INTO GOD'S MIRROR, BECAUSE IT'S TOO PAINFUL.

Deep down, I think we do yearn for the truth. Philosopher Peter Kreeft puts it this way: "Truth (our head's food) and happiness (our heart's food) are the two things everyone wants, and not in crumbs but in great loaves; not in raindrops but in waves."[2]

We all want happiness and truth, but we hide the fact that we don't have them. We give people the impression that we're almost always right and almost always happy, but we're neither. It's all an illusion. Smoke and mirrors.

When we finally admit that we're not as happy or as right as we'd like, God can begin to point us toward the ultimate happiness and truth for which we were created. Honesty is the first step.

PORTRAITS OR MIRRORS?

Nine out of ten HIV-positive individuals don't know they're infected.[3] The Center for Disease Control estimates that 25 percent of those who get AIDS tests (about 10,000 people each year) never come back for the results.[4] Why not? Traffic patterns? No. Prior commitments? I doubt it. They don't come back for the results because they don't want to know the results. They don't want to know the truth. Because if they knew the truth, they'd have to deal with it. They'd have to come to terms with their lives. And most of us prefer just about anything to that.

Whether it's the truth about AIDS, cancer, bad breath, cholesterol, foot odor, or our percentage of body fat, we'd rather tell ourselves that we're probably OK—or better than most people, or doing alright for our age—than have the truth hit us squarely between the eyes. That's why we don't like to step on the scale. Because it tells us the truth about what we weigh, and the truth isn't always easy to swallow.

The last thing an ego wants to do is look closely into a mirror. Instead, it paints flattering portraits of itself and hangs them everywhere in the chambers of the heart. It tries to convince itself that every portrait is really a mirror. "Ah, I'm so beautiful," it says. "Look at me! Look at me!"

As long as we live for accolades or applause, we're in trouble. As Dag Hammarskjöld, former United Nations secretary-general and winner of the 1961 Nobel Peace Prize, wrote, "I pity the man who falls in love with his image as it is drawn by public opinion during the honeymoon of publicity."[5]

I used to work as a wilderness guide for at-risk youth. We took ten to twelve delinquent teens on twenty-eight-day wilderness trips to teach them about choices, consequences, and responsibility. These students were some of the most troubled teenagers in the state of Illinois. For many of them, our course was their last chance before going to juvenile prison. Part of the process was to force those teenagers to peel away their excuses, get past their rationalizations, pull down their defenses, and confront themselves.

The ones who refused to be real didn't change. Those who wouldn't go through the tough process of admitting who they really were and what they'd really done stayed the same and kept falling into the same traps.

Jesus would have done well leading one of those trips. After all, he was a master at unmasking people. He did it to the Pharisees when he pinpointed their pride. He pulled off Judas's disguise when he whispered to him, "Friend, do you betray me with a kiss?" Jesus never let people hide from him.

Jesus acted like a mirror to the Pharisees, reflecting the true state of their souls. And he acted like a window to the people who knew they were hopeless, revealing the frontiers of God's grace. To the one he gave clarity, to the other comfort.

He exposed the sin of some and showed the way to heaven for others. He had a way of uncovering people's inner motives and true intentions. And it either brought them close to him or turned them off completely.

And Jesus has the same effect today.

Some folks just don't like the idea of being real, of looking closely at the truth. They hide their dark and secret thoughts where they think no one will find them. They hide their true selves and think that if they can only hold out the image of having it together long enough, everything will be OK. Everyone will like them. They're so used to hiding that they refuse to step out and be found.

SURGERY OF THE SOUL

Some of us spend our whole lives hiding, avoiding spiritual surgery. After all, those who think they're fine won't ever enter the operating room. Jesus knew our world would be like this. He told Nicodemus, "The light from heaven came into the world, but they loved the darkness more than the light, for their actions were evil" (John 3:19). People prefer hating Jesus to loving him because they prefer hiding in the darkness to standing in the light.

When our actions (or thoughts) are evil, we don't want them exposed. And the light always exposes reality. It reveals things for what they really are. It reveals us for what we really are.

In God's light we finally see the truth: "For with you is the fountain of life; in your light we see light" (Psalm 36:9 NIV). All of us commit deeds that are evil, and until we desire truth more than comfort, we'll stay in the darkness. Truth is brutal and naked and raw and exposes us to a reality we'd rather avoid.

That's why so few people find the narrow road. Most people prefer the easy pathway of illusion to the soul-awakening and lie-shattering words of truth. It's much easier to coast than to climb. So those who walk the easy way have lots of company, and those who choose the narrow path have lots of challenges.

But truth is always brighter than illusion, and it melts through our lies like sunlight cutting through the rising mists of early dawn.

God knows who we really are. The tricky thing is revealing it to us. Most of the time we'd rather do almost anything than admit the truth about ourselves. Our egos dread the mirror.

François de Salignac de la Mothe Fénelon, a seventeenth-century French theologian, observed:

> As long as the least bit of self-love remains in the secret parts of your heart, God will hunt it down, and, by some infinitely merciful blow, force your selfishness and jealousy out of hiding. The poison then becomes the cure. Self-love, exposed to the light, sees itself in horror. The flattering lifelong illusions you have held of yourself are forced to die. God lets you see who you really worship: yourself. You cannot help but see yourself. And you can no longer hide your true self from others, either.[6]

DEADENING THE PAIN

We're good at deceiving ourselves and hiding from God. But why?

Well, because honesty hurts.

When I was in graduate school, I had three of my wisdom teeth taken out. After the oral surgeon injected a syringeful of medication into my jaw to kill the pain, he handed me a prescription for some pretty powerful painkillers.

"Now, be sure you fill this right away," he said. "You don't want those drugs to wear off."

I was feeling pretty good about then. I think I saw two or three doctors handing me that prescription. "OK," I said as best I could, with no feeling from my neck up. I deposited a pint and a half of drool onto my shirt with that one word.

When my wife, Liesl, picked me up, she asked if I needed anything.

I shook my head no.

"Are you sure? We could stop by the pharmacy on the way home."

I shook my head again. I wasn't in any pain. Why would we need to stop at the pharmacy? I just wanted to lie down and rest.

Finally, she shrugged. "OK. But don't say I didn't warn you."

We drove home, I laid down, and everything felt fine.

Until about an hour later when the painkillers began to wear off.

That's when I remembered my doctor's advice. *"Be sure you fill this right away."*

Since I was still too medicated to drive, I drooled my way over to my wife and handed her the prescription form. She smiled and herded the kids into the car.

Five minutes later I thought I was going to die.

The pain began as a dull throb in the back of my throat. With every breath, I felt like a lowland gorilla was trying to strangle me, slowly, with its bare hands. I considered not breathing for a few hours. It seemed like a reasonable alternative at the time.

Then the pain began to radiate across my shoulders. I lurched through the house, trying to get to the couch to lie down. As I stumbled forward, knocking over furniture, sharp blasts of agony shot through my skull.

It can't get any worse, I thought. *It can't get any worse!*

I was wrong.

Because that's when my mouth began to hurt.

Although the word *hurt* doesn't really do justice to what I was experiencing.

Each tooth felt like it was exploding, one at a time, like miniature grenades embedded in my gums. I tried to scream, but all that came out was another gallon of drool. I knew I would die any moment.

Or at least I could only hope.

Then the door opened and my wife appeared. (Insert Hallelujahs! and heavenly sounding music.) Actually, several wives appeared, and I wasn't sure which one to take the medication from. I tried grabbing it from all of them and fell on the floor writhing and moaning, slobbering great waves onto the carpet.

My two daughters watched me quietly.

"I think Daddy's mouth hurts," said the youngest. At least I think she did. I was fading in and out of consciousness by then.

"Hmm, the medicine is starting to wear off, is it?" Liesl said as she melo-dramatically unscrewed the bottle cap.

Finally, as I took the medicine, all the wives merged into one. "Waited a little long before sending me to the pharmacy, huh?" she said.

Why does she always have to be right?

THE SHARPEST PAIN OF ALL

Sometimes it's a gift to deaden the pain, and sometimes it's a curse. It all depends on what's causing the pain and what we use to deaden it.

The pain that wells up in our souls is the sharpest pain of all. Many people spend their whole lives trying to deaden it. Some turn to drugs or drinking. Others to eating more than they should. Still others to careerism. Or to an affair. Or religion. All means of escape. Ways to deaden the pain.

The pain in our hearts shows us that something is wrong in our souls. We know that. But we prefer to deaden, deny, or distract ourselves from the pain rather than confront it head on.

Some of us try to fill our lives with one relationship after another, like the woman Jesus met at the well (see John 4:1–42). She couldn't relieve her loneliness with her string of affairs. No one except God could fill her deepest longings.

Truth and happiness. We want them. We long for them. We're so desperate for them that we'll look almost anywhere—anywhere that promises fulfillment or deliverance or joy.

Anywhere but the place we need to look: into the eyes of Jesus.

LOOKING IN THE MIRROR

Most of us spend too much time trying to direct the spotlight of every conversation and situation on ourselves. We verbally maneuver our way into looking good. We pat ourselves on the back, and we jockey for position by comparing ourselves with those who are less fortunate or successful than we are. And all of these ploys are part of the lifelong struggle to get people to like us, to make ourselves look good, and to get ourselves to feel good about whom?

Ourselves.

The first step on the road to becoming real is being honest with ourselves. And that means admitting those things about our lives that fly in the face of all the warm, fuzzy little lies that feed our egos. It means refusing to conceal ourselves from ourselves.

But it's gonna hurt. It's going to take courage to admit that some of the things we typically take for granted are, really, illusions.

Becoming real requires that we ask ourselves questions we typically avoid.

I did that recently and found these twelve attitudes lurking in my heart. As you read these admissions, search your own soul. Look in the mirror. Study your reflection. See which of them are true about you too.

1. I sometimes stretch the truth to serve my own needs and to protect my reputation. By doing this I prove I'd rather have people think well of me than live in a way consistent with those thoughts. I'd rather deceive them into thinking I'm good than actually be good, regardless of what they think.

2. I'm quick to tell other people I'm not all that great, but I'd be horrified if they actually believed me. When it seems they do believe me, I find myself manipulating circumstances and conversations to make them like me more. Because I want to be wanted. I love to be loved. And I can't stand the thought that people might not respect and admire me, even though I tell them I don't deserve either their respect or their admiration.

3. Even though I don't like to admit it, I prefer others' approval and honor to God's. I prove this when I spend more time and effort massaging my reputation than pursuing his will. I prefer the illusion of integrity to the real thing.

4. Even though I'm both weak and vulnerable, just like everyone else, I put on a show of strength and resolve so I don't appear either weak or vulnerable in front of anyone. And so I show that protecting my reputation is more important to me than avoiding hypocrisy.

5. I get really defensive when people criticize me, probably because I'm more concerned with defending myself and my actions than with knowing the truth about who I am, how I've acted, and how I may have hurt them in the first place.

6. I would rather people think I'm not a hypocrite than stop being one. I prove this by pretending to be happy and to have all the answers and to be "filled with joy" even when I'm not. I want

people to think that as a Christian these things are all true about me, even though, all too often, I'm scared, lonely, hurting, and sad instead.

7. I'd rather argue with someone to prove I'm right than accept that I might not be. I argue even if it hurts others' feelings because it's vitally important to me that everyone believes I never make a mistake, lose an argument, or have a prejudiced opinion—even though all of these things are true about me every day.

8. I put on a show when I'm at church because I want people to think I have my act together, even when I don't. I want them to think I'm dealing with life at least as well as (if not better than) they are. Even when I'm not.

9. I become upset and depressed when I find out someone is disappointed in me, even if that disappointment is justified by my behavior. And so I show that my image matters more to me than virtuous living. What someone thinks I am matters more to me than what I really am.

10. I want everyone to like and respect me. When someone doesn't, I feel deeply hurt or attacked, even though there are many people *I* don't like or respect. Then I hide this hypocrisy from myself because I hate to admit that I have double standards that always favor me.

11. I'm quick to notice the faults in others and slow to notice my own. I conveniently overlook my own shortcomings—except for those someone else catches me in. And when that happens, I do all I can to polish my tarnished reputation.

12. When I accomplish something significant, it's important to me that people notice. When they don't, I get offended and hurt and feel slighted and resentful. I fish for compliments because I want them to join me in patting myself on the back. I just love feeling important! By doing all these things, I show

that my heart is centered on myself rather than on God and that I long for praise more than humility.

Whew. It's rough to admit some of that stuff. But it's also freeing. It's like cleaning your glasses. Suddenly everything becomes more clear.

THE PERPETUAL ILLUSION

In one of the most insightful passages I've ever read, Blaise Pascal, the seventeenth-century mathematician and philosopher, delved into the duplicity of our lives. Look at how he described the nature of self-love as it reveals itself in each of our lives:

He devotes all his attention to hiding his faults both from others and from himself, and he cannot endure either that others should point them out to him, or that they should see them. . . .

We ought not to be angry at their knowing our faults and despising us; it is but right that they should know us for what we are and should despise us, if we are contemptible. . . . For is it not true that we hate truth and those who tell it [to] us, and that we like them to be deceived in our favour? . . . Human life is thus only a perpetual illusion; men deceive and flatter each other. No one speaks of us in our presence as he does of us in our absence. Human society is founded on mutual deceit. . . .

Man is, then, only disguise, falsehood, and hypocrisy, both in himself and in regard to others. He does not wish any one to tell him the truth; he avoids telling it to others, and all these dispositions, so removed from justice and reason, have a natural root in his heart.[7]

Pascal was saying that we crave esteem and want others to think well of us. We want respect, acclaim, fame, glory, honor, and a good reputation. Most of us would rather have people admire us than know the truth about us. We value reputation over integrity. In fact, we do all we can to hide the truth of who we really are and what we're really like so we can make a good impression. But that good impression is only the result of a false impression—one caused by deceit.

We prefer the salve of self-love to peeling back the bandage and seeing the extent of our disease. Rationalization is always easier than something radical, like repentance.

But we *must* peel off these excuses, rationalizations, and comparisons one layer at a time, or we will never experience true intimacy with God.

As Russian novelist and Nobel laureate Aleksandr Solzhenitsyn wrote after spending eight years in Soviet prison camps, "If only there were evil people somewhere insidiously committing evil deeds and it were necessary only to separate them from the rest of us and destroy them. But the line dividing good and evil cuts through the heart of every human being. And who is willing to destroy a piece of his own heart?"[8]

We refuse to look in the mirror, gazing instead at our own flattering portraits.

But there's good news. If you've read this far, you've shown that you're willing to pull down the self-portraits and face the truth. Even if it hurts.

Becoming real means we'll have to agree with God about who he is and who we are. We'll need to admit that we're not as good as we'd like to believe. Only then can we accept ourselves just as he does and let his acceptance and forgiveness begin to set us free.

STEPPING OUT OF HIDING

Camouflage means "concealment by means of disguise." And though we can hide ourselves pretty well from other people, we cannot hide from God. We can't impress him with our accomplishments, and we can't distract him from our imperfections, no matter how religious or clever we may be. All of us stand naked and exposed before the Almighty. The Danish philosopher Sören Kierkegaard wrote, "The sooner I realize that I stand naked before God, the more authentic I will become. . . . To see yourself is to die, to die to all illusions and all hypocrisy. It takes great courage to dare to look at yourself—something which can take place only in the mirror of the Word."[9]

There's no way to camouflage our souls. God's Word is our souls' mirror, and when we look deeply into it, we won't find flattering praise but reality and truth. As the apostle Paul noted, "No one will be declared righteous in his sight by observing the law; rather, through the law we become conscious of sin" (Romans 3:20 NIV).

God's laws and commands were not given to show us the road map to heaven so we can find our own way there; they were given to prove to us that we really are lost.

Yet God has the power both to show us our chains and to set us free. As John Bunyan, author of *The Pilgrim's Progress*, wrote:

"Run, John, run," the Law commands,
But gives us neither feet nor hands.
Far better news the Gospel brings,
That bids us fly and gives us wings!

That's what the truth will do. That's the road we need to walk.

If you want to know yourself, don't look at yourself. Look at Jesus. He'll show you the true condition of your soul, and he'll reveal the full extent of God's love. The best way to get to know yourself is to get to know him.

HONEST TO GOD?

A friend of mine who was serving as a youth pastor once told me about a discussion he'd had with one of the students in his youth group.

The student said, "I just told God today that I like pornography. I don't want to like it. I want him to help me stop. But I finally told him today that I really like it."

My friend looked at me and shook his head. "That was the most honest thing I've ever heard anyone say. I wasn't surprised at what that teenager said, but I *was* surprised he was honest enough to say it."

Most people aren't honest enough to say it. To God. To a pastor. To a friend or a spouse or anyone. We tell ourselves we're not as bad as most people—that we're only human after all. That we have good intentions, and that's what matters most anyway.

And all the while, God desires our honesty.

Jesus saved his harshest words for the people who refused to be honest with God: "These people honor me with their lips, but their hearts are far away. Their worship is a farce" (Mark 7:7).

I think Jesus wants us to tell him about our struggles with pornography or gossiping or envy or jealousy or speeding or prejudice or anger or whatever, because honesty with God paves the way to true spiritual freedom.

Take a minute right now. Pause and reflect on where you are spiritually. Tell God what you need to. Open up to him. Be honest. Ask him to reveal himself—and yourself—to you. Ask him to help you become more real. You may even want to pray something like this:

> my, how i like to play these games
> of hide-and-seek.
> at least i tell myself i like to play them,
> but down deep
> i know i've hidden long enough
> behind my carefully constructed life
> and my carefully crafted image.
> right now, today, Lord, i ask that you would uncover me.
> all of me.
> reveal yourself to me.
> reveal myself to me.
> touch me where i hurt the most,
> find me where i hide most often.
> pull back the covers and see me trembling
> and hold me.
> because i'm afraid,
> both of being real by letting you love me
> and of hiding any longer.
>
> find me and hold me.
> here i am.

Chapter 2

THE GAME YOU CANNOT WIN

Walking the Road to Humility

*O Fountain of All Good, destroy in me
every lofty thought, break pride to pieces
and scatter it to the winds.*

—A Puritan prayer

The comparison game starts early.

In kindergarten the teacher reads to us, in first grade we start reading by ourselves, and by second grade we're in reading groups.

There was the Shark Group: they were the really good readers—eight-year-old kids who could decipher medical textbooks and encyclopedias. Then there was the Barracuda Group. They could handle the chapter books and some of the Dr. Seuss classics. Next came the Goldfish. They tackled easy readers with the smallest words.

Me? I was a Carp. We looked at pictures.

And no matter what the teachers called the groups or how they tried to disguise them, we all knew where we stood. There was no hiding it. Every one of us knew where we fit in. We could have told you who the Sharks were without the help of any achievement tests or school psychologists.

But I worked at it. I practiced my reading and climbed up the food chain until I could look down on all those Carp on the other side of the room, struggling to make sense of the words. Because isn't that the whole point of the comparison game? To be able to look down on others and for them to look up at us?

But reading groups were just the beginning.

The comparison game continued all through school. After a test the first thing we did was turn to the people next to us and ask, "What'd ya get?" Not because we really cared about how well they did, but because we wanted to see if we did better.

We played the comparison game during tryouts for soccer and band and choir and drama and cheerleading. We played it on awards nights and at graduation services. And then it continued into college and drifted into our careers.

Now we look at the cars and clothes and lifestyles of others. We compare waistlines and performance reports and sales records and quarterly earning statements and casseroles and hairstyles and nose jobs.

We've never stopped playing. We just have more sophisticated ways of asking, "What'd ya get?"

How do I measure up? Where do I fit in? How many people have I beaten? The more people we've beaten, the better we feel about ourselves. The more people we clobber, the better we think we are.

Each of us wants to be number one.

We live our lives as if when we die God is going to hand us a giant report card with all the categories of our lives listed—work, family, church, relationships—and then we'll peek over everyone else's shoulder and whisper, What'd ya get? . . . Whoa! Look, everybody! I beat Betsy in Showing Compassion!

And all the while, God is saying, "You've got it all wrong. It doesn't have to do with how well you compare with others, it has to do with how well you compare to me."

COMPARISON PRAYERS

Yeah, we're good at the comparison game. But that's nothing new. It's been going on for a long time. In fact, Jesus told a parable about it. Maybe you know the story. It starts like this . . . A Pharisee and a tax collector went into the temple to pray . . .

> The proud Pharisee stood by himself and prayed this prayer: "I thank you, God, that I am not a sinner like everyone else, especially like that tax collector over there! For I never cheat, I don't sin, I don't commit adultery, I fast twice a week, and I give you a tenth of my income."
>
> But the tax collector stood at a distance and dared not even lift his

eyes to heaven as he prayed. Instead, he beat his chest in sorrow, saying, "O God, be merciful to me, for I am a sinner." (Luke 18:11–13)

If we've heard this story before, it probably doesn't impact us like it should. It probably doesn't shake our world, because we know who the good guy is and who the bad guy is.

Bad Pharisee.

Good tax collector.

But hold on a second. Something we're quick to forget is that the Pharisee really was an upstanding guy. Most of what he said in his prayer was true. And the tax collector really was a dishonest sinner in need of God's mercy. Everything he said in his prayer was true. People in Jesus's day would have known that right off the bat. They would have reversed the roles.

Good Pharisee.

Bad tax collector.

Let's sink our teeth into this story for a minute, because it's not just a story about how to pray or even just about how humility affects prayer. It's a story about how humility affects everything.

Imagine yourself in the Pharisee's shoes. People respect you. People listen to you. You obey the law, you drive the speed limit, you don't get drunk, do drugs, or get involved in shady business deals. You're not addicted to pornography. You don't cheat on your spouse. You attend church regularly and lead a small-group Bible study on Wednesday nights. You emcee for civic events and play a mean game of golf.

And you can't help but notice that some of the people you pray for each week just don't seem to be making any spiritual progress. So one day you say this prayer: "God, thank you that I'm not cheating on my wife or my taxes. Thanks for keeping me pure. For providing for me so I'm able to tithe and sponsor that child in Argentina. I'm grateful that, compared with most people, I don't have that many problems. Amen."

That doesn't sound too bad, does it?

Come on, fess up. Doesn't that hit a little too close to home?

Ah, yes, but there's more to the picture. I know.

This Pharisee was proud. He looked down on the other guy. He didn't confess anything to God because he didn't think he really needed God. So he just listed all the wonderful things about his life (I count six compliments he gave himself in this prayer). Actually, his prayer wasn't a prayer at all. It was an acceptance speech for Citizen of the Year.

JUST AS I AM, WITHOUT ONE PLEA

The man Jesus called "a dishonest tax collector" was a real scumbag, and everyone knew it.

In today's setting he's the guy who doesn't go to the altar. He doesn't even raise his hand during the invitation, because he knows what he's really like. How bad he really is. He just crumples to his knees in the back of the church. As he lowers his head, tears well up in his eyes. "Oh God," he cries, "be merciful to me, a sinner." The words are barely recognizable.

But Jesus turned the tables on his audience. He said something that must have really shocked the crowds. After all, these were people who had great self-confidence and looked down on everyone else (see Luke 18:9). He was talking to people like us. Experts at the comparison game. All-stars. I'll bet you can even guess which reading group they were in as kids.

Jesus said that this tax collector, not the first man, went home justified by God.

Only the humble man was forgiven.

And that's the way it always is. Only the humble soul can be forgiven because only the humble soul believes he needs to be forgiven.

In God's kingdom, pride is the most fatal sin because the proud person will never admit his wrongs and find forgiveness. But the humble person will.

The Pharisee preferred patting himself on the back to reaching out for God. He flattered himself before God. The crook flattened himself before God—and went home forgiven.

We'll never find forgiveness until we find humility, and we'll never find humility while we're busy comparing ourselves with others. Humility only comes when we see ourselves in the light of God's Word.

"God sets himself against the proud,
　　but he shows favor to the humble."
So humble yourselves before God. (James 4:6–7)

Humility before God is the key to spiritual intimacy with God. We'll never learn to love God while we're in love with ourselves. We'll never learn to worship God until we learn what it means to be truly humble.

The key to becoming real is humility. It unlocks all the doors beyond itself. It swings them wide open and allows us to live with authenticity. For when we're humble, we finally realize who we are.

Humility is knowing ourselves for who we really are and refusing to hide behind the illusions of who we desperately wish we were.

KILLING THE HYDRA

In Greek mythology the Hydra was a creature that grew two new heads every time one of its existing heads was chopped off. It was fearsome and terrible and deadly. And, obviously, it was extremely hard to kill.

Well, the Hydra may have been mythical, but it's still alive today.

I'll tell you its real name.

Pride.

And every time we get touchy or temperamental with others, it rears another head. Every time we're jealous for attention, every time we feel slighted or overlooked, every time we get envious or impatient or sensitive or moody or defensive, every time we play the comparison game, our pride reveals another of its many heads.

This may sound contradictory, but even low self-esteem is prideful because self-absorption in any form is pride. Of course God wants us to take care of ourselves and respect ourselves—after all, we're made in his image. But if we're constantly belittling ourselves (I'm too fat . . . too lazy . . . too short . . . too ugly . . . too much of a failure . . . no good), we're exhibiting another face of pride, because we're overly concerned with ourselves. God wants us to focus our thoughts and minds on him, not on ourselves.

When we get angry at red lights and busy signals and long lines and packed parking lots and traffic jams and clogged sinks and burned-out light bulbs and road construction and delayed flights and computer problems, we reveal our pride.

Is impatience really a symptom of pride? Yes. We typically lose our patience when we can't get what we want when we want it in the way we want it, and to our egos, that's unthinkable. Because pride sees the universe revolving around itself.

We're impatient with others while expecting them to be patient with us. We're slow to admit our wrongs and quick to cover them up. When we look at others, we're filled with envy or derision but rarely with simple, unadorned admiration or compassion. We bounce back and forth between shame and arrogance, between over-confidence and fear, rather than simply accepting ourselves, accepting others, and accepting God "as is."

And of course, we never stop playing the comparison game.

Pride even invades our worship and our prayers, just as it did for the Pharisee. If we're busy trying to "get something out of the service" or planning where to go for lunch or looking around at what everyone else is wearing or wondering what people would think of us if we raised our hands or went up to the altar, we're not offering that time to God. Instead, we're concerned about our goals and our image and our reputation.

That's self-concern. And self-concern is the opposite of worship. True worship only comes when we forget ourselves and become immersed only in thoughts of the Father. When God becomes more important to us than our reputation, when thoughts of him crowd out thoughts of ourselves, then, and only then, are we on the road to true worship.

Until then we're just playing games with appearances and pride.

And the Hydra lurks, ready to grow another head.

THE DIVINE SABER

The ego, the self-will, is fiercely territorial. If anything encroaches on it or threatens to forget it or overlook it or fight against it, it will claw its way to the throat of the intruder and fight it to the death. Whether the intruder is Humiliation or Confession or Repentance or God Almighty.

If it could, the ego would slay God and bury him in the sands of time. For God is the ego's greatest competitor for our hearts.

This Hydra is indeed a fearsome beast, and we can't kill it by ourselves. I've tried, but the swords I typically use aren't strong enough to pierce my pride. They snap off in the leathery skin of my ego before doing any real damage. We need a sword fashioned in another realm—a sword that will not bend or break. We need a mightier blade to fight this foe.

Or perhaps we shouldn't be fighting it at all. Maybe we should let a stronger warrior fight in our place, as Paul did when he struggled with sin: "Oh, what a miserable person I am! Who will free me from this life that is dominated by sin? Thank God! The answer is in Jesus Christ our Lord" (Romans 7:24–25).

When Hercules battled the Hydra, he burned each neck after he cut off a head. But the hero of our hearts has another strategy. Jesus aims his sword at the very heart of our pride. He doesn't want to merely wound our pride. He wants to kill it.

God is love, and in 1 Corinthians 13:4 we read, "Love is patient and kind. Love is not jealous or boastful or proud." Love is not proud; love is at war with pride. God's love fights for us and within us to conquer the pride rooted so deeply in our hearts.

The truth of God's holiness and the realization of our wretchedness work together to slice away at our pride. Both must be present. Both were in the heart of the tax collector who cried, "O God, be merciful to me, for I am a sinner."

THE GREAT UNTANGLING

Image and appearance and reputation and the affections of others have become reins on our necks. They control us and drive us here or there or wherever they like. Snipping those reins is the only way to be truly free and to roam the expanse of God's grace.

As long as we wrap our feelings of significance around what we do or don't do, what we have or don't have, what we wear or don't wear, what we buy or don't buy, we'll evaluate our self-worth with a measuring stick that changes moment by moment like a black, writhing eel. We'll never be happy or satisfied or free.

When we gauge our worth by what we assume other people think about us, we'll never be at peace. For one word can shatter that peace and leave us withered, raw, and alone. One insult can take us down. One look can bring us to tears.

If we depend on the comparison game to feel good, we'll lose. We will never, never, never win the comparison game. It'll swallow us right up.

The only way to win is to stop playing altogether.

As long as we remain entangled in our desire for the admiration of others, we won't experience the fullness of intimacy with Christ. We need to stop jockeying for position. We need to step out of the race.

A great freedom sweeps through our souls when we stop living for the praise of others and start living solely for the will of God.

The humble soul doesn't try to impress or control or seduce or acquire. He is content. Humility doesn't brag or boast or pose or pretend. Humility accepts humiliation.

The humble spirit is careful not to call attention to himself in either direction—neither by wearing the finest designer clothes nor yard-sale hand-me-downs.

He is content to be forgotten. Glad to be passed over. Thankful to live and serve God in obscurity. He's incognito. Unobtrusive.

But he isn't hiding. The humble person has finally come out into the open. Only the proud hide, for only the proud are afraid of what others will think of them if they finally stop hiding. That fear holds them back.

But the humble soul has lost all fear of others' opinions. He no longer plays the comparison game. He's honest about his pride and about how easily and often it raises its head. He's honest about how deeply he desires to be remembered and how often he calls attention to himself. And because of this honesty, he can finally seek to be forgotten.

If we cling to the hope that we'll be remembered, if we try to establish a legacy, humility will never find a home in our hearts. The castles of acclaim and accomplishment don't have any rooms small enough to house humility.

If we humble ourselves hoping all the while that God will lift us up or exalt us, we'll never be exalted, for our humility is still marred by self-interest. But if we humble ourselves and seek humility for its own sake, with no hope of reward and no secret desire for honor, then God will indeed accept us and offer us an eternal reward. For on that day, our pride will finally be dead.

UNDERSTANDING TRUE HUMILITY

True humility results in a different kind of living—a different kind of life:

- True humility never points the spotlight at itself. It takes genuine pleasure in the accomplishments of others.

- True humility looks down on no one but up to all, honoring their gifts and admiring their beauty.

- True humility is quick to give credit to others because it realizes every accomplishment requires sacrifice and teamwork.

- True humility doesn't seek honor, recognition, popularity, glory, or fame, because it realizes that we are all equally loved children of God.

- True humility is honest because it has no hidden agendas or secret ambitions or ulterior motives. It has nothing to lose by telling the truth and nothing to gain by hiding behind lies.

The truly humble woman is patient with others, for she has looked closely at herself. The truly humble man doesn't complain that life isn't fair, for he knows every breath is a glorious gift, that he has already been given more than he could ever deserve.

The truly humble woman never says, I told you so. She's not smug, self-assured, or arrogant. She doesn't have a constant desire to be right or to prove others wrong. She would rather they be honored or remembered or recognized or appreciated or noticed or awarded than herself.

She never delights in the failures of others. When they're honored, she's glad. She congratulates them without secret grudges or hidden envy. When others are dishonored or humiliated, she doesn't gloat. She freely rejoices with those who rejoice and mourns with those who mourn. Rather than always competing and comparing, she practices compassion for others.

The humble man doesn't ask, how can I get ahead? because getting ahead means putting others behind. He steps back to help others reach their goals since their goals are more important to him than his own. He strives to maximize not his potential but theirs. He doesn't put them down; he lifts them up. He doesn't insult; he admires. He doesn't grumble; he encourages.

He doesn't make it his goal to be number one or make more money than someone else or become better known than another, for he desires his competitor's good over his own. He knows competition nearly always requires self-promotion, so he's careful to avoid contests in which winning would mean exalting or honoring himself above another. He doesn't want others to lose, he wants them to succeed. So when his tennis opponent hits a good shot, he's thrilled. And when the other team misses a free throw, he doesn't cheer.

The humble soul seeks to serve rather than be served, just like the Master. The humble soul knows humility isn't just a lofty goal to be discussed or debated but a way of life he can't help but pursue when he looks at his Savior's face. This upside-down attitude of honoring others above ourselves is found throughout the New Testament:

> [Jesus] said to the crowd, "If any of you wants to be my follower, you must put aside your selfish ambition, shoulder your cross daily, and follow me." (Luke 9:23)

> Honor one another above yourselves. (Romans 12:10 NIV)

> Don't think only of your own good. Think of other Christians and what is best for them. (1 Corinthians 10:24)

> Do nothing out of selfish ambition or vain conceit, but in humility consider others better than yourselves. (Philippians 2:3 NIV)

Is it even possible to live like this?

Rather than pursue self-promotion, self-love, self-esteem, self-gratification, self-affirmation, self-exaltation, self-confidence, self, self, self . . . the humble person forgets himself in the service of others. He denies himself . . . he loses himself . . . he hates himself . . . Just as Jesus told him he must do if he is ever to have true life with God.[1]

For the humble person knows that any focus at all on self, any concern for the honor of self, any love that he still harbors for himself, is robbing him of a wholehearted love for God. As Andrew Murray noted in his book, *Humility: The Journey Toward Holiness*, "Humility is nothing but the disappearance of self in the vision that God is all."[2]

That is what the humble soul looks like.

So here's the question: where can the humble soul be found in this frenzied world of billions of "me's" all trying to put themselves first?

SOUL SURRENDER

The road to humility is really the road to the cross. It's marked by humiliation, foolishness, and surrender. This kind of life could never make sense to someone drenched in self-love or enslaved by pride.

But it does make sense to Jesus. And it should make sense to us. As Paul wrote, "Your attitude should be the same that Christ Jesus had. Though he was God, he did not demand and cling to his rights as God. He made himself nothing; he took the humble position of a slave and appeared in human form. And in human form he obediently humbled himself even further by dying a criminal's death on a cross" (Philippians 2:5–8).

Our pride is put to death on the cross. The nails are sharp enough to pierce its heart.

Humility is the key to all other virtues. Without it they would all be tainted with pride. Even love can be made rotten by an infusion of pride. Even charity cannot stand up against the weakening tremors of pride. A proud love is a selfish love, a conditional love, a careful love. But a humble love is a giving love, an unconditional love, a reckless love, a godly love that gives all and risks all and offers all and does not hold anything back (see 1 Corinthians 13:4–5).

It's not safe to love like that. We might get hurt in the process.

So the proud heart holds back to protect itself. But the humble heart gives all, for it does not consider the risks of love to itself, only the benefits of love for the beloved.

That's how Jesus loves us. That's where his humility led him: all the way to the cross.

The first step to becoming real is the painful process of admitting the truth to ourselves about who we really are. Flawed and wrinkled. Selfish.

And proud.

Make no mistake, humility before God means there's no place left to hide. There are no more excuses, no self-congratulations. Only honesty and brokenness and faith. That's what the tax collector had. That's why he was forgiven.

Over and over again in Scripture, it is those who are the most broken (like the tax collector) who become whole, while those who think they are whole (like the Pharisee) remain broken.

Humility does not strive for itself but forgets itself as it strives for the good of others. And so, in one of the grand paradoxes of life, humility achieves all that pride seeks. The very things humility does not care about, it receives—respect, recognition, honor, and the like. The very things pride cannot stand to live without, it loses the more it exerts itself.

ROOTS OF TRANSPARENCY

"Humility is not so much a virtue along with the others," wrote Andrew Murray, "but is the root of all, because it alone takes the right attitude before God and allows Him, as God, to do all."[3]

The root of all sin is pride. The soil in which it grows is self.

The root of all virtue is humility. The soil in which it grows is God.

So how do we achieve this kind of humility? This attitude? How does God's Word work to remove our pride?

The answer is simple, but it's not easy.

The closer we walk with God, the more we'll forget ourselves. The nearer we are to Jesus, the more we'll notice our sin. The bigger God appears to us, the less significant we'll appear in our own eyes.

The more we understand God's character—all-powerful and mighty and glorious and good; all-perfect and pure and true—the more we'll realize we have every reason to be humble. For we are much less important than we claim to be, and far less good than we try to be, and compared with a glorious and giving God, we are terribly worthless and tiny creatures.

Let the Spirit of God sweep through your soul. Let him show you the many heads of pride. Let him fight within you to give you the victory.

Go to God now, not like the Pharisee who was so busy congratulating himself and complimenting himself that he missed his meeting with the Almighty. Go instead like the tax collector who was overwhelmed by God's holiness and the awareness of his own failings. As Jesus said, "I tell you, this sinner, not the Pharisee, returned home justified before God. For the proud will be humbled, but the humble will be honored" (Luke 18:14).

Chapter 3

THE JOURNEY OF NO RETURN

Being Honest about Life and Death

Who knows when the chains will be off,
and the boat, like the last glimmer of
sunset, vanish into the night?
—RABINDRANATH TAGORE, *GITANJALI*

TODAY (A FABLE FOR OUR TIMES)

In the center of the throne room of heaven sits an angel with a singular and most important job. She is called by the name Giftgiver. Every day, in the still of dawn, she checks a list and smiles. Then she wraps a special package and sends it down to billions of skin-covered spirits.

They don't earn it. They don't deserve it. Yet every morning another new package arrives.

It is the gift of a day. A crystal-clear package placed gently by their beds. With many deep folds and secret corners and hidden surprises, it is perhaps the most precious and lovely and glorious gift of all.

But most of the people never take time to explore the depths of their gift. They just rip it open in the morning and hold it loosely in their hands until it slips away.

Yet when they lie down to sleep, they expect another gift to be set out for them the next morning. As if they'd earned it. Or deserved it. Most of them never stop to consider that Giftgiver is there or that she has given them another gift.

Or that one day their name won't appear on her list.

■

One night when my daughter, Ariel, was five years old, I walked past her bedroom door and heard her sobbing.

I pushed open the door and walked in. "What's wrong, honey?"

She could barely say the words. I had to have her repeat them several times so I could hear them between her sobs. "I . . . don't . . . want . . . you . . . to die . . . Daddy!" Then she threw her arms out to hug me.

And I almost said it.

I almost said what all parents are tempted to say in those moments: I'm not going to die, sweetheart. Don't be ridiculous. Now roll over and go to sleep so I can finish watching my TV show.

I almost said it, but then I caught myself.

Because perhaps I would die that very night. Maybe on my way back to the living room. And then she'd be right.

In any case, someday I will die. I know that. And that night she knew it too—for the first time.

So she wept with a broken heart.

I didn't know what to say. I don't typically weep when I think about death. I just change the channel or go shopping or shoot some baskets at the gym. Sometimes I go running. Or I just roll over and go back to sleep.

But I don't just lie in bed and think about death and weep.

Weep.

So I told her I wouldn't die until God knows she's ready for me to go to heaven, and I hugged her until we both felt better.

Yet now that I think about it, maybe her response to death is the best one, the only one that's really honest after all.

REMINDERS OF THE GRAVE

Some years ago I took a First Responder course to learn emergency first aid. The instructor started the first class by saying, "The first rule of emergency medicine is that everyone is going to die. The second rule is, you can't do anything about it."

I guess I'd never thought of it like that before.

Both he and my daughter were right. Both of them were saying, in their own way, the thing we dread acknowledging and avoid saying: none of us gets out of this alive.

LORD, remind me how brief my time on earth will be. Remind me that my days are numbered, and that my life is fleeing away.

34

My life is no longer than the width of my hand. An entire lifetime is just a moment to you; human existence is but a breath. (Psalm 39:4–5)

Everyone dies in the midst of something.

People die in the midst of going to the dentist's office or driving home from vacation or taking a shower or watching TV or mowing the lawn or barbequing ribs on the back deck or enjoying a good night's sleep. People die in the midst of arguments, grudges, dreams, plans, careers, headaches, heartaches, and courtships. People die in the midst of marriage and puberty and old age. Some die in the midst of being born. Or even before that.

We all die. And we don't die when we expect to die or after our dreams have all come true or when we've finally made it in the world.

No, most of us die in the midst of pretending we'll never die. We die living as if tomorrow were guaranteed and our lives will last forever. Blaise Pascal put it bluntly: "The last act is bloody, however fine the rest of the play. They throw earth over your head and it is finished forever."[1]

> MOST OF US DIE IN THE MIDST OF **PRETENDING** WE'LL NEVER DIE.

The mystic poet Rumi wrote, "Six friends hoist your handsomeness and carry it to the cemetery."[2]

All of us know we're going to die, yet we act as though we were going to live forever, as though death were not the guaranteed outcome of life. When death stalks us or claims a close relative or friend, we weep in shock. How could this happen? It's so out of the blue!

Death is never out of the blue. It's always there, right before our eyes, but we close them so we don't have to look into its face and see our name written on its forehead.

And soon after the tragedy, we go right back to living as if each moment didn't count for eternity.

Death always seems to take us by surprise. But why? It's guaranteed. We will all be lowered into the grave and disappear into dust. We hate to admit it. We don't want to think about it. But it's inevitable. Life is a gift. Death is a certainty.

The most fatal condition of all is life. It has a 100 percent mortality rate—always has, always will. Dying is one thing we're all capable of, one thing we all ultimately succeed at.

35

Once I was talking with my father, and he mentioned all the stuff he'd accumulated, having lived in the same house for more than thirty years. "I guess you'll have to get rid of it all if I die," he said.

I looked at him and said, "What do you mean 'if'?"

FUNERALS OR FESTIVALS?

I've often heard people say things like, you've got your whole life in front of you!

That's simply not true. We don't have our whole lives ahead of us. We have our whole lives behind us. What we have in front of us is a mystery that could be over at any moment.

It's sobering to reflect on the brevity and frailty of our lives.

As far as we know, we're all the same age. Not that all of us are the same distance from birth, but we are the same distance from death. We're all one heartbeat away from eternity. Sure, some of us have lived longer than others, but for all we know, we're one breath away from the end of our journey.

Maybe we think that if we don't mention it—if we're quiet enough about the whole enterprise, if we keep our distance from it by hushing ourselves up about our mortality—death won't track us down.

If only it worked that way.

But it doesn't.

Here are some sobering thoughts: When I die the universe won't even blink. Only a handful of its nearly seven billion people will even notice. The number of people who show up at my funeral will depend on the weather. And within a week, my obituary will be lining someone's litter box.

That puts things in perspective.

Life is a vapor. We hold it in our hands, and it curls through our fingers, and before we know it, it's gone.

Yet in our culture, those who think about or talk about death are labeled grim or deluded or deranged. Or worse.

"I've been thinking a lot about death lately."

"That's macabre. Is something wrong?"

"No."

"Oh . . . you wanna go see a movie?"

It's almost as if we think we can ignore it into oblivion. Yet the one un-deniable, inescapable truth is that we will all die. A sane person acknowledges

36

the inevitable and prepares for it. And nothing is more inevitable than death. A wise person asks, where am I going when I die, and what am I going to do until then?

The wise ponder death and the meaning of this brief life we've been given. Only fools are content to distract themselves and ignore the fate that awaits us all. Perhaps that's why Solomon wrote, "It is better to spend your time at funerals than at festivals. For you are going to die, and you should think about it while there is still time. . . . A wise person thinks much about death, while the fool thinks only about having a good time now" (Ecclesiastes 7:2, 4).

There's nothing like facing death to give us a clearer perspective on life. Ask anyone who has just found out she has breast cancer or AIDS or a heart condition.

At least it should give us a clearer perspective.

But sometimes we manage to ignore that death is coming for us, even when we stare it right in the face.

THE GIFT OF AWARENESS

One day I was transporting two six-foot-tall office dividers on top of my car. I'd tied them on with some leftover rope I carry in the trunk. The rope was old, but I figured it would hold, since I was only going across town.

Ten minutes later, as I merged onto the highway, I heard a gut-wrenching *SCRAPE* and *CLANG!* A cold hand of terror gripped the back of my neck. I knew immediately what had happened.

In the rearview mirror, I could see one of the dividers twisting in midair like a dancer tapping a foot off the ground and then two-stepping backward down the highway toward oncoming traffic at forty-five miles per hour.

Cars were all around me.

I pulled over, breathing heavily. My palms were sweaty. My chest was heaving. Cars kept zooming past. A few people honked at me.

At least one of them is still on the car, I thought.

But when I looked again, I saw that it wasn't. They were both in the middle of the road.

So I carried the two dividers to the side of the road, dodging traffic while my six-year-old daughter sat in the car asking me if everything was OK. If everything was OK . . .

The dividers weren't destroyed like I thought they'd be. Just twisted a little. Whew.

Just then a fellow walked up to me. He'd pulled to the side of the road in front of me.

"Man . . . I thought I was gonna die," he said. One of the dividers had just missed smashing through his windshield and had knocked the side-view mirror off his car instead. He told me what it was like to see it peel off my car and fly toward him. "I thought it was gonna go right through my windshield."

"Oh my," I whispered. "I'm so glad you're alright."

And then he said, "We can take care of this right now."

Huh?

He said it again. "We can take care of this right now." I still didn't get it.

He held out his hand.

Then I understood.

It was money. He wanted some money to pay for the mirror without getting the insurance people involved.

I pulled out my wallet. "This is all I've got," I said, handing him forty dollars. His eyes lit up.

A fraction of a second or a puff of wind, and he would have been dead. And now he was satisfied with forty dollars.

"Alright, I won't bring this up again," he said.

I felt dirty handing him the money. Like I'd just bought him off. For forty dollars I'd bought his silence, and the insurance company would never even know.

He might have been killed. I might have gone to jail or been sued by his wife and lost everything. Who knows. I might have gone bankrupt. Instead, I handed him forty dollars to fix his side-view mirror.

Across the street was a hardware store where I bought fifty feet of *very strong rope.* I tied the dividers onto the car really securely this time and drove home. My hands were still shaking when I pulled into the driveway and hid in my basement, away from the world—a world where our lives might be snatched away while we drive across town to look at used furniture. Where someone is happy to walk away from a moment saturated with revelation with nothing but forty dollars. Where a gust of wind can either rip our lives from us or hand us a gift called awareness.

All he wanted was a little money.

And Giftgiver shook her head and checked her list again.

FOSTERING AN ETERNAL MIND-SET

That man walked away for the same reason people turn off their alarm clocks and go back to sleep. He didn't want to wake up.

We are so short-sighted and misguided and blind and deceived and unaware. How do we so successfully hide the proximity of our deaths from our minds? How do we so constantly and completely deceive ourselves? Why are we so slow to become aware of the brevity of our lives?

I'll bet I know what you're thinking. Alright, already, Steve. I get the drift. I'm going to die. I admit it. So what? Why are you bringing this up, anyway? You're getting me all depressed here. Why are you hammering away at it so much?

Because I'm trying to wake you up.

Of course you know you're going to die. We all do. What I'm trying to get you to do is believe it.

And there's a big difference.

We know it but don't live like it. We acknowledge it but don't believe it. And knowledge alone doesn't change us. Only those things we believe change us. If we truly believed we were going to die someday soon, it would change the way we live today.

We need to stop simply *knowing* we're going to die. We need to start *believing* it. Until we come to grips with our own mortality, we'll never make choices that reflect the reality of life, see things in their proper perspective, or value each day as the nonrefundable gift it is.

Take this moment, right now, and thank God that you are a member of history's most elite club—the group Annie Dillard calls "the now-living." Then acknowledge that soon you will join the billions of corpses littering our planet. Pause and reflect on the brevity of your life. Ponder the miracle that at this moment, you are alive and have the chance to experience the glory of God.

You are present. You are here. You are alive.

It changes everything when we admit that we're not going to live forever—that we might not even live until suppertime. If we really realized how brief and fleeting our lives are, we would invest in different things. We would value different things. We would pursue different things. And we would be more thankful for each year. Each day. Each moment.

If we want to journey toward becoming real, we need to be honest about death. We need to let the fragility of life inform our decisions, priorities, and outlook on life.

In light of these truths about life and death, here are seven practical steps all of us can take toward becoming more real.

1. Admit That We're Human

Wisdom, clarity, and a proper perspective only arise when we're aware of our mortality. They only grow when we admit the truth that none of us gets out of this alive.

In heaven there is no more dying or pain or loss. There are no more good-byes. But in this world, we are always surrounded by skid marks and scars.

We desperately want to be secure—physically, financially, emotionally. So we build walls around our cities. Around our portfolios. Around our hearts. But to become real, we must admit that our bodies are mortal, our lives are brief, our world is fragile, and our dreams are easily shattered. None of us is indestructible, none invincible. Our hearts are not impenetrable. And our journeys across this planet are only temporary.

2. Accept the Uncertainties of Life

On September 11, 2001, the mask of invulnerability was ripped from the face of the United States. As hard as we tried to pretend that we were still untouchable, as much as it hurt to say it, we finally had to admit that we're not 100 percent secure and will never be 100 percent secure from terrorist attacks or other kinds of tragedies.

In the wake of 9/11 and the war in Iraq, I heard someone on the radio say we live in uncertain times. But when have the times ever been certain? Never.

This is (and has always been) an uncertain world. James, the brother of Jesus, put it this way: "How do you know what will happen tomorrow? For your life is like the morning fog—it's here a little while, then it's gone" (James 4:14).

Everything we trust in for security is prone to let us down except for those things that rise above and do not depend on the circumstances of this world. So we should be prudent about how much we plan for the future, for we don't even know if the future includes us. We can't let ourselves become enticed by the promises of a better life someday. The commercials are lies. There's no such thing as a safe investment. There's no such thing as a secure future on this planet. Security comes only from the hand of God.

Let's not invest too much time and energy in plans that may never even come about. Let's live today while we have it and let God be the master of our tomorrows.

When we come to grips with our mortality and vulnerability, we can find the strength to face each day, not by pretending we're untouchable, but by relying on the strength of an awesome, eternal, untouchable God.

After all, our God is a fortress that death cannot destroy, terrorists cannot topple, and time cannot erode.

3. Embrace This Moment as a Gift from God

During our brief lives, we rarely live. Instead we pass through each day or month or year or decade drowning in busyness and distraction and worry and regret. Time washes over us and floats away past our awareness.

Yet this moment, right now, is all God has given us. He may give us tomorrow, or another decade, or another fifty years. But he hasn't yet. All he has given us is this present moment. All he asks of us is this moment. It's all we have to give him. It's all we can ever give him.

So embrace it. Accept it. Don't waste it. Throw your arms around it, and live it for him. I'm not talking about indulging yourself or living merely for the moment. I'm talking about freeing yourself to actually live the moment.

This moment. Right now.

Drink it in. Experience it. Absorb it. Take care of today. Enjoy the pleasures of today. See the sights and taste the flavors and smell the fragrances that are only being served today. Listen well to the music played by the musicians of this moment, for they will never play it again.

Someone who refuses to dwell in the moment is only looking forward to life, never experiencing it. He's preparing to live but not living.

Someone once told me, "Do what you're doing and be where you are." It sounds simple, but it's not easy. Often we don't really do what we're doing because we're busy thinking about something else. We don't experience life where we are, as we are, because we're so distracted thinking about yesterday or tomorrow that we never enter the present.

Resting in God's presence is a choice. It doesn't happen by accident. We need to create space in our lives for God to talk to us, lead us, and comfort us. Peace in the present only comes when the flow of regrets has stopped and the torrent of worry has not yet begun.

Here's our challenge: to do what we're doing and be where we are, and do it and be there with God. Those who let the moment sweep over them and embrace them and wash through their souls, they—and only they—can be said to have truly lived. All others skirt on the periphery of life and dwell in possibilities and dreams. Those who are immersed in the now are truly alive and enter into the realm of the God who is.

The God who always is. Not simply the God who was or will be.

The God who is, right now. Right there with you.

4. Change Our Perspective

We need to let the knowledge of our imminent death help us reprioritize our lives. We have to stop spending our precious little time in pursuit of useless cargo that's just going to get thrown out when we die. We're blind about the brevity of our lives and mixed up when it comes to priorities. Too many of us spend our whole lives in pursuit of trinkets and trophies and never find true treasure at all.

Let's store up treasures in heaven by living for God and pursuing the things of God. As Jesus said, "Wherever your treasure is, there your heart and thoughts will also be" (Matthew 6:21). It's time to admit that the things that fill our lives are not as important as the things that will fill our eternity. And then let that admission change the way we live, the priorities we set, the goals we pursue, and the treasures we seek.

5. Unpack for the Trip Home

Rather than packing for eternity, we need to unpack. We must get rid of all the things that weigh us down and get ready for the trip to the greatest homecoming of all.

Is it wrong to love things in this world? Not necessarily. God created this world and called it good. And God loved the world so much that he sent Jesus (see John 3:16). It's not wrong to love what God values and loves. But we have to be aware of how easy it is to form attachments to the things of this world and to become entangled in them rather than breaking free from their control.

There are things about this world we shouldn't love. The apostle John listed them in 1 John 2:16 (NIV): "the cravings of sinful man, the lust of his eyes and the boasting of what he has and does." Our worldly cravings, lusts, and boastings have nothing to do with God.

We can't allow ourselves to get too comfortable here. We should never let the things of this world become entrenched in our hearts and draw us away from God. For as C. S. Lewis pointed out in *The Weight of Glory*, to be satisfied by the things of this world is to be too easily pleased: "Our Lord finds our desires, not too strong, but too weak. We are half-hearted creatures, fooling about with drink and sex and ambition when infinite joy is offered us, like an ignorant child who wants to go on making mud pies in a slum because he cannot imagine what is meant by the offer of a holiday at the sea."[3]

And it's not just a holiday at sea awaiting us; it's actually moving in forever with the Creator himself.

6. Admit We're Nomads

Why would you spend all weekend remodeling a hotel room if you knew you were going home on Monday? Why would you burden yourself with extra baggage if you were only staying overnight at a friend's house? This world is not our home. We're only here for a short visit before moving into our permanent residence. We shouldn't try to move in here. We're not home yet.

The Bible calls believers strangers, foreigners, aliens, nomads. Let's start living that way by traveling lightly on this planet and focusing our attention on home. That's what the Bible heroes listed in Hebrews 11 did: "All these faithful ones died without receiving what God had promised them, but they saw it all from a distance and welcomed the promises of God. They agreed that they were no more than foreigners and nomads here on earth. And obviously people who talk like that are looking forward to a country they can call their own" (vv. 13–14).

As long as we remember we're on a pilgrimage, we'll travel lightly. But as soon as we think this planet is where we're supposed to stay, as soon as we try to settle down here, we'll begin to pursue the wrong priorities, set the wrong agenda, and make foolish choices.

Heaven is our home. Let's live like it.

7. Look beyond the Grave

Death snaps at our heels and hunts us down. And it never returns home empty-handed. But Christ did a strange thing. He allowed himself to be conquered by death so we wouldn't have to be. As Jesus told Martha, "I am the resurrection and the life. Those who believe in me, even though they die like everyone else, will live again. They are given eternal life for believing in me and will never perish" (John 11:25–26).

To the Christian, death is not the end but the transformation from all that is temporary to all that is eternal, from all that is passing to all that is lasting. Death is the great beginning of our final journey—the trip Job called "the journey of no return" (Job 16:22 NIV).

Death is the end of a breath and the beginning of eternity. When believers die, we're not conquered by death; our dying itself is swallowed by life in the biggest gulp of all: "Our dying bodies make us groan and sigh, but it's not that we want to die and have no bodies at all. We want to slip into our new bodies so that these dying bodies will be swallowed up by everlasting life" (2 Corinthians 5:4).

We need to reprioritize our lives in view of these truths. We don't walk through the valley of death but the valley of the shadow of death. It's only a shadow. We walk through the valley of life, but every step of the way, death's shadow looms closer.

Death dogs us. But we need not fear. For beyond that shadow is the greatest Light of all. God has something incredible waiting for us. He "has reserved a priceless inheritance for his children. It is kept in heaven for you, pure and undefiled, beyond the reach of change and decay. And God, in his mighty power, will protect you until you receive this salvation, because you are trusting him. It will be revealed on the last day for all to see" (1 Peter 1:4–5).

Yes, our journeys here may be brief. But soon we get to head home to enjoy the greatest gift of all. And at last we get to move in for good.

Chapter 4

NO CARICATURES IN HEAVEN

Understanding What Christianity Is All About

Drive delusion from me, that I may recognize Thee.

—A PRAYER OF SAINT AUGUSTINE

Her question caught me off guard.

We'd been airborne just long enough for me to pull out my laptop computer. I'd strewn papers and notes and books across the seat beside me, and I was pecking away at the keyboard (probably close to a deadline, if I know anything at all about myself).

I'd noticed a woman in the adjoining seat glance up from her novel a few times. Finally she blurted out her question.

"What are you working on?"

I gestured toward my papers. "Well, it's a book—a collection of stories based on the parables of Jesus. It's called *JawDroppers.*"[1]

"Oh," she replied, staring blankly at my notes.

Long pause.

"The stories Jesus told shook people up," I explained. "That's where I got the title."

She obviously wasn't impressed.

"Are you a Christian?" I asked.

"Oh, yes," she said quickly.

"So am I!" I exclaimed, closing my laptop and getting ready to talk.

"That's nice," she said offhandedly and went back to her novel.

I blinked.

I had no idea what to say.

I blinked again.

Nice?

It's nice?

ANYTHING BUT NICE

Christianity, if it is anything at all, is not nice.

Radical, yes. Mysterious, yes. Wondrous, bewildering, supernatural, humbling, stunning, transforming—yes, yes, yes. But it is certainly not nice.

Can you picture Jesus explaining his mission to his disciples? "Hey, guys, I'm gonna be handed over to die. I'll be rejected, beaten, tortured, and killed—but then I'll rise from the dead!"

"That's nice."

Or the angel talking to the women at the empty tomb: "He's not here! He's alive—risen from the dead!"

"I see. That's nice."

"No, I don't think you heard me. He's risen!"

"I know, and I said it was nice."

What's nice about forsaking all and suffering for a carpenter? What's nice about picking up our cross daily and following a man to the death of ourselves? What's nice about hating our very lives? What's nice about being persecuted, rejected, and despised? (see 2 Timothy 3:12).

Even our hope of heaven isn't nice. It's glorious or it's nothing at all. For "if Christ has not been raised, your faith is futile; you are still in your sins. Then those also who have fallen asleep in Christ are lost. If only for this life we have hope in Christ, we are to be pitied more than all men" (1 Corinthians 15:17–19 NIV).

Christians are either pitiable, lost, deceived creatures, or already seated with Christ in the heavenly realms (see Ephesians 2:6). And how could either of these conditions be described by any sensible person as *nice*?

It might be nice to go to church, eat fried chicken at potluck suppers, and raise money so "the young people" can go to an amusement park, but it is certainly not nice to be a Christian.

NOT GOOD ENOUGH

I don't want to be too critical, but after listening to the sermons at some churches, I think their main purpose is to produce well-informed people— as if knowledge were an end in itself. The sermons are lectures. Doctrinally correct information oozes everywhere, but the people remain unchanged. These words of Jesus apply to them: "You diligently study the Scriptures because you think that by them you possess eternal life. These are the Scriptures that testify about me, yet you refuse to come to me to have life" (John 5:39–40 NIV).

Other churches seem to exist to make good people. They're like self-improvement centers. It's as if, once we learn to be better, more morally upright people, we can all join hands, sing "Kum-ba-ya," and create a better, more morally upright world—a heaven on earth. Even though Jesus said that's never going to happen.[2]

Other churches try to produce nice people. They talk a lot about love and tolerance and acceptance. They're so affirming. There's nothing to offend you at these churches. And nothing to transform you either.

None of this—knowledge, goodness, or niceness—is what the gospel message is all about. It isn't about what you know but whom you know. It isn't about how good you are but about how good God is. And it isn't about becoming nice people but about becoming new people altogether.

Christianity isn't about making dumb people smarter or bad people better or mean people nicer; it's about making dead people alive.[3] Notice the emphasis on new life in these verses:

What this means is that those who become Christians become new persons. They are not the same anymore, for the old life is gone. A new life has begun! (2 Corinthians 5:17)

God is so rich in mercy, and he loved us so very much, that even while we were dead because of our sins, he gave us life when he raised Christ from the dead. (It is only by God's special favor that you have been saved!) (Ephesians 2:4–5)

He saved us, not because of the good things we did, but because of his mercy. He washed away our sins and gave us a new life through the Holy Spirit. (Titus 3:5)

This new life occurs when repentance and faith intersect in our hearts. When that happens, believe me, it never feels nice. Because repenting means admitting we need God. And no one likes doing that.

The central truth of the Christian faith is that Jesus Christ died in our place, not because it was the nice thing to do, but because it was the only thing he could do to rescue us from hell. He took on himself the punishment we deserve so that, through faith in him, we could have peace and eternal life with God.

Somehow this message has gotten lost, muddied up, and watered down by well-meaning people who've forgotten that Christ will offend—must offend—us, or he can't help us. It has to hurt, or no spiritual surgery is occurring. Kierkegaard emphasized this: "Woe to him, therefore, who preaches Christianity without the possibility of offence. Woe to the person who smoothly, flirtatiously, commandingly, convincingly preaches some soft, sweet, something which is supposed to be Christianity."[4]

Without sin and a savior, you don't have Christianity. You don't even have a bland imitation of it. You have the opposite of it altogether.

You see, God isn't in the home-improvement business. He isn't into remodeling. He's into demolition and construction. New life in Christ means death to the old life in self.

It's not safe to be a believer. It's not nice.

Becoming a Christian is dangerous to our pride, to our ego, to our self. Because in order to help us, Jesus must first slay us. Not our bodies but our pride. The gospel has the power to "kill us to life."[5] For after the bad news of the cross comes the good news of the empty tomb: "Since we died with Christ, we know we will also share his new life" (Romans 6:8).

It's also dangerous to our reputations and our lives. Faith in him will mean persecution from the world. In many countries (yes, even today), it means imprisonment, torture, and death.

Jesus's life wasn't nice. He was homeless, despised, full of sorrow, hunted down, and unjustly killed. And in no way was his death nice. It wasn't nice, it was necessary. He is our only hope, and without him there is no hope.

Before we can discover new life, before we can become believers, we must realize the hopelessness of our lives without Jesus and then set aside both our preconceptions about the Christian life and our misconceptions about God.

CARICATURES OF GOD

Isn't it odd that the most religious person of all time was never accused of being religious? That the holiest person in history was never considered (by the religious teachers) to be all that holy but rather a nuisance, a hack, a drunkard, and a glutton?

Either we've got the wrong idea of religion, or we've got the wrong idea of Jesus. My guess is we're a little off base on both counts.

I'm impressed by how Eberhard Arnold described encountering Jesus through conversion:

Our life will become not narrower, but broader; not more limited, but more boundless; not more regulated, but more abundant; not more pedantic, but more bounteous; not more sober, but more enthusiastic; not more faint-hearted, but more daring; not more empty and human, but more filled by God; not sadder, but happier; not more incapable, but more creative. All this is Jesus and his spirit of freedom and peace. He is coming to us. Let us go into his future radiant with joy![6]

Our culture and our world are pretty friendly to a generic god we can all feel nice about, but not to the truth that we desperately need a savior.

No wonder the world isn't very Christian-friendly.

Jesus didn't come to lead peace marches or preach tolerance or show us how to live gently on the planet—he came to accuse people "of sin and evil" (John 7:7).

No wonder they didn't like what he had to say.

No wonder they don't like what we have to say.

Our world has created caricatures of God: The Granddaddy in Heaven. The Big Guy Upstairs. The Cosmic Cop. The Black-Cloaked Judge of the Universe. And we've created caricatures of Jesus: The Limp Little Lamb. The Nice Friendly Guy. The Good Teacher. The Political Visionary. The Martyred Prophet.

Like all caricatures, these images contain just enough truth for us to recognize whom they represent, but not enough truth to be true.

Because the real Jesus is not so easily stepped over. The real Jesus mystifies us.

Everyone was attracted to him—families, single women, prostitutes, supreme court judges, crooked lawyers, the intellectual elite, soldiers, home-makers, the terminally ill, social outcasts, religious leaders, political freedom fighters, and blue-collar workers. They all sought him out, even if he bewildered or confronted them. For Jesus's presence was always comforting, even though his words were not.

Jesus cared about people too much to be nice to them. Yes, he was kind to them. But kindness does not equal niceness. He loved them so much he had to be real with them. He had to tell them the truth, even when it hurt. Because according to Jesus himself, he came to seek the lost, find the lost, save the lost, and then party with the saved (see Luke 15:7, 10, 32; 19:10).

Seek. Find. Save. Celebrate. That was his mission.

But first he had to convince them they were lost in the first place. That's why he had to tell the truth.

And that's why people hated him.

It's time to get rid of the picture of Jesus as a warm and fuzzy, back-slapping buddy in heaven. That's not the Jesus of the Bible.

Jesus is not a gentle breeze blowing through history but a tempest raging across the ocean of time. Jesus said he came not to bring peace but division. If we look anywhere in the world where people have heard about him, we can see that his words were right on the nose. Nobody is neutral when it comes to the name of Jesus Christ. We don't get to abstain. He's drawn a line in the sand of eternity, and everyone stands on one side or another. Either we're on his side, fighting for him, or we're on the other side, fighting against him.

KINDNESS DOES NOT EQUAL NICENESS.

He is a poet and a mystic and a storyteller and a rebel. He is a tradesman and a lover and a spy sent from heaven to infiltrate our souls' most elaborate defenses. The one who slept through the storm is the one who storms into our sleep. He is the peace that only exists in the surrender of the soul. He was meek enough to hold a child's hand and man enough to grab a whip and cleanse the temple of those who would desecrate it.

He is sweet. He is sour. He is the emptying of the self and the filling of the soul. An enigma. A mystery. A speaker of riddles and solver of the mysteries of the universe. He is vulnerable yet impenetrable. A victim, a victor, a conqueror, and a comforter. A king and a peasant. He is wonder and joy wrapped around steel and sadness. How can we adequately describe the Nazarene, the Master? How can we touch someone so distant and yet so approachable?

Through faith. By pulling down the caricatures and saying, "Jesus, reveal yourself to me. I want you to be real in my life."

Most people won't say that because most people don't want that.

They prefer the caricature to the real thing.

THREE DOLLARS' WORTH OF GOD, PLEASE

Most people today can identify well with these unsettlingly honest words of Tim Hansel: "I'd like to buy $3 worth of God, please. Please, not enough to explode my soul or disturb my sleep, but just enough to equal a cup of warm milk or a snooze in the sunshine . . . I want ecstasy, not transformation, I want the warmth of the womb, not a new birth."[7]

In other words, I want a nice, safe Jesus and a nice, safe faith.

But it doesn't work that way.

Once, on a bus, I got into a conversation with a college student. "So, who do you think Jesus really is?" I asked.

He thought for a moment and then said, "A man of his word."

His response surprised me. It was actually a very good answer. I pointed out that Jesus said no one can come to God except through him (John 14:6). He also said if we don't believe that, we'll die in our sins (John 8:24). So if he really was a man of his word, he's the only way to God and our only hope of heaven.

If he really was a man of his word, he is much more than a man.

My young friend was silent. If he agreed that Jesus really was a man of his word, he would have to accept the consequences of Jesus's words. But he didn't want to do that.

He didn't want to acknowledge that Jesus is really God (as Jesus claimed to be), but he didn't want to go so far as to say Jesus isn't who he claimed either. He wanted a nice, safe, harmless little Jesus.

Three dollars' worth of God, please.

He preferred the caricature to the real thing because the real thing meant real consequences for his life. As John R. W. Stott observed, "You cannot fix God at the end of a telescope or a microscope and say, 'How interesting!' God is not interesting. He is deeply upsetting."[8]

THE PROBLEM WITH THE WORLD

Every religion, every philosophy has a way of looking at the world—the way it is and the way it should be. Some religions note that things aren't the way they should be. Some just tell us to try harder or to desire less or to ignore it or accept it or pretend everything is OK.

But everything's not OK. Our world is not the way it should be.

So what's the answer?

Christianity says things aren't the way they should be and will never be the way they should be because the problem is not a lack of effort or education or desire (or an abundance of desire) but a state of being. Our failings are wrapped up in our being fallen, sinful, and rebellious humans. And until our essence changes, our world will not change.

The problem stems from our choices and our nature. We are not and have never been (at least since the Garden of Eden) all God intended us to be. Early in his preaching ministry, the crowds began to follow Jesus, but "Jesus didn't trust them, because he knew what people were really like. No one needed to tell him about human nature" (John 2:24–25).

The world is not the way it should be because we are not the way we should be.

At its heart Christianity is all about removing our excuses and opening ourselves up to intimacy with God. And true intimacy with God can only come when we acknowledge our failures and shortcomings to him, then believe in his glorious promises to us.

Intimacy with God ultimately depends on our honesty with him. Yet most of us spend our lives covering our mistakes, hiding our failures, comparing ourselves favorably with others, and making up legitimate-sounding excuses for our moral meltdowns. We spend so much time hiding that we never approach God with the openness, honesty, and brokenness that leads to a deep and authentic spiritual life—and so we never become real.

REAL PROBLEMS, REAL SOLUTIONS

Unlike other philosophies and religions, Christianity tells the truth about our human condition: we often do what we don't want to do and what we know is wrong, and no amount of education, self-control, or moral training changes us. Why? And more importantly, what can be done about it? [9]

Christianity, above all other religions and philosophical systems, tackles the most searching questions humans have ever asked and offers not only answers but solutions. Blaise Pascal wrote: "What religion then . . . will, in fact, teach us our good, our duties, the weakness which turns us from them, the cause of this weakness, the remedies which can cure it, and the means of obtaining these remedies? All other religions have not been able to do so." [10]

Some religions offer solutions; others, explanations for our current situation. Christianity offers both. It honestly acknowledges our sin and provides the way of salvation. Christianity addresses guilt, loneliness, death, and despair head-on instead of sidestepping the issues like other religious systems:

You're not really a bad person, just try harder (denial).

Don't think about how bad you are (diversion).

If you feel good about yourself, your problems will all go away (disguise).

You're not as bad as most people (dilution).

You're really a god yourself (deification).

The solution for our human condition offered by Christianity is unique. It's not based on human effort or accomplishments but on God's efforts and accomplishments. Christianity says heaven cannot be earned, only given: "God saved you by his special favor when you believed. And you can't take credit for this; it is a gift from God. Salvation is not a reward for the good things we have done, so none of us can boast about it" (Ephesians 2:8–9).

The bridge between God and man does not reach from earth to heaven but from heaven to earth.

No other religion says that the only way to life lies in a person rather than in a set of religious principles, rites, or requirements. No other religion claims heaven is out of reach and can only be attained by grace. No other religion teaches that people are born sinners and should hate themselves for it. No other religion has a founder who claimed to not only know but to be the way to eternal life; who claimed to be God and backed that claim with miraculous signs; and who offered empirical evidence for his resurrection from the dead.[11]

Somewhere along the line, many of us have started associating Christianity with what we do rather than who we become. But Christianity is not a to-do list. It's a to-be list. It's not a religion of offering plates, pot-luck dinners, and sing-alongs. It's a journey of pain and of joy and of hope and of mystery.

Yet we've convinced ourselves that it's simply nice.

When we invite people to enter into the Christian life, we're inviting them into a war zone, not a vacation villa. It's a spiritual battlefield: "For we are not fighting against people made of flesh and blood, but against the evil rulers and authorities of the unseen world, against those mighty powers of darkness who rule this world, and against wicked spirits in the heavenly realms" (Ephesians 6:12).

Maybe if we made that clearer to new believers and stopped pretending that the Christian life is like a Norman Rockwell painting, they'd be more prepared for the wounds and heartaches of life on this fallen planet. Maybe they wouldn't feel so betrayed by God when life doesn't turn out to be a bed of roses.

No wonder so many people have become disillusioned with Christianity. They aren't getting the real picture anymore. We've pretended our way right into a subculture that seems about as relevant as the Stone Age and as attractive as a platypus.

It's a war zone. And nobody pretends in war. They become incredibly transparent with others and real with themselves.

NO PLACE TO HIDE

Christianity is not a crutch for the weak, it's the answer for the honest. No other religion calls people to such gut-wrenching honesty. There's always a place to hide in man-made religions, because we can't stand the thought of being in the place of no excuse and no escape and yet being offered love and relief because of the grace of God. So we invent religions with loopholes and back doors while God offers a grace with no fine print, no hidden costs, no strings attached.

The message of Christianity is simple, but it is not easy to accept. It's offer is free, but it was not cheap.

Christianity calls us to a transparency and an authenticity that will transform our lives and our relationships with others and force us to be honest with God about who we are. This honesty and vulnerability paves the way of conversion, creates the path of intimacy with God, and leads us by the hand along the narrow way of life. It is the one road to true and lasting freedom.

To become Christian we must love the truth more than we love ourselves. We must admit who we really are and accept God for who he really is.

Because there are no caricatures of God in heaven. Just the real thing.

READY TO HEAR, WILLING TO SAVE

Conversion is a matter of honesty with God. It's not just an intellectual acknowledgment that God exists; Romans 1:18–20 says that's simply common sense.

Conversion is the movement of a soul through the transformation of grace. It's a metamorphosis. A complete change. An entirely new birth and new life that results when we're finally honest to God about our failures. There can be no conversion without honesty. And there can be no conversion without a change of heart.

When we become believers, we are actually rescued from sin, Satan, and self. Saint Teresa of Avila described her conversion as being "snatched from the throat of the fearful dragon."[12] One puritan writer put it this way: "O happy day, when in thy love's sovereignty thou didst look on me, and call me by grace. Then did the dead heart begin to beat, the darkened eye glimmer with light, the dull ear catch thy echo, and I turned to thee and found thee, a God ready to hear, willing to save."[13]

Ready to hear. Willing to save. That's God.

God sees us as we truly are. Conversion occurs when we begin to see ourselves as he does rather than as we want to be seen. And each step we take toward repentance leads us closer to life-changing transparency. As we walk that road, we need to do three things.

1. We Need to Take God Seriously

One of the seven deadly sins of the medieval church was sloth, which is more than laziness. It's spiritual indifference. It's deadly because the apathetic never even seek, let alone find, Jesus.

The first step toward God is to care what happens. God says, "Turn to me. Turn your back on your old lifestyle. Let's start fresh." If we're determined to do things our own way rather than God's—regardless of what his Word says—we have no repentance in our hearts. We need to take him seriously and accept what he has to say about our lives. No matter how much it might hurt. Or where it might lead.

2. We Need to Agree with God about Our Lives

Coach John Wooden led UCLA to ten NCAA Division I national titles between 1964 and 1975. As the most successful college basketball coach of all time, Wooden had a simple philosophy: "Make no excuses and accept none."

Most of us would have had a rough time playing for Coach Wooden, because we don't like to be in that place where we can't make any excuses for what we've done. But the day the excuses fall away is the day honesty and openness with God finally unfold.

God never accepts our excuses. But he always accepts our repentance. He always accepts our honesty.

Repentance means to stop pretending, to change our minds, and to finally agree with God. To turn to him. Only the man who is aware of his sin gets close to God. Only the woman who discovers she is lost can ever be found.

If we've never acknowledged our sin to God, we've never become Christians. We might be faithful churchgoers, but we've never become children of God. But we can have new life with him. By turning to him right now. Right here. Today.

3. We Need to Turn Our Hearts toward God

Turning to God is a process that affects all of life.

When we cling to God, we let go of sin. When we love God, we hate sin.

When we follow God, we walk away from sin. We can't be pursuing both at the same time, because they lie in opposite directions. And to finally decide to walk the road to God is the most momentous decision of our lives.

Conversion occurs in a moment of clarity, submission, and honesty. It's the beginning of a long and difficult divorce with ourselves.

Repentance involves being honest to God and admitting that we've let him down, sinned against him, and are indebted to him. It's admitting we've hurt him. And how does he respond?

He forgives.

When we pray with David, "Create in me a clean heart, O God. Renew a right spirit within me" (Psalm 51:10), we're asking God to destroy our old hearts and to create responsive, new hearts that lean on him and learn from him and trust in him and love him more than anything else. We're asking for hearts of faith that follow Jesus.

Church isn't about guilt trips and bake sales and fund-raising campaigns. It's supposed to be a place where real people come to grow in a real, vibrant, living relationship with the real Jesus.

THE VIBRANT LIFE

The truly religious life is one marked by freedom rather than compulsion, love rather than ritual, and peace rather than guilt.

Jesus never once told people to be more religious, but he did invite them to come to him: "Are you tired? Worn out? Burned out on religion? Come to me. Get away with me and you'll recover your life. I'll show you how to take a real rest. Walk with me and work with me—watch how I do it. Learn the unforced rhythms of grace. I won't lay anything heavy or ill-fitting on you. Keep company with me and you'll learn to live freely and lightly" (Matthew 11:28–30 MSG).

Isn't that what we yearn for? A faith that frees us rather than enslaves us? A spirituality that's real rather than artificial? A place to get refreshed rather than dried out?

It all comes from Jesus. And it changes our whole lives. He came to give us richer, more vibrant lives than we could ever imagine: "I came so they can have real and eternal life, more and better life than they ever dreamed of" (John 10:10 MSG).

Religion wears me out; relationships fill me up. Jesus never intended for Christians to live with those constant, vague feelings of guilt that linger over us or with the fear that we might not be doing enough to earn God's favor. That's why he described Christianity as a relationship that cannot be severed rather than a set of requirements that must be kept (see John 8:34–36).

Accepting that, believing that, and living it out will lead you further and further away from religious posturing and closer and closer to the heart of God.

None of this is nice. But it leads us to something that is indescribably better than nice, better than all we could ever hope or dream or imagine— life with God. Peace with God. The freedom to finally pursue true intimacy with God. And a glorious inheritance that lasts forever and can never, never, never be taken away from us.

Come to think of it, that part does sound nice. Very nice.

Chapter 5

PSST . . . I'VE GOT A SECRET

Getting Real with God

The Master said, "In vain I have looked for a single man capable of seeing his own faults and bringing the charge home against himself."
—CONFUCIUS, *THE ANALECTS OF CONFUCIUS*

A few years ago, I met my wife and daughters at an ice-cream shop after I'd been gone all weekend. I thought it would be a fun, lighthearted homecoming party.

But as we were walking into the restaurant, the first thing my wife said was, "Ariel doesn't get any ice cream this afternoon."

Now, when those are the first words you hear after being gone for three days, it's a good clue that "Home Sweet Home" was not so sweet while you were gone.

Ariel was five years old at the time.

"Oh? Why not?" I asked.

"Ariel, tell your daddy."

Oh boy.

"I want you to tell him," Ariel said.

This was big.

"Go ahead, tell your father what happened to your cheeseburger."

Really big.

As we got in line to order our cones, my daughter mouthed her confession. It was her way of obeying in the letter but not the spirit of the law. Finally, after my wife did the Furrowed Brow Look along with the Stern Hands on the Hips Pose and the Intimidating Eyebrow Raise, my daughter said, "I put it somewhere."

At this point in the conversation, it doesn't take a rocket scientist to figure out that she probably didn't put it in her mouth.

"Where did you put your cheeseburger?"

She looked around at all the people in the restaurant who were staring our way by now. "The toilet."

"You put your cheeseburger in the toilet," I said, letting the words sink in. I even said that with a straight face. You can tell I'd been a dad for a while by then. I was used to things like this.

She nodded somberly.

Then I said the next thing that popped into my mind, and I made sure I said it loud enough that all those strangers listening in on our conversation could hear. "And why, exactly, did you put your cheeseburger in the toilet?"

"Because I didn't like it."

Did you think that would improve the taste? I thought. But I didn't say it. I held back. In my mind I could picture that cheeseburger stuck in the pipes, the water backing up and flowing over the top of the toilet, and my wife plunging until she discovered an intact (albeit soggy), medium-rare cheeseburger floating to the surface.

I just shook my head, and as I ordered the ice cream, I said something wise and fatherly, like, "Well, I hope you've learned your lesson."

But of course, all the time I was thinking, *The toilet, huh? I wish I'd thought of that when I was a kid. I always tried to hide stuff in my pockets.*

Kids, huh?

Always covering up the things they've done wrong and trying to hide stuff by flushing it down the toilet, slipping it into their pockets, tossing it to the dog, or sticking it under their beds.

That's kids for you. But certainly not us adults.

No, we're much more sophisticated. We have much more elaborate schemes for covering our tracks and keeping our secrets. Pick up a paper or turn on the news any day of the week, and you'll find stories of companies that have cooked the books, celebrities who've had their hidden trysts exposed, sports heroes who've failed to live up to our expectations, or politicians who've been caught red-handed in some kind of double-talk. Whether it's corporate lawyers shredding papers or upper-level executives stating phony earnings figures, the story is always the same—someone has gone to great lengths to cover up a wrong and conceal it from others.

But actually we don't need to open up the newspaper or turn on the evening news at all. We don't have to look any farther than the mirror to find someone who is a master of disguise.

SECRET IDENTITIES

Every summer a new batch of superhero movies draws huge crowds to theaters. Whether it's the latest adventures of Spider-Man, Superman, Batman, X-Men, the Hulk, or another in the endless stream of comic books come to life, we can't seem to get enough of those crime-fighting good guys with their secret identities, the secret lives they can't risk exposing.

I'd venture to say that even if you don't have a skin-tight, form-fitting, polyester, crime-fighting jumpsuit hanging in your closet, you have a secret identity too. Just like I do.

But as much as we're able to hide our true selves from other people, there is no hiding our real identities from God. "The LORD's searchlight penetrates the human spirit, exposing every hidden motive" (Proverbs 20:27). He knows about every cheeseburger we've ever tried to flush away from view. There are no secrets, and there are no secret lives before God.

And unlike the superheroes we admire in the movies, our secret lives are anything but heroic.

A singer and songwriter friend of mine lives in Nashville, Tennessee. One night when I was attending a conference there, I stayed overnight at his house. In the morning he got up to make me breakfast. When I was ready to leave, he mentioned that his wife was upstairs but didn't want to come down because she didn't want me to see her without her makeup on.

I looked around at my friend's house. It was immaculate. Everything was exactly where it was supposed to be. There were no toys scattered across the floor to indicate that two boys lived there. The couch was color-coordinated to match the carpeting and the wallpaper. Unburned candles decorated the shelves. And every clock in his house was set to exactly the same time. A picture of my friend and his wife lay on the end table. She was gorgeous—perfect. Everything was perfect.

But she wouldn't come downstairs to meet me. So I went on my way, and I've never met my friend's wife. Why? Because she didn't want me to see her without her makeup.

She would rather not meet me at all than let me see her when she looked like the person she really is, before she could make herself look perfect.

I suppose, though, that I shouldn't come down too hard on her.

Because I do the same thing.

WE'VE GOT A WHOLE ARSENAL OF ELABORATE DISGUISES TO COVER OUR FLAWS.

No, I don't wear makeup, but I don't especially want people to see me for who I really am. So I decorate my life to create a certain impression. Just like everyone does. Whether it's the kind of cars we drive, the cool sunglasses we slip on, the three-piece suits we wear, the leather jackets we pull out for the weekend, the hairstyles we have, or the fake smiles we paste on our faces, we're all good at hiding.

We've got a whole arsenal of elaborate disguises to cover our flaws and hide our wrinkles and mask the less-than-picture-perfect selves we are. Psychologist Dr. William Backus nailed us when he wrote, "Many Christians think they must be nice fellows—always-smiling, above-it-all, super-people who are perpetually happy no matter what. When they are hurt and react with genuine anger, they hide it and cover it up with various shrouds, such as religious-sounding words, smiles, grins, shrugs, silence."[1]

Yet God sees beneath those religious-sounding words, smiles, grins, shrugs, and silences. He sees inside our hearts. He knows us for who we really are. He knows about our wounds and our mistakes.

So why do we spend so much time hiding? Why do we wear so many masks?

I know for myself, sometimes I'm afraid of what people will think of me if they find out the truth. Other times I want to avoid the consequences of my double life's being revealed. And of course I want to protect my reputation.

INSIDE OUT AND UPSIDE DOWN

Each year Americans spend billions of dollars on designer clothes, weight-loss programs, plastic surgery, exercise equipment, and skin-care products.

We tune in to reality shows by the millions to watch normal people like us get transformed into magazine-cover models. Why are we so obsessed with our outward appearance and so lax at developing (and noticing) inner beauty?

We're overly concerned with outer-impression management and not all that excited about living lives of inner beauty or integrity. Our prayers should echo the Puritans who prayed, "Raise me above the smiles and frowns of the world, regarding it as a light thing to be judged by men."[2]

When the prophet Samuel arrived in town to crown the new king of Israel, he was impressed by the appearance of Eliab, one of the sons of a man named Jesse. Samuel knew one of the boys would be the next ruler and thought Eliab looked like king material. "But the LORD said to Samuel, 'Don't judge by his appearance or height, for I have rejected him. The LORD doesn't make decisions the way you do! People judge by outward appearance, but the LORD looks at a person's thoughts and intentions'" (1 Samuel 16:7).

Truth be told, we're not much different from Samuel. We still look at the outward appearance of the people we meet. We're still impressed by the rock-hard body or the sparkling wit or the stunning figure or the designer wardrobe. And we know that people judge us by our appearance too. So we do all we can to make sure it's as impressive as it can be. We don't want anyone to see us without our makeup.

But there are no secrets and no secret lives before God.

In Matthew 23 Jesus called the prominent religious leaders of his day hypocrites (meaning they were two-faced, or stage actors). Why? Because they didn't practice what they preached. They were only acting a part. They loved attention and prestige more than humility and were more concerned about image than substance. They locked people out of God's kingdom by their false teachings. They prioritized earthly things above heavenly treasures. They nitpicked about religious rituals but forgot about living lives of justice, mercy, and faith. Their purity was counterfeit because their motives and intentions were rotten to the core. And they showed how two-faced they were by venerating saints of the past while acting like the people who had persecuted those saints.

Here's what Jesus said to them:

> You're hopeless, you religion scholars and Pharisees! Frauds! You burnish the surface of your cups and bowls so they sparkle in the sun, while the

insides are maggoty with your greed and gluttony. Stupid Pharisee! Scour the insides, and then the gleaming surface will mean something.

You're hopeless, you religion scholars and Pharisees! Frauds! You're like manicured grave plots, grass clipped and the flowers bright, but six feet down it's all rotting bones and worm-eaten flesh. People look at you and think you're saints, but beneath the skin you're total frauds. (Matthew 23:25–28 MSG)

Talk about God's searchlight penetrating the human spirit—"people look at you and think you're saints, but beneath the skin you're total frauds."

Ouch.

We don't show people our whole selves. We let them see only the carefully edited version of our lives. We leave out the unsavory parts and embellish the complimentary ones.

But God reads the unabridged version. He sees it all. Every soul stands naked before him. There is no hiding, no covering ourselves up. No makeup will disguise our thoughts or intentions. And we can't stay upstairs when God comes over. Even if we could, it wouldn't matter because he's already seen us without makeup. He's seen our hearts.

Even though no one else may see our thoughts or hear about our secret fantasies, God knows all about them: "You spread out our sins before you— our secret sins—and you see them all" (Psalm 90:8). "I, the LORD, search all hearts and examine secret motives" (Jeremiah 17:10). "God . . . knows the secrets of every heart" (Psalm 44:21).

Nothing gets past him. No cheeseburgers get away unnoticed. In the end, nobody really gets away with anything.

THE INVISIBLE TOP TEN

What are some of these secret sins God sees? The things we hide so well? Jesus explained it this way: "From within, out of a person's heart, come evil thoughts, sexual immorality, theft, murder, adultery, greed, wickedness, deceit, eagerness for lustful pleasure, envy, slander, pride, and foolishness. All these vile things come from within; they are what defile you and make you unacceptable to God" (Mark 7:21–23).

All of these things bubble up from the bottom of our hearts. They aren't dropped in from somewhere else. The source of these sins is ourselves.

Colossians 3:5 says, "So put to death the sinful, earthly things lurking within you."

Some people say, Be true to your heart. But if all of those things Jesus listed dwell in the human heart, why would anyone ever want to be true to that?

No, we shouldn't be true to our hearts, for our hearts aren't true.

Becoming real doesn't mean following our hearts or being true to ourselves. If the human heart is truly deceitful above all things (see Jeremiah 17:9), and if we need to deny ourselves to find the truth (see Luke 9:23), then why would anyone want to follow his heart or be true to himself? Why would anyone want to follow something that's deceitful or be true to something that's false?

Trusting in our own desires will only lead us astray, further and further from God's plan for our lives. The only way to find ourselves is to let his truth shape, mold, and guide us. Shaking off the fetters of our own hearts before God is the beginning of finding truth. "Fear of the LORD is the beginning of wisdom. Knowledge of the Holy One results in understanding" (Proverbs 9:10).

When people look at our lives, they see the surface sins—things like stealing or murder or sleeping around. But God sees below the surface, to the underlying currents. He sees what goes on in our hearts and minds. That's his specialty. Because that's where most of our problems begin.

Let's take a look at a few of the most common invisible sins and hidden currents that flow through our lives. We'll call this list The Top 10 Invisible Sins.

10. Prejudice: Looking Down on Others before Getting to Know Them

We're subtle and elegant in our prejudices. We call the teenagers at our churches "the young people," but we would bristle with indignation if they called us "the old people." We avoid certain parts of town because "those people" live there. But no one else sees our prejudices. We keep them carefully hidden. And they quickly lead to number nine.

9. Hatred: Harboring a Bitterness that Blossoms into Loathing

Harboring hatred against anyone is comparable, in God's eyes, to murder (see 1 John 3:15) and keeps us from really loving God. Anytime we think, *I hate his guts, I wish she were dead,* or *I can't stand her,* we're letting our hearts murder people God loves. As the apostle John wrote, "If someone says, 'I love God,' but hates a Christian brother or sister, that person is a liar; for if we don't love people we can see, how can we love God, whom we have not seen?" (1 John 4:20). The answer is, we can't.

8. Envy: Desiring Someone Else's Position in Life

Envy is closely related to jealousy (desiring someone else's affection) and coveting (desiring someone else's assets or belongings). But is that really so bad? And is it really that common?

Actually, coveting is so prevalent and so unconscious that in Romans 7:7 Paul said he wouldn't have even known it was wrong if God's Word hadn't told him not to do it.

Anytime we wish we had someone else's job, body, looks, smarts, money, spouse, waistline, house, clothes, biceps, car, or position in life, we've begun walking a slippery slope that has three deadly valleys of desire: envy, jealousy, and coveting.

7. Greed: Lacking Contentment and Always Wanting More

Greed gives birth to envy, jealousy, and coveting. Colossians 3:5 puts it this way: "Don't be greedy for the good things of this life, for that is idolatry."

That's pretty blunt: Greed = Idolatry.

But why would greed be idolatrous?

Because when we're greedy, we seek fulfillment from something other than God, and we set our hearts on something other than him. Greed is our way of saying, "God, you're not enough for me; I need something besides you to be satisfied." And anytime something other than God fills our hearts and our dreams, we've become ensnared in idolatry.

Of course, our culture has put a positive spin on greed by renaming it *ambition*. Well, call it what you will, in God's eyes greed, by any name, is just another form of idolatry.

6. Unforgiveness: Clinging to Past Wrongs and Continuing to Take Offense at Them

Oh, we're good at holding grudges.

But according to Jesus, if we want to hold on to our grudges against others, we shouldn't expect God to forgive us: "If you refuse to forgive others, your Father will not forgive your sins" (Matthew 6:15). Too many people are unwilling to let go of past wrongs, and that shuts them out of receiving God's forgiveness and leads to the next invisible sin.

5. Resentment: Nurturing Feelings of Bitterness against Others

When unforgiveness is given a chance to germinate, it soon grows into resentment. When other people receive favors, promotions, blessings, opportunities, or get breaks that we wish we had, we get resentful. There's nothing pure driving feelings like that. It's simply selfishness rearing its head.

4. Anger: Losing Our Patience When We Shouldn't

Anger isn't necessarily wrong. Jesus became incensed when people made a mockery out of the sacred offerings of his day. But here's the question—are we getting angry at the things that anger God or just at the things that inconvenience us?

Most of the time our anger comes from the things that annoy *us,* not the things that annoy God. And how do we deal with our anger? Do we let it simmer, or do we let it go? Clinging to anger leads to sin. Paul said, "'Don't sin by letting anger gain control over you.' Don't let the sun go down while you are still angry, for anger gives a mighty foothold to the Devil" (Ephesians 4:26–27).

3. Unbelief: Trusting in Ourselves Rather Than in God for Salvation

Some people hide for years in a church. We can't see their unbelief on the surface; they go through all the right motions—Bible studies, prayer meetings, choir rehearsals, baptism, worship services. They know all the right words. But deep down, there has never been any faith in their hearts at all. Sometimes they may even fool themselves into thinking they truly are believers: "On judgment day many will tell me, 'Lord, Lord, we prophesied in your name and cast out demons in your name and performed many miracles in your name.' But I will reply, 'I never knew you. Go away; the things you did were unauthorized'" (Matthew 7:22–23).

People may be able to hide their unbelief from us, but never from God.

2. Lust: Fostering Sexual Desire for Someone Other Than Your Spouse

There's a difference between being attracted to someone and fantasizing about sleeping with him or her. Physical attraction or admiring someone's beauty isn't wrong. After all, God designed us as sexual beings—that attraction is part of our makeup. But those leering looks and suggestive thoughts have got to go. There's a time and a place for sexual gratification, and that time and place is within the covenant of marriage.

Some people toy with lust all the time, and no one ever knows. Well, let me correct that—one Person knows.

1. Pride: Thinking More Highly of Ourselves Than We Should

Pride is really the soil from which all other sins grow, as we learned in chapter 2.

■

Whew.

If we read through a list like that a couple of times, we'll begin to see the stuff that lurks beneath the surface of our own lives. God wants us to honor him not only when people are looking or when we might get caught, but also when it seems totally safe to sin. And Jesus doesn't just ask us to control only our bodies but our imaginations as well (see Matthew 5:22, 28, 44). Self-control extends to every area of life: deeds, words, and thoughts.

It's no fun to look at all the secret sins that have slithered into our lives, but according to Paul, revealing our secret sins to us can be God's way of drawing us closer to him (see 2 Corinthians 7:9–10). When we stop trying to hide and strive instead to be found out, we're on the right track.

When Job asked God why bad things were happening in his life, he appealed to his authentic living: "I have never turned away a stranger but have opened my doors to everyone. Have I tried to hide my sins as people normally do, hiding my guilt in a closet?" (Job 31:32–33).

Job didn't try to hide. No toilet is ever big enough, no closet wide enough for our sins.

God doesn't just want us to say no to sin. He wants us to say yes to him. That means pursuing purity with our bodies and with our minds. It means living honestly before him, owning up to the invisible sins we've let creep into our lives, and asking him to rescue us. From ourselves.

THE FINAL DISGUISE

OK, time to be honest.

What's in your closet? (I won't ask what's in your toilet—I don't even want to go there!) What sins are lurking beneath the surface of your life? What secrets is God's searchlight exposing?

I've gazed into my heart. I've seen what his searchlight has revealed, and it's not pretty. "It is shameful even to talk about the things that ungodly people do in secret" (Ephesians 5:12). I was ungodly for a long time, and my thoughts all too often still wander back into their old haunts.

We have to strip all the masks and disguises away and talk to God about our secret identities. Why? Because he doesn't know?

Of course God knows. He sees everything. He isn't up in heaven saying, "Gosh, I wonder what Steve is struggling with down there," or "Gossip! Breanne struggles with gossiping? I had no idea!"

Repentance is nothing more than agreeing with God about who we really are and desiring him to change us into who he wants us to be: "Finally, I confessed all my sins to you and stopped trying to hide them. I said to myself, 'I will confess my rebellion to the LORD.' And you forgave me! All my guilt is gone" (Psalm 32:5).

He forgives and he forgets when we finally stop hiding.

That day at the ice-cream parlor, my daughter told me she was sorry about the whole cheeseburger incident. I nodded and smiled. Then I handed her the ice-cream cone I'd ordered for her while she was staring down at the floor.

"I forgive you," I said.

And we sat down to enjoy our ice cream, together.

If you've been hiding something from God, fess up. He's waiting to forgive you. And he's waiting to welcome you to the greatest homecoming party of all.

Chapter 6

LETTING GO OF THE BOAT

Learning to Live by Faith

*The steps of faith fall on the seeming void
and find the rock beneath.*

—JOHN GREENLEAF WHITTIER

August 18, 1899
Somewhere off the coast of North Carolina

Wind lashed at their faces. Water sprayed across the deck. The *Priscilla* tipped dangerously to the side and then came to rest on the reef off a deserted portion of North Carolina's coast. As the minutes passed, the wind did not stop. Little by little the boat began to break apart.

The crew and the captain's family (who had decided to join him for this trip) shouted into the darkness, hoping beyond hope that someone, anyone, would hear them. But who would hear them in the middle of the night, in the middle of a hurricane, in the middle of nowhere?

Rasmus Midgett would. He worked for the United States Life-Saving Service, an organization that eventually gave rise to the U.S. Coast Guard in 1915. It was Rasmus's job to patrol on horseback the remote North Carolina coastlines. If he found any evidence of a stranded ship, he would return to the life-saving station several miles away and alert the other members of his crew. Then they would rush back and either row out to help the stranded sailors or use an elaborate rope-and-pulley system to rescue as many people as possible.

On that particular night, Rasmus was riding his horse along the coast when he saw debris washing up on shore. Boards. Planks. Pieces of a ship. And he knew.

He knew a ship was being destroyed by the waves. Pounded to pieces by the roaring surf.

That's when he heard the desperate cries of the stranded men cutting through the night. And because of the amount of debris and the fierceness of the storm, Rasmus knew that if he took the time to return to his life-saving station, by the time he and his partners returned, there wouldn't be anyone left to save.

ONE AT A TIME . . . JUMP!

So Rasmus Midgett dismounted and ran toward the ocean. He timed the pulsing, beating waves, and as they receded into the frothy sea, he sprinted out across the wet sand and screamed into the storm, "One at a time . . . Jump, and I'll save you!"

Then, as the waves rushed toward him, he raced back toward the safety of the shore.

Now, I'm not sure what those ten men on the boat were thinking when they heard his voice. But I know what I would have been thinking. *What was that? I must be hearing things. A voice? Is there someone out there? Did you hear that? Did you hear that voice?!*

A few moments earlier, the men had watched as Captain Springsteen's wife and two sons were overwhelmed by the waters and washed overboard to their deaths. All the sailors knew this was a deadly storm. Yet a voice was floating up through the darkness, promising salvation to all who would let go and jump.

Could it possibly be? Leap from a boat into the middle of a churning sea? But that would be insane! Wouldn't it?

As the waves rushed out into the ocean again, Rasmus ran out toward the hulking mass of the doomed ship. He yelled for the first sailor to jump.

And, wonder beyond wonders, the man did.

He walked to the edge of the deck and leaped into the darkness toward the waiting arms of a man he could not see. A man whose voice had pierced the storm. As the waters swept toward them to devour two more lives, Rasmus Midgett and this sailor struggled to the beach. One man's life was saved.

Six more times Rasmus returned to the sea that night. Each time he called out, another man jumped, until Captain Springsteen and two of his crew were left. All three were too weak to even stand up. So three times Rasmus Midgett climbed a rope hanging from the edge of the boat, hoisted a man onto his shoulders, climbed down the rope, and headed for safety.

On his final trip, while rescuing the captain, (who weighed over two hundred pounds), Rasmus was too slow to make it to shore. This time the waters roared over him and swallowed both him and the captain as the rescued sailors watched in horror.

But when the waters receded, the men saw Rasmus still standing, his feet planted firmly, their captain on his back. He struggled up the beach and deposited the captain on the sand.

That night, without a rescue boat or a team of trained Life Savers, Rasmus Midgett rescued ten men.

For his courage he was awarded the highest medal in the United States Life-Saving Service, the Gold Life-Saving Medal.[1]

Ten men were alive because one man had the courage to brave the storm, and they had the courage to let go of their doomed ship, to trust in the voice of a savior they could not see, and to step out in faith.

"One at a time . . . Jump, and I'll save you."

EVIDENCE OF THE UNSEEN

The author of the book of Hebrews wrote one of the most concise and memorable definitions of faith ever: "What is faith? It is the confident assurance that what we hope for is going to happen. It is the evidence of things we cannot yet see" (Hebrews 11:1).

Did you catch that? Faith doesn't need evidence, it is evidence. Faith is the evidence of things we cannot yet see. Faith proves the invisible.

The life of faith is not the life of logic but of trust. Since God desires our faith rather than simply our acknowledgment, he chooses to remain out of sight.

Yes, he calls to us. Yes, he gives us hints of his presence. But he doesn't overwhelm us with evidence. He whispers to our souls rather than shouting in our ears. He assures us in our spirits rather than appearing to our eyes.

For even physical proof will never convince the hardhearted (see Luke 16:31).

Besides, God doesn't want reasonable religionists, he wants faith-filled followers. And if we can prove something, we don't need faith.

So the life of a believer is marked by faith in the unseen, not the seen. The invisible, not the apparent. "We fix our eyes not on what is seen, but on what is unseen. For what is seen is temporary, but what is unseen is eternal" (2 Corinthians 4:18 NIV). But how do we fix our eyes on the unseen?

Through faith.

Remember Thomas? He didn't believe Jesus had risen from the dead. He said, "I'll believe it when I see it!"

Well, after Jesus let him touch his hands and side, Thomas finally believed. And Jesus told him, "You believe because you have seen me. Blessed are those who haven't seen me and believe anyway" (John 20:29). In essence, Jesus was saying, "I finally convinced you, and that's good. But it's even better if I don't have to prove myself. You thought seeing was believing, but I'm telling you that seeing isn't believing, believing is seeing when there's nothing there to see. Those with that kind of faith are the most blessed of all."

MOST OFTEN PEOPLE'S REASONS FOR REJECTING THE IDEA OF GOD'S EXISTENCE AREN'T INTELLECTUAL BUT EMOTIONAL.

Most often people's reasons for rejecting the idea of God's existence aren't intellectual but emotional. Psalm 14:1 doesn't say, "Only fools say in their heads, 'There is no God.'" It says, "Only fools say in their hearts, 'There is no God.'" People don't want to admit God exists, because if he does, they know they'll be accountable to him. As Helmut Thielicke once said, "In countless talks about Christ it has been my experience that what stands between men and Christ is not intellectual arguments but sins. They are not willing to give up this or that. They want reservations and privileges before God. Hence they will not accept Christ as such because of the consequences."[2]

Faith always requires letting go of what we do see and clinging to what we don't. To live a life of faith, we must let go of our security and cling to a promise. We must let go of our safeguards and trust in a Savior.

If we are ever going to grab hold of an authentic spiritual life with God, we must learn to live by faith, not by sight (see 2 Corinthians 5:7).

Sometimes all we can hear is a voice calling through the darkness. We want to see, God wants us to believe. We want things proven, he wants faith in the unprovable. We wonder about tomorrow, he wants us to trust him today. If the left section of the mind prefers intellect and the right half imagination, then faith is a meeting of the minds. Faith is where imagination and intellect hold hands.

"One at a time," Jesus says. "Jump! Let go of your inhibitions and fears and hesitations! Step to the edge of your reason, jump, and I'll save you."

LIVING BY FAITH

A friend of mine named Mike watched his life get dismantled one plank at a time by the storm of cancer. When I asked him how he felt toward God, he told me that at first he was angry. One day he stood in his apartment with the shades drawn and clenched his fists and wept and shook and shouted at God.

"But finally," Mike said, "I realized two things: Either God is in control or he's not—and he is. And either I trust him or I don't—and I do. After that, my attitude changed."

Mike had found the secret to true peace: true trust. He saw clearly how fragile his boat was. He saw the storm raging around him, but he was willing to step off this life into the darkness of faith—where he found God's waiting arms.

A couple of months after we talked, Mike arrived on the shore of eternity, carried home in the arms of Jesus.

Mike had learned to live out these words of Peter: "You love him even though you have never seen him. Though you do not see him, you trust him" (1 Peter 1:8).

Faith changes the way we live.

If we don't believe the chair will hold our weight, we won't sit down. If we don't think the medicine will help get rid of our cold, we won't take it.

On the other hand, if we believed we could fly, we'd jump off a skyscraper. The stronger our beliefs, the more likely we'll act in accordance with them. Our actions serve as evidence of what we believe.

God calls us to begin a life of faith at conversion and to continue a life of faith through submission. Both faith in Christ and faithfulness to Christ are essential. But neither is easy to live out. Here are five practical guidelines to help us live out our faith.

1. Faith Accepts the Mysteries of Life

Experience doesn't always have a lesson embedded in it. Sometimes God allows stuff to happen to us not to teach us a specific lesson but to grow us into his kind of children. He's more concerned about our character than our cleverness, our integrity than our ability to siphon meaning from the things that happen in our lives.

Even Jesus questioned why God had forsaken him. Remember? On the cross? "My God, my God, why have you forsaken me?"(Matthew 27:46). Bible scholars may debate about the theological implications of these words, but it sure seems to me that at this point in his suffering, even Jesus couldn't decipher the big picture. I know his faith in God never wavered. But when the questions loomed larger than life, Jesus cried out, "Why God? Why have you done this to me?" I find that reassuring. Because I know Jesus can identify with me when I ask the same question.

Think about this—if God is truly fighting for us, if he is really on our side, then what's the danger of putting ourselves completely in his arms? Even when we don't understand his ways or his reasons?

Total trust will free us from worry. For if we dwell in God through faith, the uncertainties of life can never touch us, because our souls reside in the heart of God—and what can harm us when we dwell there? Not hardships. Not problems. Not heartaches. Not troubles.

Nothing can separate God's children from his love.

Nothing.

Imagine how much peace we could experience if we really believed that.

God never asks that we understand him, only that we love him and trust him. We need to learn to hang on to our faith and stick with God. Even when he doesn't explain himself. Even when life doesn't make sense. Life isn't a puzzle to be solved, it's a gift to be enjoyed. So let's accept the questions in life and let go of our need to know all the answers.

We won't always know God's motives, but we do know his heart. And that's enough. For when we realize the depth of his mercy and the height of his love, we can live at peace with our circumstances, no matter how inexplicable they are. We know he is only handing us blessings, however painful they may appear or how hard they are to swallow.

Living by faith means we won't always have all the answers, so we might as well stop trying to understand everything. Accept the mysteries of life. Trust in God. Rely on him.

His arms are strong enough to hold us, even when the waves wash over our heads.

2. Faith Takes Risks

Over and over again, Jesus emphasized the pleasure God takes when we risk our all to increase his kingdom.

In a story Jesus told in Matthew 25:14–30, a landowner put three servants in charge of different amounts of money while he went on a journey. Two of the men invested the money while the third guy buried his cash because he was afraid he might lose it. When the landowner returned, he congratulated the two men who had invested their money and berated the man who had buried his. The landowner offered this summary to the men: "To those who use well what they are given, even more will be given, and they will have an abundance. But from those who are unfaithful, even what little they have will be taken away" (Matthew 25:29).

Did you catch that? The guy who played it safe was called unfaithful. That means being faithful to God doesn't mean socking away what he gives us for a rainy day but risking all in our daily quest to be faithful to him.

But doesn't it seem reasonable to bury someone else's money? I mean, otherwise it could get lost, right? Doesn't it seem a little risky to invest another's money, since there's a chance we could lose it?

Yes. That's the point.

God is into risk taking. He's not into playing it safe. God wants us to live out on a limb, not just step out there once in a while. We have to let go of the boat and step off the deck, not hold on with one hand, trying to play it safe.

God is looking for people who are interested in risking everything to follow him. So ask yourself:

Am I playing it spiritually safe, or am I going to the place where I have to rely on God?

Am I stuck in a rut, or am I focused on the frontier?

Am I doing only the stuff I'm good at, or am I attempting more than I think I can accomplish?

Am I indulging in myself, or am I walking in obedience?

If we really believe God desires what's best for us and has the power to orchestrate our lives in a way that brings us blessing, why would we ever hold back? There's a reason we use the phrase *stepping out in faith*. Faith always involves stepping out, letting go, risking something. Those who hold back reveal their lack of faith.

According to Jesus the life-graspers will be the life-losers: "Whoever clings to this life will lose it, and whoever loses this life will save it. . . . Those who love their life in this world will lose it. Those who despise their life in this world will keep it for eternal life" (Luke 17:33; John 12:25).

The life-losers will be the life-receivers. Those who play it safe with their souls will lose all, while those who risk everything will be welcomed into the throne room of the King.

3. Faith Focuses on Faithfulness

Following God and living a faith-filled life are not intellectual exercises. It's not logical, sensible, or practical to live for Jesus. How could faith be sensible when the message of the cross is foolishness? (see 1 Corinthians 1:18). How could faithfulness be practical when we're called to sacrifice everything and follow Jesus? (see Luke 14:33). If we're interested in what's safe, predicable, and popular, we shouldn't sign on with Jesus Christ.

Life is a journey, and living a life of faith requires not just the faith to begin the journey but also the faithfulness to complete it. God wants both our faith and our faithfulness—and faithfulness means risking all to serve him. But think about it. What's the bigger risk: investing our lives in following God or going our own way instead?

Life is a brief and wonderful flicker of hope leaping up through the mists of eternity. Some choose to dive into the mystery of it all; others choose to pull back where it seems saner and safer. They never leave the boat. Then one day it splinters to pieces all around them, and they're swept out to sea rather than carried safely to shore.

4. Faith Looks beyond the Circumstances

Faith is forward-looking. "We don't look at the troubles we can see right now; rather, we look forward to what we have not yet seen. For the troubles we see will soon be over, but the joys to come will last forever" (2 Corinthians 4:18).

In an Ethiopian folk tale, a rich merchant bets his poor servant that he can't survive a night on top of the country's tallest mountain without food, shelter, companionship, and clothing. The young man readily accepts the challenge, excited about the promised reward.

But as the night draws near, he's filled with anxiety. What if he can't make it? How will he survive?

Finally his friend offers to build a campfire on a neighboring mountain. "Then, throughout the night," he explains, "as the frigid winds bite into your face, you can look across the valley and see my fire. You'll be warmed by the thought of it. When you feel lonely, look through the darkness and think of me."

So during the night, the young servant gazes through the darkness and is comforted by the glow of his friend's fire. He survives and receives his reward.[3]

The way to rise above your circumstances is to look beyond them to the future we have with God and the promises that are ours through Christ. When loneliness grips us or the darkness closes in, he lets us glimpse a fire burning on a distant hill. A fire we see by faith.

And all the while, our Friend is waiting, and dawn is drawing near.

5. Faith Is Ready to Respond to God

I once met a pastor who'd "settled in." He was certain God had called him to that place—permanently.

"But what if God calls you to someplace else?" I asked.

"He won't."

And even if he does, I thought, *you won't hear him.*

God may call any one of us to move. Tonight. Across the globe. He may ask us to change career paths tomorrow. Will we do it? Or are we too tied to places and positions and prestige to follow him?

Are we willing to heed his voice? Are we ready to roam the planet? Are we ready to leave everything behind?

Locations, jobs, obligations, commitments, and possessions can entangle us. A responsive faith is marked by a freedom that comes from living lightly as pilgrims on this planet.

Without a responsive faith, we'll become like that comfortable pastor who'd settled in.

Abraham might have settled in rather than embrace his life's true journey. Imagine if God's conversation with him had gone like this:

"Abe, I want you to leave all of this and go to a place I will tell you about."

"No thanks, God. I'm retired."

"Not any more, Abe. I'm calling you to something new."

"Maybe you didn't hear me, God. This is my home. We've settled in here. Trust me on this one. I know what I'm talking about."

Instead Abraham stepped out, lived by faith rather than by sight, and risked all to follow God. And his faith still shines as an example for us today: "It was by faith that Abraham obeyed when God called him to leave home and go to another land that God would give him as his inheritance. He went without knowing where he was going. And even when he reached the land God promised him, he lived there by faith" (Hebrews 11:8–9).

Let's be ready to go wherever God leads. Just like Abraham was.

LEANING ON THE UNSEEN

On August 18, 1899, Captain Springsteen and the crew of the *Priscilla* found that their only hope of survival was to trust in a mere voice floating up from the waves: "One at a time . . . Jump, and I'll save you!"

When they did, they were rescued from their stranded and battered ship in the midst of a dark and deadly sea.

God first calls us to leave the boat and become his children through faith. Then he asks us daily to set our minds and hearts on him, to see beyond this life to eternity, and to trust him as he carries us safely to shore.

It's not easy. It's not safe. It's not practical.

The storm is raging. Life surrounds us with uncertainties, pain, sadness, questions, heartaches, and setbacks. It's easier to cling to what we've known than to let our lives be guided by faith. It's much easier to fix our eyes on the seen than on the unseen.

But, oh! To fall into those waiting arms and say, "Take me wherever you will, Jesus. I put my life in your hands!"

In the end, there's really nothing freer, safer, saner, or wiser than that.

PART 2
AWAKENING

One night on his way to a city called Paran, Jacob set up camp and fell asleep in a field. The Bible tells us he used a rock for a pillow. That's a great little detail. It was a normal field. On a normal night. With a normal rock.

But that night Jacob dreamed a magnificent dream that God was speaking to him, promising him great things. "Then Jacob woke up and said, 'Surely the LORD is in this place, and I wasn't even aware of it.' He was afraid and said, 'What an awesome place this is! It is none other than the house of God—the gateway to heaven'" (Genesis 28:16–17).

Imagine waking up one day with that revelation—God was right next to you, and you weren't even aware of it. God himself was in that normal-looking place, and you didn't realize it.

Now think back to this morning when you opened your eyes. When you flopped out of bed and headed to the bathroom to take your shower. Waking up from a normal night. Just like Jacob.

And guess what? The Lord was in that place. Were you aware of it?

He was at the breakfast table with you. He was with you at work. In the car. At the coffee shop, the golf course, and the soccer game. Were you awake to his presence? Or have you been asleep the whole time?

Too many people will awaken in eternity to the revelation that God was right beside them their whole lives, but they didn't realize it. They'll lower their eyes and whisper, "Oh, what have I done . . . The Lord was in that place, and I didn't even know. God was always beside me, but I acted as if he were on vacation or in exile or dead and buried in the distant past . . . Oh, what have I done . . ."

God is in this place, and most of us aren't even aware of it.

God is by your side. And if you're a Christian, he is actually dwelling within your heart.

"What an awesome place this is! It is none other than the house of God—the gateway to heaven!"

I heard someone say that the average Christian spends only seven minutes a day with God. While I understood what he was trying to say, I think he missed the main point. The average Christian spends twenty-four hours a day with God. It's just that we may only be aware of it for seven minutes. Or less.

God is right by your side—"For in him we live and move and have our being" (Acts 17:28 NIV)—but too often we don't look far enough past our own selves to see him.

To become real we need to be honest enough and courageous enough to look past ourselves and our circumstances, see God in the everyday details of life, and say, "Since you are in this place, Lord, I'll live like you're here. I want to walk with you today."

It is a little like waking up, as Jacob did that morning. He awoke out of two kinds of sleep: his body's sleep and his soul's sleep. He set up that rock pillow as a pillar—a memorial to God—and called that place *Bethel*, which means "house of God." And Jacob was never the same man again.

Becoming aware of God's presence in our lives can be the greatest awakening of all.

> oh Lord,
> i am so often asleep to your presence;
> asleep to your love, asleep to the truth.
> how i like to invent cool, soothing excuses
> and surround myself with subtle lies.
> i am a sedative to myself, and my soul is fast asleep.
> awaken me.

Chapter 7

WORSHIPING GOD BY DOING THE DISHES

Discovering an Authentic Spiritual Life

*My prayers are nothing other than a sense
of the presence of God.*

—BROTHER LAWRENCE

Imagine if God were so big that he could fill all of our moments and dreams and ambitions. So extreme that he could bring meaning and glory and worship and hope to even the most mundane and routine chores. Imagine what that would be like.

If God could do that, he could redeem not just our future but our days, not just our souls, but ourselves. Every moment would hold the potential for union with the supernatural; for experiencing ultimate joy, acceptance, belonging, and love.

Imagine a God who not only saves but inhabits; who not only exists but permeates. He would be the ultimate redeemer. He would bring purpose and fulfillment and significance to all of life—waking, sleeping, eating, yawning, brushing our teeth. We could do these things not with reluctance, as necessary distractions, but with a realization that they are powerful opportunities for honoring Jesus.

Well, that's precisely what Jesus promises. That's exactly what God intends.

God's presence isn't some remote possibility offered only to the most dutifully religious people. It's the assurance God gives to all who believe. The

Spirit fills us. The Son lives in us. The Father surrounds us constantly with his love. We dwell in him, he dwells in us.

> When I [Jesus] am raised to life again, you will know that I am in my Father, and you are in me, and I am in you. (John 14:20)

> Christ lives in you, and this is your assurance that you will share in his glory. (Colossians 1:27)

> Since Christ lives within you, even though your body will die because of sin, your spirit is alive because you have been made right with God. The Spirit of God, who raised Jesus from the dead, lives in you. (Romans 8:10–11)

> For you died when Christ died, and your real life is hidden with Christ in God. (Colossians 3:3)

Jesus told his followers, "Be sure of this: I am with you always, even to the end of the age" (Matthew 28:20). He never leaves us. Our peace comes from his presence. It isn't the kind of peace the world can give. It's deeper and richer. And it's available moment by moment as we dwell with the God who has loved us forever.

That's God's desire for each one of us. Paul summarized it like this: "So here's what I want you to do, God helping you: Take your everyday, ordinary life—your sleeping, eating, going-to-work, and walking-around life—and place it before God as an offering. Embracing what God does for you is the best thing you can do for him" (Romans 12:1 MSG).

The New International Version translates this offering of ourselves to God as our "spiritual act of worship." Offering ourselves to God (not just going to church or reading the Bible) is our spiritual act of worship.

All of life is worship. The act of living is an act of worship.

As Christian mystic Francois de Fénelon wrote, "Do not seek God as if He were far off in an ivory castle. He is found in the middle of the events of your everyday life."[1]

When we make tea, the tea permeates all of the boiling water so that we can no longer separate them. The tea changes the water for good—in both senses of the word.

That's what God wants to do in our lives.

He wants to permeate all of our thoughts and dreams and desires and aspirations and motives and moments. He will immerse himself in us when we immerse ourselves in him.

NO TRIVIAL PURSUITS

Life is saturated with holiness and the potential for revelation. Yet we swim through it unaware that the moments flowing past us are holy, so holy, drenched in the garb of the familiar.

So often we don't reach out and touch the moments we live through. We don't even notice them because we've been underwater so long, and we only come up long enough for another gulp of air before diving down into the boredom or the busyness of our lives again.

Yet all the while, God wants to saturate our moments with his presence.

God doesn't fill a place, he fills people. When he's living in us, breathing in us, possessing us, then everywhere we go is holy. Every step we take, divine. Each moment can be one of praise; each act, one of worship. Everything we do can be an expression of living life fully and sacredly.

It isn't the big things that make for a life well lived. It's the acceptance of the small things. Life is lived in the details, and we can bring every aspect of our lives to God without trying to "spiritualize" everything.

God doesn't ask us to do great things for him; he asks us to do everything with him—in his presence, aware of his glory.

Most of us don't see anything spiritual about picking up the kids from school or vacuuming the living room or pouring a bowl of cereal. It's just stuff we have to do.

But in the kingdom of God, there are no trivial pursuits. Every act, every moment, every detail is imbued with meaning if it's part and parcel of a life lived for God. Changing a dirty diaper, sharpening a pencil, boiling water, mowing the lawn, driving to work, signing a check, playing Chutes and Ladders with our kids—all of these daily events are saturated with holiness when they're lived out not as means to an end but as ends in themselves. When they're offered up to God because of his love and in honor of his glory.

We can worship God not just *while* we do the dishes but *by* doing the dishes.

A REVOLUTIONARY WAY OF LIVING

In God's eyes, living our lives moment by moment and fulfilling the work he has given us to do is our calling. It can be just as spiritual to kneel down and wrestle with our kids as it is to kneel down at an altar to take the Lord's Supper.

This is a radical change of view for most of us—to think that all of our lives can be lived in the presence of God, moment by moment. Can we really swim through the ocean of our days immersed in his love? Could this moment—right now—be holy? Could it carry eternal significance and the evidence of God's presence in our lives? Thomas R. Kelly wrote in *A Testament of Devotion*, "I am talking about a revolutionary way of living. Religion isn't something to be added to our other duties, and thus make our lives yet more complex. The life with God is the center of life, and all else is remodeled and integrated by it."[2]

We're told to give God all of our lives, even the details. Even eating a carrot or drinking a cup of iced tea can be an act of worship: "Whatever you eat or drink or whatever you do, you must do all for the glory of God" (1 Corinthians 10:31).

All for the glory of God.

All.

We worship God with our lives, not just with our prayers. Not just with the tiny portion we may label religious or spiritual.

Everything we do can be done for the glory of God.

Think about that.

God awaits us in this moment. In the routines and the duties and the obligations and the chores of life. Every moment he is available. Every moment he is here.

Apart from sin, no activity is holier than another. Take Jesus, for example. He immersed all of his life in the service of his Father—whether he was preaching a sermon, sitting around a campfire with his fishing buddies, casting out demons, having a glass of wine at a wedding, or joining a bunch of crooked accountants for supper. He honored God while he was a carpenter, not just when he became a preacher. Sawing a board in half honored God just as much as breaking the loaves of bread in half to feed five thousand families. During all of his life, he never wavered from doing his Father's will.

That's refreshing and freeing. We can honor God by doing anything the Bible doesn't tell us brings him dishonor. It isn't a certain activity that brings God honor, it's the condition of our hearts—no matter what the activity. We worship God whenever we do things for his glory and according to his will. No activity can compare with pursuing holiness and union with him. Nothing is more holy than a life lived in God's presence.

Let him saturate your moments and fill your days. Open every corner of your life to God. Make every moment available to him. And then live the lives he has crafted for you. Jesus said, "I have come that they may have life, and have it to the full" (John 10:10 NIV). And the fullest life of all is the one filled with him.

Rather than spending so much time trying to surgically separate our lives into "spiritual" and "secular" activities, we should strive to offer all of ourselves, all of our time, all of our activities, all of our lives to God.

That's real worship. That's real living.

WORSHIPING IN SPIRIT AND IN TRUTH

Too often churches have become places to hide, not to be found. Some people hide in the programs, others hide behind fake smiles and superficial grins, and still others hide in the obligations of the little church or the anonymity of the megachurch. They go to church but never become part of God's family. They attend but are never transformed. They're still playing at religion, poking at God from a distance, like someone trying to nudge coals around in a fire without getting close enough to get burned.

When you're ready to come to God, he won't let you get away with simply prodding him from a distance; he'll set you right down in the middle of the flames. You can't just warm your hands on the edge of his love. He consumes those who seek him.

He sets your life on fire.

If reading the Bible has become just part of your daily spiritual checklist and prayer has become a repetitive ritual, you're not worshiping anyone. You're just spinning your wheels, not moving any closer to experiencing God's presence. You may be saying your prayers, but you're not praying. You may be going to church, but you're not worshiping. Real worship is more than a sing-along. Real prayer is more than a bunch of words. As Saint Teresa of Avila prayed,

> O Lord,
> do not then ever allow those who talk to you
> to think it sufficient to do so
> with their lips alone.[3]

If prayer were really limited to folding our hands or closing our eyes or saying certain words, how could we possibly pray without ceasing? (see 1 Thessalonians 5:17). We'd only be able to pray for a small portion, a sliver, of our lives. God would be confined to a corner of our existence, compartmentalized away into that little section reserved for religion.

God wants to permeate all of our lives. He wants to be the one who fulfills all of our deepest desires and dwells in the corners of all of our dreams.

All of life can become worship. All of our moments can become prayers. But genuine worship only occurs when we worship God in spirit and in truth.

One time, when a woman tried getting into a debate with Jesus about where different groups of people were supposed to worship God, he made it clear that God isn't nearly as interested in where we worship as he is in how we worship. Jesus told her: "The time is coming when it will no longer matter whether you worship the Father here or in Jerusalem. . . . The time is coming and is already here when true worshipers will worship the Father in spirit and in truth. The Father is looking for anyone who will worship him that way. For God is Spirit, so those who worship him must worship in spirit and in truth" (John 4:21; 23–24).

The place doesn't matter to God. It can be a temple in Jerusalem, a street corner in New York City, a beach in Belize, a hillside in Tennessee, or the backseat of a Volkswagen Beetle. To God, one place is no more sacred than another.

What does matter to God? That we worship in spirit and in truth.

But what does that mean?

Well, we worship God in spirit when our souls come to him in faith and connect with him on the deepest level. Prayers aren't performances but gut-level, soul-to-soul communication with the Almighty—our spirits talking to his Spirit. Here's how Eugene Peterson paraphrased the words of Jesus to that woman at the well: "It's who you are and the way you live that count before

God. Your worship must engage your spirit in the pursuit of truth. That's the kind of people the Father is out looking for: those who are simply and honestly *themselves* before him in their worship. God is sheer being itself—Spirit. Those who worship him must do it out of their very being, their spirits, their true selves, in adoration" (John 4:23–24 MSG).

And we worship God in truth when our worship is rooted in reality, not in opinion or illusion. It's pretty easy to make up a god we can feel comfortable with, but true worshipers of God must worship him in truth, believing what he says, accepting who he is.

God doesn't allow us to worship caricatures of him. He doesn't want us to worship him based on what we want him to be but rather on who he really is.

We need to come to terms with this and abandon any misconceptions we have of God. Let God be God.

My friend Aaron Wymer pointed this verse out to me: "Leaving the crowd behind, they took him [Jesus] along, *just as he was*, in the boat. There were also other boats with him" (Mark 4:36 NIV, emphasis added).

They took Jesus "as is."

That's what we need to do with Jesus too. Let's not be too quick to say, "My God would never do (this or that)," because God isn't ours. He's his own. He is the way he is, and he does the things he does because he is God. And we are not.

We need to come to God as is and accept him as is. Then—and only then—will he begin to change us into who we could never have become on our own.

SECRET SPIRITUALITY

Our lives are always on display, but our worship must never be. So Jesus gave advice when it comes to letting others see our good deeds, our prayers, and our spiritual practices:

When you give to someone, don't tell your left hand what your right hand is doing. Give your gifts in secret, and your Father, who knows all secrets, will reward you. (Matthew 6:3–4)

When you pray, go away by yourself, shut the door behind you, and pray to your Father secretly. Then your Father, who knows all secrets, will reward you. (Matthew 6:6)

When you fast, comb your hair and wash your face. Then no one will suspect you are fasting, except your Father, who knows what you do in secret. And your Father, who knows all secrets, will reward you. (Matthew 6:17–18)

We're not to put our spiritual practices on display. God knows our hearts. If we deserve any rewards, he'll give them to us. But we shouldn't try to impress others with our spirituality.

God wants us to be less concerned about others' opinions and more concerned about his. He is the only audience we should have when we pray, when we worship, and when we give.

In his warnings about avoiding audiences, Jesus was saying, "It's so vital that you not get caught up in religious posturing that you ought to take practical steps to make sure your relationship with me doesn't turn into a spiritual sideshow."

Preoccupation with the opinions of others can lock us out of true faith. Jesus made that clear when he said, "No wonder you can't believe! For you gladly honor each other, but you don't care about the honor that comes from God alone" (John 5:44). True believers step out of the back-patting long enough to see how fruitless it all is. And they bare their hearts to God.

Humility is simply being honest with God. Humble worshipers don't want accolades, they want authenticity. So they worship and pray and live in spirit and in truth.

Don't draw attention to spiritual practices, because those activities aren't what attest to our faith. It's the love that flows out of our lives (not the cash that flows out of our wallets or the prayers that pour out of our mouths) that reveals our faith to the world. Love, not religious rituals, draws people into the kingdom of God.

TRANSPARENT PRAYERS

If we want to know God intimately, we must be totally honest with him. And if we want to know ourselves, we must be totally honest with ourselves about who we are.

But what if I don't know who I am? you may say. What if I'm still trying to find myself?

According to Jesus, every one of us is lost. The goal isn't to find ourselves but to find him.

We just need to tell God what we know of ourselves. Admit our mistakes to him. Hold nothing back. That's the way we should pray—in specifics. No one is inspired by vague descriptions, it's the details that bring writing to life. No one is swayed by vague promises, it's the specifics that give validity to what we say. And no one is redeemed by vague guilt, it's the actual admission of specific sins that brings us closer to Christ. True prayer is the removal of all masks.

And as we reveal ourselves to God, he'll reveal not only himself to us but ourselves to us as well: "Those who obey my commandments are the ones who love me. And because they love me, my Father will love them, and I will love them. And I will reveal myself to each one of them" (John 14:21).

Love and obedience toward God will result in a clearer revelation of who he is. God discloses himself to those who love and obey him.

PRAYING FROM THE GUT

I was talking with two of my friends recently, both of whom are strong believers and respected leaders in regional ministry organizations. One of them, I'll call him Barry, said, "A friend of mine just got a call from a local pastor who asked him, 'Can I be completely honest with you?'

"'Sure,' he said.

"And the pastor yelled into the phone, 'S—!'"

We chuckled a little, and I said, "I feel like saying that sometimes."

Both of my buddies said, "I do say that sometimes."

"Yeah," I mumbled. "I guess I do too."

Barry smiled and concluded, "I haven't met that pastor yet, but I like him already."

What are we to make of this story? Some of you are probably shocked that we would even joke about saying a profane word. (And some of you are relieved!) So what's my point?

Well, obviously, God doesn't want us to pepper our speech with obscene language.

But he does want us to pepper our prayers with honesty.

And to pretend that we don't ever lose our patience or feel like cussing or get totally fed up with life is simply denial. To act as if the harshest thing we ever think is, *Oh phooey!* is absurd. It's ignoring the raw realities of life in this imperfect world.

There's a story that when Saint Teresa of Avila was crossing a river, her horse threw her off into the muddy water, and God said to her, "This is how I treat my friends."

And she told him, "No wonder you don't have very many!"

That's being honest with God.

Frustration is natural. Jesus got frustrated with the inane questions of his disciples, with the unbelief of the people in his hometown, with the hypocrisy of the religious leaders, and with the duplicity of the people who tried to trap him with their questions.

And he let them know it. When Jesus got frustrated, he didn't hide it. Sometimes his language was blunt and harsh and confrontational. Because burying our feelings or problems won't solve anything. Honesty just might.

So when we get frustrated, let's stop acting so happy! When we're sad, let's not pretend we're not. Especially when we talk to God.

But I couldn't talk like that to God! If he knew what went through my mind sometimes . . .

I've got news for you: He already knows what goes through our minds. He already knows what we feel like saying. He's just waiting for us to acknowledge it.

BURYING OUR FEELINGS OR PROBLEMS WON'T SOLVE ANYTHING.

God knows when we've reached the end of our rope and the end of our patience and the end of the line. And he loves us anyway.

Hiding from him by reciting "proper" prayers or simply saying the things we think we're supposed to say will never lead us closer to his heart. God isn't impressed with long prayers, with spiritual-sounding prayers, with thee-and-thou prayers, or with our ability to chant a foreign language.

More than anything else, God longs to hear us say the things we hide from him. He's waiting for the phone in heaven to ring and for us to say, "God, can I be completely honest with you?"

"Sure," he'll say. "I've been waiting a long time for this call."

PRAYERS WITH TEETH

Let's be done with these tidy, packaged, sacred-sounding speeches once and for all. Real prayers are unvarnished. They're not soft, cuddly little kittens. They're more like thunderstorms, windy and ragged.

They flash with insight and rumble with complaints. Wet and soggy sometimes, but opening to rainbows at the end. Real prayers express inspiration and drudgery, fear and glory, joy and praise and roaring truth. With God in the middle and all around.

Real prayers are not flimsy and weak but big and round and bold. They don't worm their way into heaven, they pound on the door and knock it down. A thousand dull, timid, pale, lifeless prayers will never move the heart of God like a single sentence exploding from the honest places of our souls.

"How could you let this happen!" we scream.

"Why, God?" we weep.

"Are you there?" we shout, shaking our fists at heaven. "Are you even listening to me?!"

"I failed you, God. I don't deserve your love."

"So you are real—and I am so small," we whisper in a moment of revelation.

"God, show me your mercy," we beg. "I'm so, so sorry for what I've done."

"God, can I be completely honest with you? . . ."

Those kind of prayers have teeth. And guts. And heart.

Sometimes we throw our hands up in wonder. Other times we cry and pound the table. We're broken. We're angry. We're amazed. We're lonely. We're inspired.

And we're changed. Because something happens during the storm. We're washed clean again, shocked by the cold, but thankful for the reality of being alive in the middle of God's love.

We can't escape the raw experiences of life. Real prayers ache with the truth and pour from our hearts with agony and awe.

That's why prayers, true prayers, reveal both God and ourselves. We stand naked and honest before him and become clothed and real. No more masks. No more gentle, rational excuses piled on top of each other like coats of paint. Prayers scrape us clean and bare before God, where we can finally rest as calm and unashamed as a child in the arms of her father. In the arms of our Father. Who wipes every tear from our eyes.

GROANING TO GOD

Tell God your secrets. Show him your shame. Shout out his praises. Beg for his presence. Bring him your questions. God cares about the details of your life. Nothing is too big for him to handle, and nothing is too small for him to be concerned about.

Our prayers can be a way of letting joy dance in our hearts. And in those times when we need to give voice to our pain, we don't have to worry if we don't know the right words to say. We can just open our hearts up to God, and his Spirit will do the rest: "The Holy Spirit helps us in our distress. For we don't even know what we should pray for, nor how we should pray. But the Holy Spirit prays for us with groanings that cannot be expressed in words. And the Father who knows all hearts knows what the Spirit is saying, for the Spirit pleads for us believers in harmony with God's own will" (Romans 8:26–27).

If the Holy Spirit himself groans when he prays, why are we so concerned with sounding articulate and eloquent to God? We don't need the right words. We just need the right attitude.

Prayer is the process of shedding our lies, our masks, and our inhibitions, and standing in God's presence as we really are—neither proud nor ashamed, simply accepted and loved and heard.

Talk about becoming real!

That's how Job prayed. It's how David and Paul prayed. It's how Jesus prayed. And that's how we need to pray.

For then, in the midst of the turmoil, suddenly, taking us by surprise, comes the calm we longed for. Peace within the storm. Within ourselves. Comfort from the Spirit. A calmness and stillness we wouldn't have noticed if it weren't surrounded by the gusts of hardship and drenched with the sheets of slanted, cleansing rain we call prayer.

God dwells there. Where all of life is sacred. All of life is worship. And where every moment can be spent dwelling in the center of a prayer.

Chapter 8

IN SYNC WITH THE SPIRIT

Walking Intimately with God

*You breathed your fragrance upon me,
and I drew in my breath and now I pant
for you; I tasted you and now I hunger
and thirst for you; you touched me, and I
burn for your peace.*

—SAINT AUGUSTINE, *CONFESSIONS*

Lovers find it easy to walk in step with each other. Just watch a couple strolling through the park or walking along the beach. They walk side by side, hand in hand, arm in arm. Leaning on each other. Enjoying each other's company. Together.

If you watch carefully enough, you'll notice that nearly always, one of them (let's pretend it's the woman) has to change her stride to match the stride of her beloved.

But does she mind?

Not at all. Because she just wants to be close to this man. She wants to be by his side.

She doesn't want to walk in front of him or behind him or away from him. She wants to walk with him. In step with him. Because she loves him.

Sure, she could walk off and leave him there. She could walk her own way—but why would she want to? Intimacy is more important to her than the freedom to walk at her own speed or pursue her own path or go her own direction. Because then she would miss enjoying this moment with him. She would miss his presence, his touch, his company. She chooses intimacy over independence.

IN STEP WITH GOD

A short word of advice nestled in Paul's letter to the church at Galatia really impacted my life. I'd read it dozens of times and never noticed it. Then one day it hit me like a fist in the gut and woke me up to what it really means to walk with God. Here it is: "Since we live by the Spirit, let us keep in step with the Spirit" (Galatians 5:25 NIV).

That's it. One simple thought: keeping in step with God.

But here's what hit me—I don't usually keep in step with the Spirit at all. I tend to head wherever I want to go and tell God, "Hey, if you wanna tag along, that's fine. But you're the one who's gonna have to change your stride to stick with me. I just hope you can keep up."

Of course I don't actually say those words, I just reveal that attitude by the way I live.

And this verse says I've got it backward. It doesn't say God's Spirit should keep in step with me, but that I must keep in step with him. I'm the one who needs to change my stride to match his.

"Since we live by the Spirit, let us keep in step with the Spirit."

Walking in step with God means giving up our own goals and making intimacy with him our only goal. It means giving up the right to walk our own way in favor of walking stride by stride with him. It's a moment-by-moment process.

Step by step.

His yoke is easy and his burden light, but still, when we're yoked to someone, we have to go where he goes. If we try going our own way, we'll only stumble and fall. Spiritual intimacy with God will never come when we're running off in our own direction. It only comes when we submit and surrender and keep in step with him.

That wouldn't be too much fun if God weren't our intimate ally. If we thought God was a cosmic cop who's always out to get us, or a black-robed, gavel-wielding judge of the universe, hoping to accuse and condemn, we'd never want to walk with him.

But walking with him isn't a burden at all if God is our beloved. If we're in love with God, it's a joy to change our stride to match his. Because then we get to enjoy his presence every step of the way.

Paul wrote, "I advise you to live according to your new life in the Holy Spirit. Then you won't be doing what your sinful nature craves" (Galatians 5:16). The new life and the old life are in stark contrast to each other, for the Spirit and the sinful nature head in opposite directions.

Walking in step with the Spirit means going his direction rather than the one our sinful nature craves. It means making this our soul's goal and our sole goal: to walk moment by moment, step by step with God.

So what does it take to walk in step with God? (1) The humility to admit we don't know the best paths, (2) the faith to follow wherever he leads, (3) the submission to change our stride to match his, and (4) a greater desire to be close to God than to go our own way.

MY WAY OR HIS WAY?

As we seek to change our stride to match God's, we may feel overwhelmed. But there's good news. Walking with him is our way of expressing our love for him, and showing love isn't a burden but a joy: "This is how we know that we love the children of God: by loving God and carrying out his commands. This is love for God: to obey his commands. And his commands are not burdensome, for everyone born of God overcomes the world. This is the victory that has overcome the world, even our faith" (1 John 5:2–4 NIV).

Obedience isn't a burden? No, not when we walk step by step in faith. Our faith overcomes the world because it sees past this life and touches on eternity. That's where our strength comes from. Obedience means walking in step with the Spirit, not fretting about following a set of rules.

It isn't a burden, but it's not always easy.

Even Jesus found it tough in the Garden of Gethsemane. "If there's any other way," he prayed. "If there's any other path . . ." But there wasn't. So finally he said, "Not my will but your will be done." Yet it wasn't a burden for him. His love made the choice. He was totally in step with the Spirit. All the way to Calvary. His faith overcame the world.

Jesus had a simple agenda—to submit moment by moment to the will of his Father.

Moment-by-moment obedience is our one way of expressing love for God. There's really no other way to show God that we love him. Would cheating on our spouses show our love for them? Would we feel loved by our children if they ran away from home? Can we really claim to love God if we're constantly running away from him or chasing other lovers?

Jean-Pierre De Caussade, a Jesuit priest in the early eighteenth century, wrote: "Every moment of our lives can be a kind of communion with his love. . . . This tremendous activity of God, which never varies from the beginning to the end of time, pours itself through every moment and gives itself in all its vastness and power to every clear-hearted soul which adores and loves it and abandons itself without reserve to it."[1]

This moment, right now, ask yourself: Is my life in step with God's Spirit, or am I walking off in my own direction? Are my thoughts in step with him? Are my choices in step with his? Are my dreams in step with God?

If not, hand them to him right now. Let God pave the way to a new way of living—where he calls the shots and you change your priorities and make your choices and shape your dreams around one thing, and one thing only: being in sync with the Spirit. David prayed this: "I run in the path of your commands, for you have set my heart free" (Psalm 119:32 NIV). God had set him free, and at last he could run in the path of the Lord's commands. And so can we.

STRIDE BY STRIDE

Obedience and love for God go hand in hand. Obedience without love is legalism. Love without obedience is sentimentality. True love expresses itself in tangible ways. If it doesn't, it was only a masquerade to begin with.

Look at how David prayed that God would guide him step by step throughout the day as he placed his hope in the Lord: "Show me the path where I should walk, O LORD; point out the right road for me to follow. Lead me by your truth and teach me, for you are the God who saves me. All day long I put my hope in you" (Psalm 25:4–5).

God will guide. God will direct. God will lead. But we must be willing to go where he leads.

The goal is not to find out God's will for our lives but to submit to God's will whenever we find it out. God doesn't usually dump the road map for the rest of our lives into our laps and say, "See you at the finish line!" He wants to walk beside us and call out directions all along the way—"Turn right here! Let's go check out the waterfall up ahead!"

"But God," we stammer, "that's not in the itinerary. It's not even on the map!"

And God smiles. "I know. I've been keeping it a secret. But wait till you see the view!"

It takes great humility to say, "Lead on, Spirit! Even though I can't see far down the road or understand why you chose this road rather than another one, lead on. For you are my soul's most beloved, and all I desire is to walk with you along the shore of life, arm in arm, enjoying each step of this journey together."

THIS SACRED MOMENT

I like to think of worship as the soundtrack of my life. It's always there in the background, yet sometimes it bubbles up and takes over, and it's all I notice.

A movie soundtrack accentuates everything that happens on the screen. It's always there, even when we're not aware of it. Just like the beating of our hearts or the flowing of blood through our veins or the exchange of oxygen in our lungs. These processes happen naturally, all the time, within our bodies—not just when we notice them.

In the same way, worship happens naturally, all the time, within the spirits of those who believe in Christ.

When I was talking about this with my small group Bible study, my friend Grant Miller nodded in agreement. "Yes, and I can picture two competing soundtracks. Two volume knobs—one that plays the music of worshiping God, the other filled with the noise of self. And suddenly you look at them and you say, 'How did that one get turned up so loud?'"

So that's what we must do each day—tune back in to God. Get back in step with him. And then walk together in submission and synchronicity.

Jesus never taught people to abandon life but to embrace it. Never to divide the secular and the spiritual as if we were separating the food on our plates into the stuff that tastes good and the stuff that's good for us. Yet we divide life so distinctly between the secular and the sacred that we have Christian bookstores, Christian fiction, Christian music, Christian yellow pages, Christian radio stations, Christian coffeehouses, Christian T-shirts, and Christian schools. I even saw a "Christian family haircutters" shop recently! Instead of saturating our world with salt and light, we've retreated into the cupboard and shut the door.

Life isn't split between the secular and the sacred. Life can only be split between worship and sin, between righteousness and rebellion, between light and darkness. Jesus never taught that some things are outside the realm of the holy, and he didn't live as though they were. He lived each moment richly, in the presence of God. His entire life was an act of worship, and he offers us the same opportunity: a life in which God is always present and lives in our hearts and directs our lives. In the words of the great hymn by Frances R. Havergal,

> Take my life, and let it be
> Consecrated, Lord, to Thee.
> Take my moments and my days;
> Let them flow in ceaseless praise.
> Take my will, and make it Thine;
> It shall be no longer mine;
> Take my heart, it is Thine own;
> It shall be Thy royal throne.
> Take my love, my Lord, I pour
> At Thy feet its treasure store.
> Take myself, and I will be
> Ever, only, all for Thee.

That's walking in step with the Spirit. That's staying in tune with the ways of God.

THE THINGS OF GOD

When the angel told Mary about God's plan to send her a son who would be the savior of the world, she was bewildered. After all, even though she was engaged, she was still a virgin. How was a virgin going to have a baby? How did God plan to pull that off? The angel assured her that nothing is impossible for God. And Mary responded by saying, "I am the Lord's servant, and I am willing to accept whatever he wants. May everything you have said come true" (Luke 1:38).

100

Mary said, "Whatever God wants for me, I want for me." Her agenda was simple—to accept whatever God sent her. To live within his will, to walk in step with God. She had in mind the things of God and not the things of men.

"I am willing to accept whatever he wants."

She submitted to God's will, God's plan, and God's agenda for her life. Whatever that meant. Wherever that took her. Whatever God wanted, she wanted.

Contrast her attitude with Peter's. At one time he told Jesus not to talk about being betrayed and killed. Jesus turned to him and said, "Get behind me, Satan! You are a stumbling block to me; you do not have in mind the things of God, but the things of men" (Matthew 16:23 NIV).

Peter's plans were too small. They were man-sized. Actually, they were Satan-sized.

Mary said, "OK, God. Let's do things your way." Peter said, "I've got a better idea, Jesus. Let's do things my way."

LIVING TO HONOR THE SPIRIT

There's a simple way to tell how tuned in you are to the things of God. Ask yourself these questions (and be brave enough to answer them honestly):

- Do I find more pleasure in the things that please God or the things that please me?
- Do I find more fulfillment in pursuing God's will or my own?
- Do I focus more on my own goals or on God's?
- Do I get more frustrated when my plans are disrupted or when his are disrupted?
- Do I laugh at the things God laughs at or at the things he weeps over?
- Do I pursue his pathways, or do I go in my own direction and hope he'll eventually follow?

It's not easy to admit that you've had in mind the things of men rather than the things of God.

I know. I've had to do it all too often.

When we walk into a situation that tests our resolve to do God's will (or that stretches us in a specific area of obedience), we face a choice: will we honor God in this situation, or will we go our own way? And if we choose to do what God desires, will it be out of obligation or out of devotion?

The lover changes her stride because she wants to, not because she has to. No one is forcing her. And she doesn't resent it, she enjoys it. Because the change in her actions grows from the love in her heart.

So how do we go about walking with God? Here are seven steps we can take to stay in sync with the Spirit.

1. Let Go of Personal Agendas

At one time the Baptist Missionary Union adopted a seal of an ox standing between a plough and an altar. Below the picture was the inscription "Ready for either." As F. E. Marsh put it, "This at once suggests that the ox is ready for service or sacrifice. Thus all who are Christ's should be ready to do His will, whether that will mean suffering or serving."[2]

That was Mary's attitude. And Jesus's too.

Like mother, like Son.

Just like them, we need to be willing to do things God's way rather than our own. That means we're going to have to let go of our own plans, stop relying on our own strength, fix our eyes and hearts on Jesus alone, and then step out of the way and let God be God. And he will work great things in our lives.

It means setting down our own goals, agendas, and dreams and picking up the cross that comes with following Jesus. The plough or the altar. Ready for either—to suffer all or give our all, whatever he asks of us.

Anyone who has given up her relationships, her dreams, her possessions, her life, has given her all. Not because she has to. Not even because she wants to. But because she can't help it—her love calls her to make choices that honor her beloved. Love calls her to sacrifice all.

2. Stop Relying on Personal Strength

Without tapping into God's strength, we're like cell phones that haven't been recharged. Or toasters that aren't plugged in. Or flashlights without batteries. We don't have the power to do what we were meant to do.

We need to depend on God for strength, answers, guidance, and results. God wants to fill, equip, empower, and guide us. As Jesus told his disciples, "Remain in me, and I will remain in you. For a branch cannot produce fruit if it is severed from the vine, and you cannot be fruitful apart from me. Yes, I am the vine; you are the branches. Those who remain in me, and I in them, will produce much fruit. For apart from me you can do nothing" (John 15:4–5).

The branches depend on the vine. They need it to grow. That's where they get their strength. We are not the source of our own strength; God is. And our lives will not bear fruit unless we are united with Christ, reliant upon the Spirit, and leaning on the Father's strength.

Of course, no one is perfect, and we fail God more often than we care to admit. But what attitude do we have toward God's commands—one of rebellion or one of submission?

By yourself, it's a losing battle. It's like getting stuck in quicksand—the harder you struggle, the farther you sink. So stop all the struggling and yield your will to God. Obedience has more to do with faith and reliance than with striving and effort.

His will, not ours, be done.

Consistent Christian living isn't a matter of effort but of submission.

3. Absorb God's Promises

I used to think of the Christian life as being like a faucet—that we should let God's Spirit pour through us to the world, that we are nothing but the channel through which he works.

And while I guess that's partially true, lately I've been thinking our lives are more like sponges. We fill ourselves with the Spirit, and then when the world squeezes us, out comes God's love: "For we know how dearly God loves us, because he has given us the Holy Spirit to fill our hearts with his love" (Romans 5:5).

At least that's what's supposed to come out. But if we're more filled with our own agendas and goals, frustration rather than love will flow out of us when we're squeezed.

So absorb him and let his love fill you up. He won't pass through you and leave you empty. He fills you and keeps you fulfilled.

Yes, we get in the way sometimes, but we're more than conduits of grace. We're called to be filled with God, and the only way to do that is to immerse ourselves in his love, saturate our lives with his Spirit, and then let him refresh the world through us.

4. Fix Your Eyes and Heart on Him Alone

The Amplified Bible paraphrases Hebrews 12:2 like this: "Looking away [from all that will distract] to Jesus." When we fix our eyes on one thing, we must divert our attention from another. When we fix our eyes on Jesus, we have to look away from the world.

When you walk with your lover, your attention is focused on her. If you're walking arm in arm with one woman while you're constantly scoping out the other women on the beach, your eyes and your heart are not being faithful to the one you're with.

We need to look away from all that will distract us and look solely to Jesus as we walk with him.

5. Consider Motives, Not Just Actions

Just as certainly as we can do either the right thing or the wrong thing, we can do the right thing for the wrong reason. Anytime we're not motivated by faith expressing itself through love, we're motivated for the wrong reason (see Romans 14:23).

Becoming real requires that we unveil not only our actions but also our attitudes—that we look closely not only at what we do but also at what we think.

Most of the time, we don't act as we do because of our love for God but because of our love for ourselves. As long as satisfaction is our desired destination, peace will remain just out of reach, just beyond the horizon. We're a bunch of donkeys with an infinite number of carrots dangling before our eyes, walking blindly toward a cliff.

We need to review our motives and bring them in line with the will of God.

6. Take God Seriously

It isn't that we suddenly begin to hate God in those moments when we disobey him. At least for me it's not. It's just that in those times, God seems irrelevant. I don't consciously think, *I'm gonna do this to hurt God and rebel against him.* I just become indifferent toward him. I ignore him.

I think the opposite of loving God isn't hating him, it's discounting him as unnecessary.

The whole book of Zephaniah is a wake-up call to the Jews. Look at how God told them he would deal with those who were complacent. It shows a different aspect of God's love—his jealous anger over those who claim to be his followers but don't take following him seriously: "I will search with lanterns in Jerusalem's darkest corners to find and punish those who sit contented in their sins, indifferent to the LORD, thinking he will do nothing at all to them" (Zephaniah 1:12).

Indifferent. Complacent. Contented in their sins. These words were written to God's people. At least they were supposed to be God's people. But they had become indifferent to God. They went their own direction.

They called God their heart's true love but pursued other lovers.

And God does not deal lightly with those who consider him inconsequential to their lives.

7. Obey God in the Little Things

Believers are in the process of being transformed. It starts in this life and ends in the life to come. This knowledge that we are God's children and are being changed into the likeness of his Son motivates us (or at least it should motivate us) to pursue purity in our lives right now. As John wrote, "Yes, dear friends, we are already God's children, and we can't even imagine what we will be like when Christ returns. But we do know that when he comes we will be like him, for we will see him as he really is. And all who believe this will keep themselves pure, just as Christ is pure" (1 John 3:2–3).

Once we become Christians, our actions and attitudes naturally begin to change. Even though we'll never become perfectly holy or completely in tune with God on this earth, we look for practical ways to demonstrate our faith. Yet it isn't what we do that saves us; Jesus already took care of that. Rather, what we believe changes us into servants.

That's why obedience to God is emphasized throughout the New Testament as the evidence of a changed life:

Not all people who sound religious are really godly. They may refer to me [Jesus] as "Lord," but they still won't enter the Kingdom of Heaven. The decisive issue is whether they obey my Father in heaven. (Matthew 7:21)

Those who obey God's word really do love him. That is the way to know whether or not we live in him. Those who say they live in God should live their lives as Christ did. (1 John 2:5–6)

Since God's grace has set us free from the law, does this mean we can go on sinning? Of course not! Don't you realize that whatever you choose to obey becomes your master? You can choose sin, which leads to death, or you can choose to obey God and receive his approval. (Romans 6:15–16)

God is working in you, giving you the desire to obey him and the power to do what pleases him. (Philippians 2:13)

Get rid of all the filth and evil in your lives, and humbly accept the message God has planted in your hearts, for it is strong enough to save your souls. And remember, it is a message to obey, not just to listen to. (James 1:21–22)

Obedience doesn't save us, make us right with God, or keep us in his kingdom. God's grace saves us, his love changes us, and his mercy sustains us. Good deeds don't get us into God's family. Good deeds don't keep us in God's family. And good deeds don't determine whether we'll go to heaven.

But obedience—walking in step with the Spirit—naturally results when we're reunited with God through faith. That's why those who say they live their lives for God should do more than just say they live their lives for God.

On our own, of course, obedience is impossible. If we depended on our own strength or our own efforts, we would constantly fail. But when we're led by God's Spirit and rely on our faith instead of our fortitude, God will give us the victory through his strength and through his Son.[3]

Commit yourself to living each moment with God. Change your stride to match his, and then enjoy his company as you walk together, step by step, moment by moment, through life.

Take his hand right now. It's stretched out for you. He's got a great adventure planned for you, his soul's most dearly beloved.

Chapter 9

TOO BUSY FOR YOUR OWN GOD?

Pursuing Peace amid Busyness

*We have only this moment, sparkling like
a star in our hand . . . and melting like a
snowflake. Let us use it before it is too late.*
—MARIE EDITH BEYNON

You've probably heard the story about Mary and Martha as many times as
I have.

Jesus and his disciples were on their way to Jerusalem and stopped at Mary
and Martha's house. Remember how Martha was so busy getting supper ready
while Mary just sat and listened to Jesus? Martha got exasperated, and Jesus
told her, "My dear Martha, you are so upset over all these details! There is
really only one thing worth being concerned about. Mary has discovered it—
and I won't take it away from her" (Luke 10:41–42).

So Martha, the busy one, got in trouble with Jesus.

OK, now—let's be honest.

Which of the two women is easier to identify with—worried, hurried,
hassled Martha (who was just trying to get dinner done on time) . . . or
peaceful, reverent, angelic Mary sitting earnestly at the feet of Jesus?

May I have the envelope, please?

Oh, sure, we know we're supposed to be more like Mary, seeing life with
a crystal-clear perspective, spiritually tuned in to God, at peace with the
moment; not frazzled and frustrated and stressed out and behind like Martha.

But come on, now. Be honest.

Doesn't Jesus seem to come down a little too hard on Martha? I mean, she was doing her work for him—isn't that what God wants? And doesn't Mary seem a little too good to be true?

It seems to me that Martha got the raw end of the deal. When she complained to Jesus that her sister wouldn't help her, I kind of wish Jesus had said something like, "No kidding, Martha. Get busy there, Mary. Are you lazy or something? Break time is over, girl!"

But of course he didn't. He had something important to teach Martha.

And us.

THE ONE THING

Some people look at this story and get the impression that we're supposed to stop working altogether or that contemplating God is better than serving him. But I think those people miss the point.

Jesus was sometimes just as busy as Martha was. I love how the apostle John offhandedly mentioned this: "I suppose that if all the other things Jesus did were written down, the whole world could not contain the books" (John 21:25). Healing. Preaching. Traveling. But there was a difference. He was at peace with God through it all.

It wasn't Martha's activity that made her miss the boat, it was her perspective. Martha could have been just as at peace as Mary was, even doing all the work she had to do, if she had only found the "one thing." The problem was that her busyness kept her from Jesus's presence.

OK, let's just say it—her ministry was more important to her than Jesus was. The tasks she was doing for Jesus took precedence over the time she could've been spending with him.

Ah, now I'm beginning to see that this isn't just her story; it's mine.

Don't get me wrong—I'm not lazy. And most of the people I meet aren't lazy. In fact, our lives are frenzied with activity. We're overcommitted and overextended and overcome with busyness. Or, sometimes, we're bored out of our wits. One or the other.

But we're rarely like Mary. Content. At peace. Fulfilled.

I don't care how busy we are doing things for God, we still might not have found the one thing that's essential. Because there's really only one thing worth being concerned about. And Mary found it.

And it wasn't even a thing.

It was a person.

Jesus.

STAYING BUSY?

People at church often smile at me and say, "So, are you staying busy?"

I'm not always sure how to respond. I've started replying, "I'm trying not to."

You should see some of the looks I get.

We don't ask each other, Are you staying faithful? Are you full of joy? Are you at peace? Are you being led by love? Are you walking in step with the Spirit?

Instead we ask, "Are you staying busy?"

I guess it shows where our priorities are.

In our culture we've made busyness the barometer of a well-lived life. It's as though the best possible response to the question of how you're doing is "I'm really busy these days."

When I tell people about my writing or speaking schedule, some folks even say, "Well, at least you're busy."

At least? Is busyness really the least we can be? Is it really the first step toward an authentic and spiritually fulfilled life? Or could it be a step in the wrong direction altogether? Could it be that busyness isn't really very good after all?

Jesus seemed to be saying precisely that to Martha.

Maybe we're under the illusion that God wants our productivity. Maybe we fill our lives with meetings and checklists and events because we think busyness equals faithfulness.

But Martha proved that wrong two thousand years ago.

We can waste our time doing spiritual things just as well as we can waste our time doing nothing. We tend to define wasted time as time when we don't get anything done or when we don't get our way, rather than when God doesn't get his way. And his way is to give us peace, joy, and righteousness. "For the Kingdom of God is not a matter of what we eat or drink, but of living a life of goodness and peace and joy in the Holy Spirit" (Romans 14:17).

We lose that joy and peace when we lose sight of Jesus.

No, productivity isn't what God requires. Obedience is. If we're disobeying

God's will, whether we go about sinning busily or lazily doesn't really matter. Lots of activity isn't what God wants. Lots of intimacy is.

Every moment contains the potential to carry us closer to God. Every moment, we have the opportunity to experience a sacred union with Jesus. His intention has always been to be present in the moments of our lives as we walk in peace with him. He explained it this way: "I am leaving you with a gift—peace of mind and heart. And the peace I give isn't like the peace the world gives. So don't be troubled or afraid" (John 14:27).

The only way to waste time is to spend it in the pursuit of our own interests rather than those of God.

NOT ON MY CHECKLIST

It seems to me that we confuse efficiency with spirituality, time management with simplicity, activity with affection, and Bible study with devotion. Instead of devotion being a way of life, it has become something to do for five minutes after supper. We say, "We're going to have family devotions," rather than, "We're going to be a family of devotion."

Because that sounds too hard.

Christianity has never been about potluck dinners, building campaigns, or choir rehearsals. It has always been about simple faith, genuine love, and heartfelt devotion to God. But these are the things that cannot be easily measured or managed or scheduled. They don't mesh well with spiritual-growth programs, and they don't fit easily into our checklists.

Stepping away from our preconceived ideas of what a "good Christian" should do, what does the life of a genuine follower of Jesus really look like? The life of a believer is certainly woven with threads of love, faith, hope, obedience, righteousness, wonder, joy, mystery, and more. But the pattern the world sees is threefold. Micah 6:8 (NIV) puts it this way: "What does the LORD require of you? To act justly and to love mercy and to walk humbly with your God."

Justice. Mercy. Humility. That's what God asks of us.

I can picture some people after reading this verse: Hmm. Act justly: check . . . Love mercy: check . . . Walk humbly: check . . . OK, what's next?

That's not Christianity. That's churchianity.

Christianity is about a change of heart, not a change of schedule. It's about refusing to get caught up in the frantic pace of accomplishments, and discovering peace instead—a peace "which is far more wonderful than the human mind can understand" (Philippians 4:7). Peace with Jesus.

It was the one thing Martha had missed. And the one thing Mary had found.

THE SOUND OF SILENCE

God's peace can pervade a full and busy life, but it cannot conquer a crowded heart.

Martha's heart was crowded with many things. And that was her fault.

Jesus didn't blame God for Martha's frustration; he pinned the responsibility back on her. As much as I believe in God's power and control over the universe, I also believe we're responsible for our choices.

God doesn't get involved in long-distance relationships. He moves into the center of our hearts because he wants to be at the center of our lives, not somewhere out on the fringes, driving around in the suburbs. And when God gets crowded out of our hearts, it's not his fault. It's ours.

The heart of the Christian life resides not in the busy fervor of the over-committed but in the simple and lovely melody of the moment when God speaks to us and nudges us and laughs with us and whispers our name. And we actually take the time to listen.

Stillness is something we're not too familiar with these days. Our entire culture is racing forward on a caffeine high, pounding away at the treadmill of life. We're some of the busiest people in the history of our planet, with to-do lists a mile long, Day-Timers, overstuffed in-boxes, and jam-packed schedules. We're always overcommitted, under a deadline, and stressed. We're a bunch of Marthas running around. We busy ourselves to death. Sometimes we complain about it, but we don't do much about it. I think we actually like it that way.

I think sometimes we're afraid to slow down because we might see ourselves as we really are—lost, lonely, longing, hurting, hurtful, and unfulfilled. We're afraid of the silences and stillnesses in our lives because we're afraid of what they'll reveal in our hearts. Because they tell us more about ourselves than we want to know. So we pack our days with commitments and cram them with so much small talk and so many entertainments and diversions

111

that we're always behind. We build noise into our routines. We fill the corners of our lives with obligations so we can always have a valid excuse to remain so, so, so busy.

We talk, not because we have something significant to say, but because we can't stand the roar of our own silence. Frank Laubach once wrote, "I disapprove of the usual practice of talking 'small talk' whenever we meet, and holding a veil over our souls. If we are so impoverished that we have nothing to reveal but small talk, then we need to struggle for more richness of soul."[1]

And we're so stuck in this mode that we don't realize we're running faster and faster, trying to escape the very thing we claim we want more of—free time.

Maybe if we fill our lives with enough distractions, we won't have to think about who we are. Or how lonely we are. Or how empty we are. Or how disappointed we are with ourselves. Maybe we can fill our lives with urgent things so we don't have to think about the important ones.

Philosopher and author Peter Kreeft puts things in perspective: "We *want* to complexify our lives. We don't *have* to, we *want* to. We want to be harried and hassled and busy. Unconsciously, we want the very thing we complain about. For if we had leisure, we would look at ourselves and listen to our hearts and see the great gaping hole in our hearts and be terrified, because the hole is so big that nothing but God can fill it."[2]

Mary looked at that hole. Martha didn't.

Until Jesus pointed it out to her.

ALWAYS ENOUGH TIME

While it's certainly true that some people hide behind their obligations, I'm not sure that's what happened to Martha. I think she just drifted into busyness one choice at a time. The same way I do. And Jesus got lost in the shuffle.

A few years ago, when I was talking with my friend John Paul Abner (who happens to have a PhD in psychology) about my schedule, he asked me, "Why do you keep saying yes to everyone?"

Huh.

Why indeed?

Because I feel like God wants me to? No.

Because I really want to do all those things? No.

Did I need the money? Sometimes, but not always.

Then why?

And then it hit me: because I'm concerned about what other people would think of me if I said no.

Aha.

Here's the truth I learned that day: unless I'm careful, I'll drift into being overcommitted because *I like being liked.*

But life is not a popularity contest. Those who lead their lives based on what they think others will think of them will never find peace. And I realized I'd rather have peace than prestige, so I've been a lot quicker to say no since that day.

Life isn't about packing in as much as we can or grabbing all the gusto we can but about letting go of more than we'd like to. I'm not talking about resignation or denial or laziness or excuses. But I am talking about an attitude of submission, surrender, and service to God.

There's always enough time for us to complete what God wants us to do. Think about that.

Would God ever ask us to do more than he gave us the time to do? Of course not. God won't require more of us than we can accomplish with his help.

God desires for us to be content, joyful, and at peace. So if we're always stressed, anxious, and behind, what's the problem?

Well, we're following the wrong agenda. We're not tuned in to his plan for our lives.

If we're always behind, we may be doing a lot, but we're not doing what he wants. We've missed the one essential thing in the array of life's busy little details. If we're too busy, there's too much of us in our goals and too little of God's agenda in our lives. If we're too busy to walk in step with the Spirit, sit at the feet of Jesus, and listen to the words of the Father, we're way, way, way too busy.

MOVING AT THE SPEED OF GOD

Jesus was never in a hurry, yet he was never late. He never rushed, yet he accomplished more good than anyone else in history. And Jesus never once apologized for taking his time.

God doesn't hurry. He does things in his own time. At the right time. If he wants a universe, he spends a week painting sunsets and shaping planets and dreaming up dinosaurs and dodo birds and forming people out of clay. If he wants a tree, he plants a seed. If he wants a savior for his people, he waits until just the right moment in history, and then he sends . . . a baby.

God does everything in the unhurried rhythm of grace.

And God is at peace with himself. He isn't distracted by ambition or envy or pride. He's in sync with the way things should be.

By pausing from our cluttered lives and focusing on Jesus, we can finally free ourselves to live in the freshness of the moment. Just like Jesus did. For when we're moving at the speed of God, why would we ever need to hurry?

Sure, Jesus had lots to do, but he was never controlled by busyness, and he was never behind. Early in Jesus's preaching ministry, large crowds showed up at sunset to be healed and freed from demons. There was certainly plenty to do that night. I guess you could even say Jesus was "staying busy."

HE DIDN'T COME TO MAKE A SPLASH BUT TO MAKE A DIFFERENCE.

But look at what he did the next morning: "Jesus awoke long before daybreak and went out alone into the wilderness to pray. Later Simon and the others went out to find him. They said, 'Everyone is asking for you.' But he replied, 'We must go on to other towns as well, and I will preach to them, too, because that is why I came'" (Mark 1:35–38).

Jesus took a timeout.

He wasn't concerned with what everyone thought of him or what they wanted him to do.

"They're all looking for you!" Peter said. "You're famous!"

"Then let's go somewhere that I'm not."

Jesus was only concerned about what God wanted of him, not what others wanted. He focused on God's will for his life, and he built times of silence into his schedule so he could stay focused on his mission. He didn't want the ministry he was doing to become a distraction from his ultimate calling. He didn't come to make a splash but to make a difference.

We should follow his example and accept each moment as an opportunity to follow God's will and worship him. Nothing more. Nothing less.

By the way, the opposite of busyness isn't boredom. The opposite of both of them is peacefulness. Boredom reveals the same lack of spiritual focus busyness does.[3] But God has a twofold prescription for stepping out from behind the twin guises of boredom and busyness. His answer is summed up in a simple and stirring verse tucked away in Psalms, the book of songs in the Bible: "Be still, and know that I am God" (Psalm 46:10 NIV).

THE HEART OF STILLNESS

Stillness isn't the same as laziness or idleness or boredom. Instead, it's a quieting of our souls before God, a refocusing of our lives on God, and a shifting of our attention away from the future (or the past) and onto the present moment.

All around the dining area at the Abbey of Gethsemani in Trappist, Kentucky, are little signs that say "Silence is spoken here." It's not that the monks think talking is wrong, it's just that they want to create enough silence in their lives to hear God speak to them.

That's a good goal for all of us.

I love how the New American Standard Bible translates this verse: "Cease striving and know that I am God."

Most of us are always striving. We don't have many moments of silence or stillness in our days. Our lives are filled with noise when God wants them filled with music.

Even when we're not doing anything, we're not still. Not really still. We're planning what we're going to do this weekend, dreaming about retirement, worrying about whether the kids will be OK on that field trip, remembering that the car needs an oil change, or whatever. But we're not still.

If we want to connect with God, we need to take the time to be still.

Some religions tell us we have to empty our minds of everything in order to be enlightened. God never says that. But he does want us to empty our lives of distractions so we can be filled with him.

Christianity has less to do with producing results than with becoming holy. It has less to do with spiritual activities than with deepening relationships.

To cease striving doesn't mean we cease serving God, just that we stop trying to please him by doing "spiritual things" and instead take the time to focus on the thing that matters most—our relationship with him.

Being still means more than refraining from movement. It also means to stop desiring movement—or even planning or hoping to move. A person who's content to be still is the person who has ceased striving. Stillness is not the absence of activity, it is the presence of peace.

It's only in those moments when we are still, perhaps out of breath, but finally looking around, pausing, just *being*, that God speaks to us. In those brief silences, when the desk is cleared and the clothes put away, when the meal is over, the exam handed in, the graduation completed, the report filed. Then listen. When the noise has quieted, listen. Be still. There will always be more work to do, but this moment will never come again. Listen.

Step off the treadmill, slow down, and take a time-out. Be still. Calm those raging, roaring waves of discontent. The shores of your heart have been ravaged long enough by your attachments to the world and entanglements in its frenetic ways.

Be still.

Cease striving.

And look to Jesus.

When you're still enough and your soul is contemplating him, you will hear God whisper words like these in your soul: "I'm in control. I'm at the helm. I haven't fallen asleep at the wheel. Don't fret. Don't worry. And don't panic. You have nothing to fear, nowhere else to be, nothing else to do but invest this moment in your relationship with me."

It starts with stillness. Stop worrying, cease striving, slow down, and quiet all the noise in your life. Consider who God is, what he's done for you, and how you fit into his plan. That's a lot to think about.

No wonder the monks like it quiet.

KNOWING GOD

The second part of God's prescription for peace is that we focus on knowing him for who he is. Stillness without spiritual focus won't draw us any closer to God.

Throughout the Psalms, believers are encouraged to meditate on the Lord. In Psalm 143:5 David wrote, "I remember the days of old. I ponder all your great works. I think about what you have done."

It doesn't take an intricate plan to do this. We just have to orient our lives on God and, in moments of stillness, consider who he is. Read or pray or think or walk or wonder or worship or imagine or reflect. Maybe take a

Scripture verse and turn it over in your mind, thinking about all the truths it contains. Just take the time to focus on God's grace and love, and spend less time worrying about how many minutes you put in praying or how many Bible verses you were able to memorize.

We can be close to God anywhere—in a monastery or a church, on a mountain, in our bedrooms or offices, or in our cars on the way to work. But the problem is that the busier we are, the more distracted from God we tend to be.

Cease striving. And know that he is God.

SPIRITUAL STRIVING

Once I attended a youth retreat in Michigan, and on the last night of camp, all the students were coming forward by candlelight and sharing spiritual decisions and commitments they'd made over the weekend.

Everyone was saying stuff like, "I'll read my Bible more," or "I'm gonna go to church and youth group every Sunday," or "I'm gonna pray for twenty minutes a day." And everyone was getting all teary eyed.

Then suddenly the camp speaker stood up and said, "It's great to hear about all these spiritual commitments, but let's remember that we can't turn our relationship with God into a bunch of spiritual activities."

It was a good reminder. Christianity isn't about what we do, it's about what Jesus did. As my friend Tom Oyler once said, "It isn't about us giving our lives to God, it's about God giving his life for us."[4]

None of those students stood up and said, "I'm gonna focus my life on getting to know Jesus more intimately," or "I'm gonna honor God and let him take control of my life," or "I'm gonna pursue purity and submit my agendas to the Spirit's leading."

Christianity isn't a bunch of activities we do. It's faith and compassion lived out in the real world. To become more spiritual, we don't need to go to church more or pray more or go on a missions trip. God isn't interested in us bringing him our prayers when we've failed to bring him our lives.

TRUE INTIMACY

At one time in his reign, King David had an affair with a married woman, Bathsheba. When the prophet Nathan confronted him, David said this to

God: "You would not be pleased with sacrifices, or I would bring them. If I brought you a burnt offering, you would not accept it. The sacrifice you want is a broken spirit. A broken and repentant heart, O God, you will not despise" (Psalm 51:16–17).

God doesn't want our religious activity if it's not brought with a humble and believing heart. God doesn't say, "I desire productivity." He's more interested in humility, brokenness over sin, and an attitude of reverence and worship and awe.

That's what Mary had. That's why she was there, at the feet of Jesus.

So let's put away the checklists and focus on deepening and developing our relationship with the Almighty. It isn't as easy as checking things off a list, but it is the way to true intimacy with God.

God knew our lives could get frantic, just like Martha's did. That's why he gave us that simple prescription to turn our focus back to what matters most: "Cease striving. . . ." Be still. Nurture substantial enough silences in your life to hear God speak. Then listen. ". . . And know that I am God." Reflect on God's character, think about his love, contemplate his grace, and ponder his plan.

Becoming real involves seeking peace amid the turmoil of life by carving out times of stillness and reflection and then immersing those moments in the pursuit of intimacy with God.

Now that I think about it, Jesus wasn't too hard on Martha after all. He was telling her the same thing he's telling us. "There is really only one thing worth being concerned about. Mary has discovered it—and I won't take it away from her."

I think I've discovered it too.

Chapter 10

AT THE FEET OF JESUS

Rediscovering Yourself and Esteem

Know that the love of thyself is more hurtful to thee than anything of the world.

—THOMAS À KEMPIS, *THE IMITATION OF CHRIST*

When my youngest daughter, Eden, was two and a half years old, she said to my wife, "I want to tell you a secret."

My wife leaned close, and Eden whispered into her ear, "I love me."

We all laughed until we realized she wasn't just being cute. She was being honest.

And my guess is, she speaks for most of us. Pop psychologists and self-help books keep giving us the same messages over and over:

"There's no such thing as mistakes, only lessons."

"Cheer up! You're not as bad as most people."

"Before you can love others, you have to love yourself."

"Feel good about yourself, and all your problems will go away."

And we've taken their advice to heart. We've become intoxicated with pumping up ourselves. We have more self-esteem, self-love, and self-infatuation than any generation before us, but has it brought us any closer to a spiritually authentic life? Or are we just more in love with ourselves?

I'm going to make a bold statement. I know this will ruffle some feathers, but here it is. The four most dangerous words in the world are these: *Feel good about yourself.*

Pretty ruffling, huh?

Well, stick with me through this chapter. Humor me even if you disagree with me. Let's explore one of the shortest stories Jesus ever told (it's only two verses long). After we've looked at what he said and what happened at supper one night, let's see what you think of self-esteem.

CRASHING THE PARTY

Here's the background of what was going on before Jesus told his brief story. Jesus had been invited to dinner by a man named Simon. As a Pharisee, Simon was very concerned about making sure he followed all the religious regulations of the Old Testament. Yet when Jesus arrived, Simon didn't offer to take his coat, give him a drink, show him around, serve him hors d'oeuvres, or anything. None of the stuff you'd expect to see when an honored guest arrives.

A bit later on, Jesus listed the specific ways Simon failed to show him hospitality: Simon didn't wash Jesus's feet (in those days people either walked barefoot or wore sandals everywhere, and a host would typically have someone waiting to wash a guest's feet). He offered no kiss of friendship (a cordial greeting, much like offering a handshake or a hug today). And Simon didn't offer oil to anoint Jesus's head (a way of showing great honor and respect for one of God's prophets).

All in all, Simon shunned Jesus. He was neither courteous nor cordial, and it wasn't an accident. He knew better. He did it on purpose. He had no respect for Jesus.

Now Simon and his friends weren't the only ones at the meal. Someone else had heard that Jesus would be there that night—a woman Luke called "a sinner." But he used a Greek word that many Bible scholars say refers not just to a sinner but to a prostitute.

So a prostitute heard Jesus would be at this elite dinner party with the prestigious religious leaders, and she showed up. Not only did she show up, she was shown in.

Nothing was going as you might expect at this meal.

In the middle of the main course, the town whore walked in and dropped, weeping, at Jesus's feet. She never said a word, but her actions spoke volumes.

She had expensive perfume that she poured on his feet. Then she started kissing and caressing his ankles. With her tears she was cleaning his feet, and with her hair, she was wiping them clean. While this was going on, all the religious leaders watched—probably with their jaws hanging to the floor in utter shock.

They didn't know how to respond. Finally, Simon shook his head. *If Jesus were really a prophet,* he thought, *he'd know what kind of a woman this is that touches him—that she's a sinner, that's she's a prostitute. It's just like I thought. He's not really the guy he claims to be. He's not really sent from God, because if he was, he wouldn't let her touch him.*

The Bible doesn't tell us if Jesus overheard Simon whispering these things to someone close by, or if (since he was God) he simply knew Simon's thoughts. In either case, Jesus said, "Simon, let me tell you a story."

Simon said, "Go ahead, Teacher."

And that's when Jesus told his story. It's recorded in Luke 7:41–42, just two verses long. Here it is: "A man loaned money to two people—five hundred pieces of silver to one and fifty pieces to the other. But neither of them could repay him, so he kindly forgave them both, canceling their debts. Who do you suppose loved him more after that?"

It's a simple story: A guy cancelled two debts—one big, one small. That's it. That's the whole thing.

Then Jesus asked Simon a surprising question. He didn't ask, "Which of those two guys was more thankful?" That would've been the natural question, but Jesus didn't say that. Instead he asked, "Which of the two will love him more?"

The question seems to have taken Simon by surprise. He was probably thinking, *What does love have to do with a business transaction?*[1] He replied, "I suppose the one who had the bigger debt cancelled."

And Jesus said, "You're right."

So far, so good. But what's the significance of all this?

Well, then Jesus turned to the woman, but he was still speaking to Simon. "Do you see this woman?"

Of course Simon saw her, that's what started this whole thing—he couldn't help but see her.

But Jesus said, "Do you see this woman?" Simon had seen a sinner. A prostitute. When Jesus looked at her, he saw a woman—a woman with great love. He saw past her sin. He saw past her past.

Jesus saw her. And he said, "Don't you see this woman? Don't you *see* her?"

Jesus saw her heart, not her sin. Simon saw her sin, not her heart.

And that's when Jesus contrasted the way the woman had treated him with the way Simon had treated him. He pointed out all those ways Simon had failed to show love and all the ways the woman had expressed her devotion to him. Finally Jesus concluded by saying, "I tell you, her sins—and they are many—have been forgiven, so she has shown me much love. But a person who is forgiven little shows only little love" (Luke 7:47).

That's the key, right there. This story is about the expression of love when a debt is cancelled. The more we're forgiven, the more we love the one who forgave us.

Cause and effect.

That's why Simon shunned Jesus: he didn't love him. And he didn't love him because he didn't think he needed to be forgiven by him. The prostitute, on the other hand, was in love with Jesus because she knew how great her debt was.

Most of us are more like Simon than the woman.

We try to minimize our debts in our own eyes: I'm a pretty good person. I follow the rules, I try my hardest, I do my best, I go to church, I do pretty well . . . We love ourselves so much because we don't see how much we need forgiveness. And because of that, we never discover true love for Jesus.

Cause and effect.

As long as our hearts are busy writing their own press releases, as long as our self-love is strutting across the stage of our souls, there won't be any room in our lives to love Jesus.

Jesus is saying, "If you want great love for me, you'll look at the depth of your debt rather than feeling good about yourself."

Cause and effect.

UNPAYABLE DEBTS

The key to understanding grace is to realize that in Jesus's story, neither person could repay the debt. The difference in the debt doesn't matter. All of us are bankrupt before God. We're all in the same boat. None of us has the ability to repay the debt we owe God. Some of us realize that and fall at Jesus's feet. Many of us don't, and we bury our love for God beneath piles of our own self-esteem.

If I don't have any money, it doesn't matter how much a car costs—eight hundred dollars or eighty thousand dollars—I can't afford it. It doesn't matter how good a swimmer I am—if I drown five feet from shore or five miles from shore, I'm still dead.

Neither man could repay the debt.

This isn't the only time Jesus talked about forgiveness and canceling debts together in the same breath. When Peter asked Jesus about forgiveness, Jesus told a story about debts being cancelled (see Matthew 18:21–35). And when Jesus taught his disciples the pattern for prayer we call the Lord's Prayer, he said, "Forgive us our sins, just as we have forgiven those who have sinned against us" (Matthew 6:12). I don't know Greek, but those who do tell me the original language says, "Forgive us our debts as we forgive everyone who is indebted to us."

THE MORE WE'RE FORGIVEN, THE MORE WE LOVE THE ONE WHO FORGAVE US.

But what kinds of debts do we have before God?

With God our debts come because of our wrongs. And "No man can redeem the life of another or give to God a ransom for him—the ransom for a life is costly, no payment is ever enough" (Psalm 49:7–8 NIV).

A ransom for life is too costly. We can't balance it out, we can't tip the scales in our favor. No payment is ever enough, that's how indebted we are. OK, I'll say it: that's how sinful we are.

Even if we're pretty good people, it's not enough. But then, a few verses later, the psalmist says, "But as for me, God will redeem my life" (Psalm 49:15). God will take care of the debt when we rely on him through faith.

He will forgive. He will cancel our debt. By paying it off himself.

There's only one way to get rid of guilt, and it's not by ignoring it or burying it under favorable comparisons, warm-fuzzy feelings, or compliments: "If we say we have no sin, we are only fooling ourselves and refusing to accept the truth. But if we confess our sins to him, he is faithful and just to forgive us and to cleanse us from every wrong" (1 John 1:8–9).

All of us have sinned. All of us are indebted. And none of us can pay the debt.

That's why the advice to "feel good about yourself" is so deadly. Because the better we think we are, the less we'll think we need a savior. If we're not really so bad, why would we need Jesus? Couldn't we just work a little harder at being good and become acceptable to God eventually?

Self-love cuts us off from recognizing and confessing our sins, placing our faith in Christ, and finding our new identities in him. Simon had lots of self-esteem. The prostitute had none. And she was the one to receive peace and forgiveness that night.

Years ago I heard Dr. Kevin Leman say (and I'm paraphrasing), "In all the history of the world, nobody ever became a Christian while he was feeling good about himself." That thought stuck with me. We only become Christians when we realize there's nothing within ourselves to feel good about. To realize the depth of our forgiveness, we must stare unblinkingly at the height of our sin.

After all, when someone pays off your debt, who do you feel good about? Who do you esteem—yourself or the one who extended his generosity toward you?

See?

Jesus said that those who've been forgiven much love much. Love who? Themselves? Of course not. They love the one who forgave their debt.

We've got it all backward. We think it's all about us, when it's all about Jesus—the one who forgave our debt. The secret is to come to him and say, "God, I have a great, great debt"—and to hear him say, "I can see, because you have great, great love."

THE KEY TO FORGIVENESS

Before we become believers, we're not good, or even neutral. We're actually enemies of God (see Romans 5:10). There's nothing good in our sinful selves (see Romans 7:18). Our old sinful natures are hostile toward God (see Romans 8:7), so when Jesus came to live among us (see John 1:14), he was going behind enemy lines.

Since by ourselves we cannot obey God at all (see Romans 8:8), Jesus didn't tell folks to feel good about their lives but rather to hate them (see John 12:25). Paul said that he counted all of his hard work at keeping the religious laws (before knowing Christ) as worthless garbage. Actually, the King James Version gives us the literal translation of Paul's word: "dung" (Philippians 3:8).

Not something to feel all that good about.

We need to stop trying to convince ourselves how great we are. As long as we're concerned about the level of our own self-love, we're distracted by the disease rather than interested in the cure. We're sipping from the poison without consuming any of the antidote. We're trying to fall in love with a steamy pile of manure.

The only way to feel good about Jesus is to feel bad about our sin. In reference to a convicting letter he sent to the church in Corinth, Paul wrote, "Now I am glad I sent it, not because it hurt you, but because the pain caused you to have remorse and change your ways. It was the kind of sorrow God wants his people to have, so you were not harmed by us in any way. For God can use sorrow in our lives to help us turn away from sin and seek salvation. We will never regret that kind of sorrow. But sorrow without repentance is the kind that results in death" (2 Corinthians 7:9–10).

Some people look long and hard at themselves and, without finding Christ's forgiveness, slip into despair—like Judas, who ended up taking his own life. Some people are aware of God's grace and forgiveness but never realize they're the ones in need of it. They don't end up changed at all—like the Pharisee in our story. Only when we see both Christ and ourselves can we begin to turn away from sin and seek salvation—like the prostitute did.

It's not comfortable to look that closely at our lives. But it is the only way to fall in love with Jesus. And it's the only way to find true forgiveness.

That woman wasn't just washing Jesus's feet, she was expressing her love for Jesus. It was all about him. She was being completely real, totally transparent. We don't drop to our knees at the feet of Jesus and burst into tears while we're busy feeling good about ourselves.

We only fall to our knees and weep when we realize the depth of our debt and the depth of God's forgiveness.

For he who has been forgiven much, loves much.

CHRIST-ESTEEM

Then Jesus turned to the woman and addressed her personally for the first time. He said, "Your sins are forgiven."

The other guests immediately started murmuring. "Who does this guy think he is, claiming to forgive her sins?"

You see, they knew something about forgiveness. They knew that only the person to whom we're indebted can cancel our debt. For example, if I walked up to you and said, "Hey, guess what? You don't have to pay the rest of the mortgage on your house. It's all cancelled. Your debt is gone." You'd say, "Great!" But unfortunately, I'm not the bank. I can't cancel that debt because you don't owe me the money. And unless I pay off the mortgage in your place, you still owe the full amount.

Those other dinner guests knew that our sin makes us indebted to God, that we've failed him. So they said, "How can you talk about forgiving her sins? Only God can do that!"

And they were right.

I have a feeling Jesus knew that and that's why he said it right there in front of them—to show them who he really is. And rather than clarify or explain himself to them, he let his words sink in even further: Jesus said to the woman, "Your faith has saved you. Go in peace."

She didn't come in peace that night, but she left in peace. Because Jesus looked at her and saw more than just her sin. He saw her faith and her love, and he said, "Go in peace, because your debt has been cancelled."

Did Jesus think it was important to raise her self-esteem? Apparently not. He had something much more important to offer her: peace and forgiveness.

The woman's problem wasn't her lack of self-esteem; her problem was the greatness of her sin. Simon had two problems: his sin and his self-esteem. And his self-esteem was so high he couldn't see over it to notice his need for forgiveness.

Peace follows forgiveness. It doesn't follow self-congratulation.

When the prostitute left that night, I don't think she had any more self-esteem than when she arrived. She wasn't esteeming herself at all. The cry of her heart was, "Jesus, I've failed you. I've messed up. Yet you accept me? You forgive me?! I don't care what anyone else thinks of me or says about me. I only care about you, Jesus. I just want my life to show you the depth of my love."

She was esteeming someone, but it wasn't herself.

THE END OF SELF-LOVE

"But, wait a minute," you say. "Aren't we supposed to feel good about ourselves? Didn't Jesus even say we should love ourselves?"

Jesus mentioned self-love (see Luke 10:27), but not to encourage us to love ourselves more; it was to exhort us to love God and others more. We already love ourselves plenty. After all, "No one hates his own body but lovingly cares for it" (Ephesians 5:29).

Nowhere in Scripture does God tell us to love ourselves more. Nowhere.

Let me mention something here: everyone is worthy of respect and dignity because people are created in God's image. But the problem with feeling good about ourselves, even because of that, is that we're focusing our attention in the wrong direction. Should the painting praise itself? Should the sculpture feel good about itself, or does the praise belong to the one who shaped it to match the dream in his soul?

> **NOWHERE IN SCRIPTURE DOES GOD TELL US TO LOVE OURSELVES MORE.**

Everything we are comes from God: "Not that we are competent in ourselves to claim anything for ourselves, but our competence comes from God" (2 Corinthians 3:5 NIV).

If we're honest, we have to admit that we already know self-love isn't the answer we're looking for.

Sometimes when I speak to teenagers, I'll ask them, "How many of you have ever been told by a teacher, a coach, or a counselor to feel good about yourself?"

Guess how many hands go up? Every one of them.

Then I ask, "How many of you know that's not the answer to life's problems?" Guess how many hands go up?

That's right. Every one of them.

Because they know (and we know too), that we've all done stuff we shouldn't feel good about. And we know that smothering our guilt with self-flattery isn't the answer.

Teenagers know that, and they're tired of the advice of the self-esteem gurus because they know it isn't true. They want truth. They want real answers. They want forgiveness.

And that's what Jesus offers. He gives us the truth and sets us free.

Jesus didn't turn to the woman and say, "Cheer up, it's not so bad. Sure, you've made some mistakes, but you're only human. You're better than most people. Stop all this negative self-talk. Feel good about yourself. Go home and give yourself some self-affirmation. Tell yourself you're a nice person. Say it with me right now, 'I'm a nice person' . . . Come on, repeat after me: 'I'm a nice person.'"

No, Jesus was honest with her. Rather than making people feel good about themselves, Jesus made them become aware of themselves. Because that's the pathway to truth, to freedom, and to him. Awareness opens us up to finally becoming real.

Jesus acknowledged the greatness of the woman's sins and offered her something far better than the salve of self-esteem. He offered total acceptance, eternal forgiveness, unfailing love, a peace that passes understanding, adoption into the family of God, and an entirely new life.

Not a bad deal if you ask me.

WORTHLESS AND NO GOOD?

A few years ago, a youth worker told me this story. He used to work at a church in the Twin Cities, and one of the students in his group had a father who yelled at him, "You're worthless and no good!" That night the kid took an X-Acto knife and carved the word *worthless* into one of his forearms and the words *no good* into the other.

Is that what our heavenly Father wants us to think of ourselves? That we're worthless and no good?

Absolutely not.

We are unworthy of God's love, but we're not worthless to God. We're precious. Believers are living paradoxes.

Because of my pride, I'm lost; because of his mercy, I'm found. Because of my rebellion, I'm guilty; because of his grace, I'm pardoned. Because of my sin, I'm wretched; because of his image woven into my soul, I'm great. I am both a sinner and a saint. Both a pirate and a prince. Both a mutineer and a son. Both a prostitute and a bride.

God loves us even though we're unlovable. He accepts us despite our failures. He gives us worth and dignity in spite of our mistakes. He equips us to serve others despite our selfishness. And he forgives our sins in spite of our rebellion.

In God's eyes there's no such thing as an insignificant person. Remember that verse about even the hairs of our heads being numbered? (see Luke 12:7). Some people think it's trite or silly that God would be sitting up in heaven counting hairs. Is that the point? That God has nothing better to do than count the hairs on our heads?

Don't be ridiculous.

That verse means that God values you so highly that he cares about every hair on your head, every dream in your heart, every yearning in your soul. He knows every freckle on your face and every scar from your past. And he cares about each one: "You keep track of all my sorrows. You have collected all my tears in your bottle. You have recorded each one in your book" (Psalm 56:8).

His love is that deep. His concern is that great. We can't even fathom a love like that.

So we're left either believing the unbelievable or rejecting God altogether because his love seems too good to be true. It's a ludicrous love. Could it really be that we matter ultimately to God? That he offers us free and full and complete forgiveness? That he would rather die than spend eternity without us?

Could God care that much about each one of us?

That truly is the question.

And the answer is yes.

And the proof is the cross. "No one is likely to die for a good person, though someone might be willing to die for a person who is especially good. But God showed his great love for us by sending Christ to die for us while we were still sinners. . . . So now we can rejoice in our wonderful new relationship with God—all because of what our Lord Jesus Christ has done for us in making us friends of God" (Romans 5:7–8, 11).

God already knows how often we doubt and fail and fear and falter and fall, and he still accepts us. He hears our cries and sees the tears we only shed on the inside, and he isn't embarrassed by them. God's love for us is everlasting, unfailing, faithful, self-sacrificing, and it endures forever.[2] When God looks down at us, he can't help but burst into song, so great is his love for us: "The LORD your God is with you, he is mighty to save. He will take great delight in you, he will quiet you with his love, he will rejoice over you with singing" (Zephaniah 3:17 NIV).

That's what God thinks of us. He breaks into song when he thinks of his children.

ACCEPTING GOD'S LOVE

If we've placed our faith in Christ, the gospel has a whole bouquet of promises for us. God chose us from before time began to spend eternity with him. He sent his Spirit to live within us, to strengthen and guide us, to comfort and protect us, to assure us of our salvation. He has guaranteed us a home in heaven where there's no more sadness, suffering, separation, or death, and the word *good-bye* is never heard. He has specifically gifted each of us for service in the greatest task the world has ever known—to tell others of his love.

Jesus died for us.

God loves us that much.

Are we worthless to God? By no means.

To God we're worth dying for. To God we're worth more than life itself. We are new creations with new lives, deeper significance, and eternal purpose. We've become part of the family of God and the body of Christ. And because of our relationship with God, we're heirs of heaven with an inheritance that can never spoil, tarnish, fade, or slip from our grasp. We're more than conquerors through Christ's love.

And since we've become children of the King of kings, we've entered a royal lineage. We are sons and daughters of the King. Nothing, not even death itself, can separate us from the everlasting, indwelling, life-changing love of God.

When we immerse ourselves in truths like these, we won't ever have to prop up our egos by trying to feel good about ourselves.

A DAUGHTER OF THE KING

You should see my daughter Eden when she puts on a sparkly, plastic princess crown. Everything about her changes. The way she moves. The way she stands. The way she talks. She's transformed by a piece of plastic.

For that moment, she believes she is a princess. She holds her head high. She has dignity and grace and poise. Because she believes she is part of a royal family.

Imagine how she'll feel when she learns that she truly is.

When we find out who we really are, it leads us to the feet of Jesus.

Those who are forgiven much, love much. We'll esteem someone, but it won't be ourselves.

"Your sins are forgiven. Your faith has saved you; go in peace."

Go to Jesus right now. Leave your self-love at his feet. He has words to whisper to you, promises of peace and forgiveness, the moment you stop saying, "I love me" and finally say, "I love you."

Chapter 11

FLIRTING WITH THE FORBIDDEN

Confronting Temptation

Let no one persuade himself otherwise—
our vicious lives alone have conquered us.
—SALVIAN, COMMENTING ON
THE DECLINE OF THE ROMAN EMPIRE

Let me get this out in the open. Let me admit something, just between you and me.

I like walking the edge. I like peering into forbidden territory. I like looking both ways to make sure I won't get caught, and then . . . I like the thrill of stepping over the line.

I admit it. Sometimes I enjoy licking the forbidden fruit.

Just like you do.

It doesn't do any good to pretend that we would never do "those things," that those things are only true for other people, that we're beyond temptation. We like to think of ourselves as immune, but the temptations we face are all too real. Of course, they differ for each of us. Some people struggle with pride, others with envy or pornography or gossip or anger, but all of us struggle.

Sometimes we give in.

And—here's the kicker—sometimes we like it when we do. We enjoy the taste of the forbidden.

Everyone is vulnerable. We just don't like to admit it. We don't like being that transparent. That real.

It's time we owned up to the truth.

TWO VOICES

Marsha winked at me as we strolled out of the workshop. September sunlight danced in her blonde hair. She was in her early twenties, had a charming smile, and was seductively attractive.

"Stop whistling," she said as she stepped outside.

"Was I whistling?"

She laughed. "Are you one of the speakers? Will you be telling a story tonight?"

"Yeah, I am." Sometimes when I speak, I share a scriptural message. Sometimes it's simply to entertain. Tonight it was to entertain.

She smiled. "Tell me a story."

"Maybe later on," I said. I was surprised by the attention but beginning to enjoy it.

"I'll look forward to it." She reached out her hand. "I'm Marsha."

I took her hand and shook it. "I'm Steve."

The conference center was a few hours from my home. Since it was going to be a late night, I would be staying over at a friend's house nearby. I travel often, and I frequently have to stay overnight after my speaking engagements. It was no big deal.

At the next session, I sat across from Marsha and found myself inadvertently glancing in her direction throughout the presentation. I studied her face. She was beautiful, and her eyes were bright and intelligent.

A conversation leaped to life in my heart.

You like her, don't you? You think she's cute.

Then another voice.

But you're married, Steve! What are you doing?

Back and forth.

You're not doing anything. You can't help but see her when she's sitting right in front of you.

That's no excuse, you're looking at her on purpose!

Toward the end of the workshop, she looked at me exactly when I was staring at her, and she smiled. She winked at me and unconsciously licked her lips.

She likes you too. She's teasing you.

No, she's not. It's nothing. Just doughnut crumbs or something.

I just smiled back at her and looked away.

I'm sure no one else noticed.

MORE WHERE THAT CAME FROM

That afternoon she filled my thoughts.

She's just being nice. It's all innocent. You haven't done anything wrong.

Stop kidding yourself. You like it, don't you? You like the attention. It's flattering, isn't it?

It's nothing. She's just being friendly.

I started getting edgy and nervous. Nervous enough to start avoiding her.

At the evening meal, I made sure I sat next to an old friend of mine. It would be much safer if I positioned myself out of Marsha's path. But then I turned to see who was sitting on my right.

"Welcome to our table," Marsha said.

Oh great.

By then the banquet had begun, and it was too late to move.

She reached into her bag and produced a peach. "I always carry fresh fruit to these things. Would you like a peach?"

It seemed innocent enough. I didn't want to appear rude, so I said, "Sure."

"There's more where that came from," she said, tucking her bag underneath her chair.

What did she just say?! What was that supposed to mean?

You're reading too much into this, Steve. Stop worrying so much. Just enjoy her company. At least there's someone here who wants to talk to you.

A little while later, her fingers brushed against mine. She held the back of my hand for a second too long before letting go. "Would you like some more lasagna?" she asked innocently.

Then, toward the end of the meal, I felt her hand on my leg under the table. I was so startled I jerked back in my chair, almost falling backward to the floor.

Everyone in our area looked over at me. "Are you OK?" someone asked.

"Yeah," I said quickly.

Marsha snickered. She put her hand up to her lips and patted them, smiling.

Oh.

She was only signaling to me that I needed to wipe my face with my napkin.

That was all.

"I was just trying to get your attention," she whispered.

Maybe I was reading this all wrong. I mean, all she'd done was start a conversation with me as we left the workshop, been kind enough to offer me a piece of fruit, passed me the lasagna, and saved me the embarrassment of having food on my face.

That was it.

Or was it?

It had been so long since anyone other than my wife had shown romantic interest in me that I wasn't sure what to think.

After the meal I escaped to a quiet place to practice my performance. But I was preoccupied with thoughts of Marsha: *Ask her to go for a walk. Come on, don't tell me you haven't thought about it. Just see what happens. No one will know. You're not even expected home until tomorrow. If you asked Marsha, I'm sure she'd offer you a place to stay tonight. After all, she mentioned at supper that she lives in the area . . . and you really don't want to have to drive all the way to Jim's house, do you?*

I couldn't believe what I was thinking! Where were these thoughts coming from?

No, Steve! What are you doing? What's going on here?

I admit it. Her attention was flattering. And exciting. I felt like I was single again.

Stop it! How dare you? What are you thinking? Think of how it would affect your wife and your daughter. And your wife is carrying your second child. Walk away!

That's when I remembered the story of Joseph in the Old Testament.

KEEPING THE DOOR OPEN

His brothers had sold him to slave traders, and he ended up working for Potiphar, an official to the king and the captain of the temple guard.

So here was Joseph, alone in a foreign land.

Soon Potiphar recognized Joseph's leadership qualities and placed him in charge of all of his possessions.

Now, Joseph was well built and handsome. It didn't take Potiphar's wife long to notice this good-looking hunk working around the house. He was an impressive guy. Potiphar thought so. And so did she.

One day she came on to Joseph and invited him to sleep with her. He refused her advances and said something you'd expect a Bible hero to say: "'Look,' he told her, 'my master trusts me with everything in his entire household. No one here has more authority than I do! He has held back nothing from me except you, because you are his wife. How could I ever do such a wicked thing? It would be a great sin against God'" (Genesis 39:8–9).

HE HAD NO CHOICE BUT TO RUN.

Those are not the words of a man in the throes of temptation. Those are the words of a man standing outside the territory of temptation. Because once we're gripped by temptation and lured into the heart of it, we don't think any longer about consequences or responsibility or about what pleases God. All we can think of is the possibility of getting away with whatever it is we're tempted to do.

But Joseph's response didn't stop Potiphar's wife. She kept talking to him day after day. And he tried to avoid her.

Well, sort of.

She began to wear him down. And I think he started to consider her offer.

How do I know? Even though Joseph told her no, he left the door open. He never brought the matter up to his master, and even though he kept refusing to sleep with her or spend time with her, he didn't change his schedule enough to avoid her, because somehow she was able to keep propositioning him day after day (see Genesis 39:10). This guy was in charge of the household staff's schedules, and yet somehow he kept ending up alone with his boss's wife in situations where she could make passes at him. How hard was he trying to avoid her, really?

Apparently he continued to let her speak to him and hint to him and flirt with him. He let her tease him.

He played along. He didn't walk away.

Until he had no choice but to run.

FATAL HESITATION

I'm sure that after a while he couldn't help but notice her taking notice of him. He probably felt just like I did at that conference. Flattered.

Day after day she lured him, winked, and licked her lips. "There's more where that came from," she whispered. She laughed at his jokes, smiled from across the room, and let her hand brush across his. "I was just trying to get your attention."

Joseph had to see where this whole thing was going. He couldn't have been that naive.

Then came the day alone in the house: "One day, however, no one else was around when he was doing his work inside the house. She came and grabbed him by his shirt, demanding, 'Sleep with me!' Joseph tore himself away, but as he did, his shirt came off. She was left holding it as he ran from the house" (Genesis 39:11–12).

What did she do, sneak up from behind and surprise him? I doubt it. Remember, they had to be standing close enough for her to grab his shirt. It doesn't take a whole lot of imagination to picture him standing right in front of her, looking down into her eyes as she whispered, "Come to bed with me. You know you want to. You've wanted to for a long time. No one will find out. No one else is here. No one will ever know."

Maybe then she reached out to wrap her arms around him. And what did he do?

He hesitated.

This man of God hesitated just long enough to realize that this time was different from the others. This time he couldn't "just say no," because this time part of him really wanted to say yes.

He hesitated just long enough for her to actually touch him, and when she clutched at his clothes, he realized he had to make a decision. What did he do? He left his shirt in her hands and ran out of the house.

I used to think about that and be impressed by his purity as he fled from temptation. What a guy! What a model of righteousness!

But that night at the conference I realized something—he ran away because it was the only thing he could do. He knew he could have gotten away with the affair. She'd been throwing herself at him for weeks. They were alone. She wouldn't have told her husband. How would any man feel?

I used to think Joseph wasn't even tempted, and to be honest, I couldn't really identify with him. Because I do know what it's like to be tempted.

But come on.

That day Joseph was in her arms, and they were alone in the house. For weeks she'd been chasing him, and now they were finally alone and together. Your shirt doesn't just fly off your body.

This guy hesitated.

Remember, he was well built, muscular (see Genesis 39:6). Did she overpower him and rip off his clothes? I don't think so. She had his help.

I'll bet I know what was going through his head. The same thing that would go through any guy's head. The same thing that was going through my head that day at the conference.

Go ahead, see what happens.

He knew if he stayed there one second longer, the sin wouldn't have been just hers; it would have become his. Most importantly, he would no longer have been able to say no.

I think his heart was beating and his head was spinning and his body was responding to her attention, and the only thing he could do was flee.

A TIME TO FLEE

I realized I needed to do the same, so I steered clear of Marsha as best I could. And when I ran into her after the program, I stuck out a stiff hand and I told her it was nice to meet her and I hoped she enjoyed the conference. She got the hint.

"OK, I get it. It was nice to meet you too."

I made a beeline for my car. As I sat down, breathing heavily, I finally realized how close I'd come to the edge of temptation.

I had flirted with the forbidden. At least my thoughts had.

"Whew, Jesus, thanks," I muttered. "Thanks that I didn't get her phone number or her address or even her last name. Thanks that I didn't bump into her on the path to my car. I wouldn't have known what to do."

As I drove home, I was humbled by how tempted I'd been.

And that's a good place to be.

Paul wrote: "If you think you are standing strong, be careful, for you, too, may fall into the same sin. But remember that the temptations that come into your life are no different from what others experience. And God is faithful. He will keep the temptation from becoming so strong that you can't stand up against it. When you are tempted, he will show you a way out so that you will not give in to it" (1 Corinthians 10:12–13).

God will show us a way out. The problem is that when he does, we tend to look the other way. These verses take away that old excuse "I just couldn't help it." We can help it. We just don't want to.

We don't suddenly fall into sin. No one does. We ease into it slowly. It isn't like we blindly topple off a cliff, it's more like we slowly inch our way closer and closer to peer over the edge until we finally lose our footing and realize one moment too late that we're slipping. We drift into sin one choice at a time. Martin Luther is reported to have said, "You can't stop a bird from flying over your head, but you can stop it from making a nest in your hair."

That day I almost had a nest in my hair. I nearly stepped over the edge.

And when I got home and told my wife all about it, we both thanked God for that little voice inside that told me to flee at just the right time.

SWEET PROMISES

When we're in the heat of temptation, we don't usually tell ourselves the truth. Instead we think of all sorts of excuses: I won't get caught. Nothing bad will happen to me. It's not that bad. No one will find out.

The irony of sin is that it lures us with sweet promises of freedom, but the further we walk into it, the more entangled we become. The alcoholic drinks because she has to, not because she wants to. The man addicted to pornography surfs the Internet late at night because he needs his fix. The gossip keeps spreading rumors because she can't stand keeping the misdeeds of others to herself. We become trapped, enchained, enslaved by our desires.

We are such poor, blind, wandering fools. How easily we're led astray— by the flash of a breast or the promise of fame or the glimmer of a few slim pieces of gold—even though we know these things often bring pleasure without fulfillment and fill our hearts but empty our souls. James had it right: "Temptation comes from the lure of our own evil desires. These evil desires lead to evil actions, and evil actions lead to death" (James 1:14–15).

It's a downward spiral. We're lured into evil desires, then evil deeds, and then, eventually, death.

When Solomon warned his son about avoiding adultery, he told the story of a young man who was enticed by a flirtatious woman. Note the similarities in his description to the path toward destruction that James outlined in the verse mentioned above:

> She seduced him with her pretty speech. With her flattery she enticed him. He followed her at once, like an ox going to the slaughter or like a trapped stag, awaiting the arrow that would pierce its heart. He was like a bird flying into a snare, little knowing it would cost him his life.
>
> Listen to me, my sons, and pay attention to my words. Don't let your hearts stray away toward her. Don't wander down her wayward path. For she has been the ruin of many; numerous men have been her victims. Her house is the road to the grave. Her bedroom is the den of death. (Proverbs 7:21–27)

Evil desires. Evil deeds. Den of death.

One subtle lie after another. We listen because we don't really think we'll get caught. How could we ever deceive ourselves so easily?

Maybe it happens because we want to be deceived.

Let's admit it—we enjoy some of the things that anger God. We like getting our way more than we like him getting his.

Or maybe I should say part of us likes it. Some people call it the "old Adam" or the "old sinful man." Whatever we call it, I know what it sounds like in my heart. I hear it whisper to me every day.

THE PATHWAY THROUGH TEMPTATION

In the prayer Jesus taught his disciples (we usually call it The Lord's Prayer), he said, "Lead us not into temptation, but deliver us from the evil one" (Matthew 6:13 NIV).

If we pray that God leads us "not into temptation," we're really asking him to lead us away from the temptation. Sometimes he may lead us up to it, as he did with Jesus (see Matthew 4:1). He may lead us into situations in which we'll be tempted in order to help us grow in faith or conviction or wisdom. But he would never force us to sin or lure us off the narrow path. God never tries to trick us into hurting him.

No, he's not in the business of deceiving his children. He just allows temptations to enter our lives to give us a chance to show him where our true allegiance lies.

So if we pray, "Lead me not into temptation" while we're busy tiptoeing as close to it as we can, we're saying one thing and doing another. We're praying one thing while desiring another. And that's the very definition of a hypocrite.

I guarantee that if we toy with temptation, temptation will make mincemeat out of us. God doesn't want us to toy with sin, he wants us to put it to death (see Romans 8:12–13). He doesn't want us to dance with the devil but to resist him. If we resist, he'll flee. If we flirt, he'll lean over and kiss us on the cheek, take us by the hand, and lead us back to his bedroom.

LISTENING TO THE SNAKE

That day at the conference, I learned that no one is immune from temptation or sin. The moment we let down our guard is the moment we'll live to regret.

We often think Bible heroes and great saints of the church were somehow exempt from the temptations we face. We act as though they never heard those little voices in their heads, luring them further than they wanted to go.

But they were just as real as we are, and they struggled with the same things we struggle with today.

David had an affair. Samson struggled with getting even. Jacob was a liar. Noah drank too much. Peter liked to brag. James and John were power hungry. Eve wanted to be like God.

They were as vulnerable as any of us. And they all listened to the snake.

Most of the Epistles of the New Testament weren't written to congratulate people who were doing pretty well. They were written to believers who were struggling to live out their faith in the real world. That's encouraging to me because they didn't have it all together either. They were just as human as I am. And that means there's still hope for me.

For all of us.

Once you admit that you're not strong enough on your own and begin to rely on God instead of yourself, he will strengthen you, help you, and direct you. Ask him for the wisdom to avoid tempting situations, the courage to resist temptation, the honesty to admit you like some things he despises, and the resolve to follow his guidance rather than be led around by your passions and desires. Then rely on God to lead you through the times of temptation.

We'll never reach perfection in this life. Let's be honest enough to admit that we're going to mess things up sometimes, but let's also be humble enough to go to God for forgiveness when we do.

Flee when you need to. Resist when you can. Either way, let's stop flirting with the forbidden. Instead of seeing how close we can get to the edge of temptation, let's see how close we can get to the will of God.

Chapter 12

SLAYING THE MONSTER

Experiencing and Extending True Forgiveness

He that cannot forgive others breaks the bridge over which he must pass himself; for every man has need to be forgiven.

—THOMAS FULLER

You're in Jamaica. It's nighttime. You hear the ocean lapping on the shore. You see the stars hanging in the raven-black sky. You smell the rich undergrowth nearby and feel the soft tropical breeze brush across your face.

It's almost midnight, but no one is asleep. The year is 1838. At the stroke of midnight tonight, July 31, all slaves on the island will be officially free.

A crowd of people is heading toward the village. You join them. Some are praying. Some are crying. Some are singing. It's hard to believe this day has finally arrived.

Great Britain has been in charge of the island since they took it by force from the Spaniards on May 11, 1655—nearly two hundred years ago. Since then, more than 850,000 Africans have been captured, taken across the seas, and sold as slaves in the West Indies.

Some 300,000 of those slaves ended up here, in Jamaica.

And now, on this night, every slave will finally be declared free.

Two missionaries, William Knibb and James Philippo, are leading prayer. Joining them are fourteen thousand adults and five thousand children. Everyone waits anxiously for the bell at the church to announce the midnight hour.

Near the missionaries is a large hole dug into the rich dirt.

It's a grave.

Next to it is a coffin. Mahogany. Made and polished and fitted by slaves skilled in carpentry.

People have come forward and placed things into the coffin. Arthur Pierson described the scene: "The whips, the torture-irons, the branding irons, the coarse frocks, and shirts, and great hat, fragments of the treadmill, the handcuffs—whatever was the sign and badge of 78 years of thralldom—they placed in the coffin and screwed down the lid. As the bell began to toll for midnight, the voice of Knibb was heard saying: 'The monster is dying—is dying—is dying' and as the last stroke sounded from the belfry, 'The monster is dead! Let us bury him out of sight forever!'"[1]

They lower that casket into the ground, burying those relics of slavery. And more than nineteen thousand people join their voices together in singing the doxology:

Praise God, from whom all blessings flow;
Praise Him all creatures here below;
Praise Him above, ye, heavenly host;
Praise Father, Son, and Holy Ghost![2]

As Arthur Pierson summarized, "This was the way in which these black slaves took vengeance on their former masters—not by deeds of violence and murder, but by burying the remnants of their long bondage and the remembrance of their great wrongs, in the grave of oblivion."[3]

THE NAME OF THE MONSTER

When I first read that story, I thought, *Whoa! That's incredible! Those people buried the monster of slavery that night.*

But then I started thinking about it.

Was slavery really the monster they buried? Those ex-slaves buried the pain of the past so they could move on and live free from bitterness and unforgiveness. They didn't bury what they'd done but rather the reminders of what had been done to them. They didn't bury slavery, they buried the remnants of being enslaved.

They chose to forgive. Their monster was not slavery. The monster they slew was unforgiveness.

I've never been in chains or enslaved, yet I face the same choice almost every day. I'll bet you do too. Maybe a family member said something so hurtful you just can't forget it no matter how hard you try. Maybe someone touched you in a way he shouldn't have when you were a kid. Maybe a friend betrayed you weeks ago and you're still holding a grudge. Or you may have scars no one else can see from your dad or your sister or the guys at work or the women at your church.

Whoever it was, whatever it was, most of us have a hard time forgiving other people when they hurt us in that tender, easily bruised place at the center of our hearts.

That happened to me early in my marriage when my wife had a miscarriage. She grieved differently than I did, and I resented it. She made some offhand comments, and I thought, *How could she be so insensitive and unloving toward our unborn child?* And those thoughts gnawed away at my soul.

Until a friend said to me, "You know what I think your problem is?"

"No, what's that?"

"You haven't forgiven your wife."

He was right. Until I forgave her, I was the one who was enslaved.

Unforgiveness reveals itself in the set jaw, the narrowed eyes, the cold shoulder, the slammed door, the premature divorce. It crawls in and makes its lair within us. It lurks in the dark corners of our memories. And we refuse to release it. Instead we feed it, finger its mane, sharpen its claws. Then, when we least expect it, without our permission or knowledge, it begins to feed on us, slowly devouring us as it grows stronger and stronger.

That's what unforgiveness does. It devours. It enslaves.

But those slaves had had enough of slavery. So they buried their bitterness and embraced the freedom of forgiveness.

THE SLAVE WHO FORGAVE

Their story reminds me of another ex-slave who forgave. His name was Joseph (we looked at part of his story in the last chapter). And he had every right to hold a grudge.

Joseph's brothers hated him and made fun of him. One day they decided to kill him but at the last minute opted to sell him as a slave instead. Huh. How kind. Joseph became a household servant in a foreign land and was soon imprisoned for a crime he didn't commit. (You remember: Potiphar's wife . . . hesitating . . . caught with his shirt off . . .)

His brothers thought they would never see him again.

But after many years, God brought them back together, and this time the tables were turned. Joseph, as a high-ranking government official in charge of food distribution, held their lives in his hands. He had the chance to get even, but he didn't. Instead of seeking revenge, he invited the whole family to move in with him.

His brothers were terrified. They knew Joseph might one day decide to pay them back for the way they'd treated him, so they begged him not to retaliate. "But Joseph said to them, 'Don't be afraid. Am I in the place of God? You intended to harm me, but God intended it for good to accomplish what is now being done, the saving of many lives. So then, don't be afraid. I will provide for you and your children.' And he reassured them and spoke kindly to them" (Genesis 50:19–21 NIV).

Joseph wasn't out for revenge. He saw a bigger plan at work. He realized God was in control behind the scenes. Because of his faith, Joseph was able to let go of bitterness and open his arms to those who had hurt him.

Forgiving others isn't easy, but it is possible. When you've been wronged, remind yourself how willing God was to forgive you, then lean on his promises and his love rather than on your own feelings.

God can remove even the most entrenched grudge, if you let him.

LEARNING TO FORGET

When it comes to forgiving others, Jesus didn't pull any punches. When Peter asked him if he should be so gracious as to forgive someone seven times, Jesus answered, "No, multiply that times seventy, and you'll be on the right track." Then he told a story about a guy who'd had a huge debt cancelled but then had someone who owed him a few dollars worked over until he could pay.

At the end of the story, the guy who refused to forgive the minor debt was thrown into prison. Jesus summed up his story: "That's what my heavenly Father will do to you if you refuse to forgive your brothers and sisters in your heart" (Matthew 18:35).

Another time Jesus said, "I am warning you! If another believer sins, rebuke him; then if he repents, forgive him. Even if he wrongs you seven times a day and each time turns again and asks forgiveness, forgive him" (Luke 17:3–4). Seven times a day? Is this guy serious?

Yes, he is. Limitless forgiveness is what we're talking about here. Refusing to hold a grudge no matter what. Even if we keep getting hurt.

Then, when Jesus was teaching his followers how to pray, he even went so far as to say, "If you forgive those who sin against you, your heavenly Father will forgive you. But if you refuse to forgive others, your Father will not forgive your sins" (Matthew 6:14–15).

I once met a girl who'd been sexually abused by her stepfather dozens of times before he was finally caught and convicted. When I asked her if she forgave him, she quoted those words of Jesus to me. She understood that refusing to forgive others locks us out of receiving forgiveness ourselves. Because we can't honor God by holding a grudge.

> WHEN YOU'VE BEEN WRONGED, REMIND YOURSELF HOW **WILLING** GOD WAS TO FORGIVE YOU.

Each of us faces the same choice the slaves faced. What will we do when someone wrongs us? Or hurts us? Or wounds us deeply? Feed on the bitterness or bury it? Cling to it or let it go? We have the power to lock up the past. That's easy. But do we have the courage to let it go?

When Jesus was laid out on the cross and the soldiers lifted the hammers to nail him to the wood, he prayed for them. He begged God to forgive them. He was willing to forgive the final and most deadly blow of all—an unjust death.

But is that practical? Forgiving people no matter what? Is that even possible?

On our own, without God's help, I'm not sure it is. I can't seem to conjure it up by myself. But with his help, I think we can begin to live that kind of forgiving lifestyle. It's not easy. No doubt about that. It's a process. But Paul gave us a blueprint for forgiveness in his letter to the believers in Ephesus: "Get rid of all bitterness, rage, anger, harsh words, and slander, as well as all types of malicious behavior. Instead, be kind to each other, tenderhearted, forgiving one another, just as God through Christ has forgiven you" (Ephesians 4:31–32).

Two things are going on in this verse—God's relationship with us, and our relationship with others. We receive forgiveness and we offer forgiveness.

We accept it and we extend it. We're even told how to forgive: "Just as God through Christ has forgiven you."

How exactly does God forgive us? Fully, completely, and forever—even if we choose to hurt him again and reject his love.

Don't throw the manipulating tentacles of guilt around the necks of those you love. Instead, cut them free with the grace of forgiveness.

REAL FORGIVENESS VERSUS SITCOM FORGIVENESS

In sitcoms, no matter what happens, by the end of the show, everyone is buddy-buddy again. But if you look carefully, no one really gets forgiven.

Sitcom forgiveness works like this: Joe breaks Bob's vase, Bob gets angry, and Joe eventually mumbles, "Sorry about that vase."

Bob says, "Oh, it's OK. No big deal. I never liked that vase anyway. Just spring for supper tonight and we'll forget about it."

Then Joe says, "Thanks, buddy! You're a real pal!" And as they head out to go the restaurant together, the credits roll.

Did Bob forgive Joe?

No, he excused him.

And there's a big difference between excusing and forgiving.

When we get excused, we haven't done anything wrong; we have a justifiable reason for our actions. When we get forgiven, we have no excuse; we actually did something wrong, but the crime isn't counted against us.

For true forgiveness to occur, three things must happen. First, a real debt needs to be owed. In other words, a real wrong needs to be done. If it's no big deal, or if no debt was incurred, there's no debt to be forgiven.

Pretending no debt exists never leads to forgiveness. Pretending we weren't hurt by someone will never lead us to forgive her. Until we're honest about it, we can neither forgive nor be forgiven.

Second, the debt must be graciously cancelled with no strings attached. If the person never liked that vase anyway, he doesn't need to forgive his friend, he needs to thank him for doing him a favor! Forgiveness acknowledges a debt and then cancels it graciously.

Finally, when true forgiveness is offered, nothing more is ever required of the debtor. If Bob makes a deal with Joe for him to pay for supper, he isn't forgiving him, he's bartering with him. "I'll forget about this as long as you . . . [fill in the blank]." That's not a canceled debt, it's simply been renegotiated.

True forgiveness never asks anything of the one who is forgiven. Nothing more is required. Ever. The one who forgives acknowledges the wrong, gives up the right to feel angry or resentful, and seeks nothing more from the debtor.

In our little sitcom, did Bob acknowledge the debt? No. He downplayed it. Did he graciously forgive? No, he told him he never even liked the vase. And did he release Joe of any future obligations? Nope. He made a deal with him to pay him back by taking him our for supper. Strike three.

None of the requirements for forgiveness were met, so no forgiveness was offered, and no forgiveness was received. That's sitcom forgiveness.

But that's not God's kind of forgiveness.

God lets us know when we've wronged him. He doesn't downplay our debts or ignore them or make light of them. He doesn't wink at our sins. If he did, he could never forgive them. Instead, he honestly acknowledges our sins, and then he completely cancels them. He forgives us and welcomes us back to himself without any resentment on his part, or any obligation on ours.

STONE THROWING

When God forgives, he forgets. He doesn't remind us of the past. He doesn't barter with us or make deals with us. He forgives completely. He pardons our past. As God told Israel, "I—yes, I alone—am the one who blots out your sins for my own sake and will never think of them again" (Isaiah 43:25).

When the Pharisees brought to Jesus a woman caught in the act of adultery, they tried to trap him into saying something they could use against him. They wanted to accuse him of being a literalist or a liberal, of either being too legalistic or too tolerant, too dogmatic or too lenient.

But Jesus didn't fall for any of that. He said, "All right, stone her. But let those who have never sinned throw the first stones" (John 8:7).

Well, they realized they were just as guilty of sin as the woman was, and they slipped away one by one until Jesus was left standing there alone with the adulteress. And it's interesting what Jesus asked her. "Where are your accusers? Didn't any of them stick around to condemn you?"

"They have all gone," she said. And she was right. Her accusers had all gone. But not Jesus. He was right beside her. You see, he never joined in with the accusing.

"Neither do I condemn you," he said. If he didn't accuse her or condemn her, what did he do? He forgave her.

He forgives me.

He forgives you.

Note that Jesus didn't accuse her, but neither did he excuse her. He didn't make light of her sin. He didn't ignore it. He looked straight at it and forgave it and gave her another chance.

HONEST ENOUGH TO FORGIVE

So forgiveness isn't pretending the hurts didn't happen. It's honestly recognizing that they did and making a conscious decision to no longer hold those wrongs against the person. It isn't ignoring the past, it's choosing to move on and face the future. It isn't about lingering guilt and festering grudges. Unlike sitcom forgiveness, which ignores the wrong, real forgiveness is refreshingly, brutally honest.

Forgiveness isn't about ignoring a wrong or telling ourselves it didn't hurt. Forgiveness is the opposite of that. It's the ability to look the person in the face and say, "You hurt me. But I forgive you."

That's speaking the truth in love.

"But when I've been hurt," you're probably saying, "don't I have a right to feel angry? Don't I have a right to be resentful?"

Yes, you do. Absolutely. That's the point.

When we forgive others, we honestly acknowledge that we have a right to be angry; but then we give up our right to bitterness once and for all. That's why forgiveness, real forgiveness, is so tough. And so rare. It's why we so often skirt around it without accepting it or offering it.

Don't miss the other facet to all this: we need to admit when we need forgiveness too.

Often we construct elaborate defenses so we'll never have to admit we've done anything wrong. Even when we ask for forgiveness, we say, "I'm sorry if I said something that hurt your feelings."

If?

That's not asking for forgiveness. There's no acceptance of responsibility for hurting the person. It's like the responsibility is placed back on the offended person: "If you felt offended, I'm sorry." What kind of an apology is that?

"I'm sorry I yelled at you, but . . ."

But?

A true apology never has a *but* in it. *But* is just another way of shifting responsibility to the other person. We shouldn't play word games to weasel our way out of a genuine confession. Truth frees; half-truths enchain.

Only when we stop playing these games of ignoring the pain, pretending the wrong didn't occur, and excusing behavior can forgiveness—real forgiveness—be offered and received. Until then no one has to feel remorse. And no one gets to feel forgiveness.

When we're hurt, treated unjustly, or wounded by others, we're given a choice: lock up the anger and bitterness behind the guise of victimization, or let God have it and move on.

What's the best way to slay the monster and bury it out of sight forever? Forgive those who've wronged you just as God has forgiven you. As hard as it may be, as tough as it may seem, forgiveness is the only way to move on to restoring the relationship.

BURYING THE MONSTER

I know what belongs in my coffin. I've thought about it long and hard. I've had to put some things in there that I've been carrying around for a long time. They were hard to bury. Hard to let go of. Because I liked playing the role of the victim. I liked fingering the mane of the monster.

I know what belongs in my coffin. What belongs in yours? What reminds you of the pains of your past? What do you still carry around that weighs you down and drains your joy and gnaws away at your soul? Is it the guilt and shame of your own sin? If so, God will forgive you. Completely. Fully. Freely. Forever. God doesn't carry a grudge, and he doesn't dredge up the past. He forgives and he forgets. And he remembers our sins no more (see Jeremiah 31:34 and Hebrews 10:17).

Or maybe you're carrying bitterness for wrongs that have been done to you. If so, let go. Forgive. Bury the monster and move on.

Those ex-slaves had a choice. They'd been freed by the government, but they could have remained enslaved by the past—shackled to their pain. Instead they chose to move on, to let God have their past, and to honestly and genuinely forgive. We can do the same thing. Right now. Right here. Today.

The monster is dying . . . is dying . . . is dying.

Let us bury him out of sight forever.

PART 3
EMERGING

Instant replay allows millions of sports fans to relive the highlights (and low points) of sporting events just seconds after they occur. The big catch, the free kick, the breakaway slam dunk, the fumbled ball . . .

Most of us will never see ourselves in an instant replay on TV, but we all have private replay screens in our minds. We replay the highlights (and low points) from the past: it might be the time that girl laughed at you in ninth grade, the time your boss chewed you out, the day you landed the big account, or the moment you proposed to your spouse. Sometimes we see the slam dunks, and sometimes the fumbles as we look back at the glories and accomplishments, wounds and mistakes, traumas and triumphs of our lives. We play those scenes over and over in our minds as we try to figure out exactly who we are and where we fit into this strange, wonderful, mixed-up world.

Some people only replay the highlights. They're the stars of their own pasts and continually say, "Remember when I . . ."

Others only replay the low points. They're the ones who convince themselves they could never be successful at anything. They think, *If only I had said or done that differently . . .*

But each, in his own way, is setting a trap for himself. For as the Chinese Christian leader Watchman Nee once said, "Our failure lies in thinking of

155

ourselves too much. We remember either our virtues or our defeats, both of which hinder Christ from being fully manifested in our lives."[1] The words of Peter Kreeft summarize nicely: "Humility is thinking less about yourself, not thinking less of yourself."[2]

All of these replayed scenes tell only a portion of the story and focus our attention in the wrong direction—on our past rather than on our future with God.

The process of becoming real requires shutting off that internal instant-replay screen. That doesn't mean denying the mistakes we've made or pretending the wounds or struggles of our pasts never happened. (It doesn't mean flattering ourselves by clinging to past successes either.)

Rather, God's grace sets us free to finally accept all of those scenes for what they are—moments that have helped to shape us but do not define us.

Our new lives are defined by Christ. Our worth and our identities don't come from our past successes or failures but from our relationship with God. For our lives are completely in his hands and no longer under the thumb of the past. We need to be able to tell ourselves, "I haven't always made good decisions, and I haven't always made bad ones. But right now, right here, this is where I am. I won't continue to relive either the glory days or the sorry days. I am who I am. I don't have unlimited potential (nobody does), and yet with God's help I can become more than I ever have been. I'll accept my past as a part of myself, but I'll also accept this moment as the first moment of a brand-new game."

I WON'T CONTINUE TO RELIVE EITHER THE GLORY DAYS OR THE SORRY DAYS.

If we can start living out those words, we'll be freer than most of the people on Planet Earth. Putting the past in its place is vital. As Paul wrote, "I am still not all I should be, but I am focusing all my energies on this one thing: Forgetting the past and looking forward to what lies ahead, I strain to reach the end of the race and receive the prize for which God, through Christ Jesus, is calling us up to heaven" (Philippians 3:13–14).

Since God forgives all wrongs, there's no reason we should dwell on the past. We're free from its grip when we're forgiven by the Master. And since God is in complete control of the universe and nothing slips through the cracks or gets past him, we need not fear or fret about tomorrow, for he holds it securely in his hands.

The past is past, the future is up to God. This moment is all we have. So make it count.

Learn from the past—acknowledge it and move on. Thank God for the lessons. Hand him the pain. Reflect on the past, but don't try to live there. It's a road that has passed under your wheels. It's countryside no longer in view. That doesn't mean you ignore the past. Let it inform you—but not distract you.

God has given you this moment to serve him. What will you do with it?

oh Lord,
find the darkened corners of my life
and bring them to light.
find the empty places in my soul
and fill them with yourself.
find the excuses i love to make
and expose them to the truth.
find me lost in the valleys of loneliness
and lead me to the mountains of communion.
let me be unashamed
to be myself in your presence
despite what i was.

as you make me into
who i am.

Chapter 13

THE MILLION-DOLLAR MAN

Exploring True Wealth and Poverty

> *No man is rich who shakes and groans*
> *Convinced that he needs more.*
> —BOETHIUS, *THE CONSOLATION OF PHILOSOPHY*

On the surface Darren's life was perfect. A beautiful wife, loads of money, a successful business. But he'd been hiding a secret life for a long time. And one day it all became public.

Listen to him tell his story.

The twin engines of our Piper Navajo whined as we skimmed less than fifty feet above the ocean, low enough to avoid getting picked up on radar. We'd been in the air for seven hours, and this was the most dangerous part of our trip. The shoreline lay two hundred miles in front of us, through the pitch-black night. Rain pelted against the plane's windows. We had to dodge oil rigs rising out of the water. The plane was overloaded and especially tough to maneuver because we were smuggling 1,300 pounds of marijuana.

I thought of my family back home in Tennessee. How long had it been now since I'd seen my daughter? Or talked with my wife? But then I thought of all the money I'd earn from this trip and from selling the marijuana to my distributors.

I smiled and stared out the window of the plane. It's worth all the danger and all the lies, I thought. The money makes it all worthwhile.

When Darren was young, his family never had much money. Even though his dad was brilliant and talented, he wasn't a very involved or responsible father. So Darren's mom had to take care of him and his five siblings. At an early age, Darren decided the secret to happiness was money—the more you had, the happier you'd be. He vowed that his family would have lots of money someday.

"But part of me knew what I was doing was wrong," he later said. "A small part that I'd learned to keep silent over the years."

For each trip we would leave southern Florida and fly seven hours to the jungles of Columbia, where we landed on a secret airstrip to pick up the marijuana. On the way back, we'd refuel mid-flight with an extra tank of gasoline we kept behind the pilot's cabin. We did the refueling from inside the cabin. There was no escape from the fumes, and if just a spark would have gone off, we would have been killed instantly in the explosion. It was dangerous and stupid, but all we could think of was the money we'd earn.

After returning to the States and eluding detection by the Drug Enforcement Administration (DEA), Darren and his crew would load the marijuana into a motor home, and he would drive it nineteen hours back to eastern Tennessee, where he sold it to his network of distributors. After four years of smuggling, he was making about $85,000 to $120,000 per flight. He had more money than he could ever spend. But he still wasn't happy.

It was on one of those flights over the Gulf of Mexico that I realized I was becoming more and more like my father—always away from my family, always making excuses. The answer to happiness must lie somewhere else. That's when I decided to stop selling drugs. Slowly I began to pull out of the smuggling business.

But it was too late. The DEA was already onto me.

A few months later, an FBI agent and a DEA agent caught up with Darren at a restaurant.

"You'll be indicted and prosecuted under the Continuing Criminal Enterprise statute, which carries up to a life sentence," one agent told him. Darren figured they were bluffing.

They weren't.

Six months later they arrested him at his health club in Huntsville, Alabama.

I figured it was no big deal. I'd just hire a lawyer again, and all my troubles would go away. I had the money. But money wasn't the solution. Not this time.

When they threw me in jail, it was all over the news. Everyone was calling me the million-dollar man because they figured if bail was set, it would be at least that much. At first I felt like a celebrity.

But then I got word that no bail had been set because the authorities thought I would flee or would try to have the informants killed. My lawyer told me, "These are some serious charges. And eleven of your closest friends and relatives have agreed to testify against you. You're looking at a minimum of forty-five years in prison."

They took me to an isolated prison in Alabama, and when the guard swung the door shut and I heard the lock clang, I realized everything was gone. The planes. The drugs. The money. Hope for the future. Even my family would be taken from me. I had nothing left. Money hadn't brought me happiness, and pursuing it had only hurt the people I loved and destroyed my life. I might never be a free man again.

When that metal door slammed, I knew I would be spending at least the next twenty to forty years in prison. As I sat there in my cell, alone and in despair, I finally asked God to forgive me.

MOMENTS OF CLARITY

Most of us don't have our secret sins revealed so dramatically. Most of us can cover our tracks pretty well and keep our lives pretty much in control. At least for a while.

But when we're forced to look deep into our hearts with clarity and gut-wrenching honesty, our lives can be changed forever.

In those moments we become real, not a little at a time but all at once. Sometimes it happens when a loved one dies. Or when we lose a job. Or when a spouse leaves. Or when a private sin we thought no one would ever discover becomes public. Some people's secrets are exposed by the media.

With others it's a husband or a child or a friend or a stranger who somehow sees past all the pretenses and excuses and double-talk.

Sometimes the revelation comes in a moment of clarity, when we ask ourselves, is this really all there is to my life? Isn't there something more? Sometimes we find regrets catching up to us, and we have to admit—even if it's just to ourselves—that we aren't as good as we make ourselves out to be. Too many of us reach the top of the ladder of success, only to realize it was leaning against the wrong building.

In those times of no excuse and no escape, we're faced with the question of who we are and what we're searching for in life. And we're given the chance to be honest with God.

It's in those moments of vulnerability that God speaks to us and offers us a different kind of living. A chance to look at life and see it, perhaps for the first time, the way God intended for us to see it all along.

That day, with everything gone except God, I felt a peace with him that I had never felt before. With nothing left to distract me, God seemed closer than he had ever been. When I had no hope, he became my only hope. And for the first time since I had become a Christian many years before, I began to pursue a relationship with God. Money was not the answer I'd been looking for; God was.

Darren was sentenced to fifteen years in prison and ended up serving forty-four months before he was released. He told me, "My time in prison was actually good for me. I drew closer to the Lord. With no future plans, no work, I had no life left. That's when my faith became real."

Did you catch that? Finally, when there was no lawyer to bail him out, no money to pay off informants, no place to go, nowhere to hide—that's when Darren's faith became real. He learned his lesson the hard way.

When Darren first told me his story, I thought, *Well, that guy had it coming to him. I mean, I'm not nearly as bad as he was. Drug smuggling. Prison. He really got off track.*

But then I started thinking about my life. How comfortable I am. How many of my decisions are based primarily on the bottom line—on the amount of money I stand to make. On the security or the benefits or the payoffs.

Hmm.

Has it ever happened to you? Where you start to ask yourself, is this really what life is all about? Just making a few more bucks? Can money ever buy me the things I yearn for most?

It's easy to get blindsided or distracted by the glitter of fame and fortune. I'll admit it. It's happened to me.

In our society, it's tough to imagine happiness apart from money. We're taught that money paves the road to contentment. And we measure worth in terms of wealth.

But when we're honest with ourselves, I think most of us would have to admit that money can't really buy the best things in life—that the best things in life aren't things at all. And money can never satisfy the deep questions and hopes and desires of our souls.

THE WORTH OF WEALTH

For his part, Jesus made people look closely at their attitudes about wealth and their priorities in life. He told the rich religious leaders of his day, "No one can serve two masters. For you will hate one and love the other, or be devoted to one and despise the other. You cannot serve both God and money" (Luke 16:13).

Service. Love. Devotion. Jesus said we can't have them for both God and money. He didn't say we *shouldn't* serve both God and money.

Jesus said we can't.

Too many people are in love with money—devoting their lives to acquiring it and serving it with their time and passion. Jesus said we can't serve both God and money. It's one or the other: an authentic spiritual life of love, devotion, and service to God, or the passionate pursuit of wealth and materialism. One or the other. Never both.

We're either slaves to God or to materialism. That's pretty eye-opening for most of us. We tend to equate prosperity with "the good life"—just like the Pharisees did.

Here's how the religious leaders responded to Jesus's little nugget of wisdom: "The Pharisees, who dearly loved their money, naturally scoffed at all this. Then he said to them, 'You like to look good in public, but God knows your evil hearts. What this world honors is an abomination in the sight of God'"(Luke 16:14–15).

163

Yikes. That's pretty blunt: "What this world honors is an abomination in the sight of God." The world honors wealth, but unless we have hearts that are yielded to God and that put him first, it's all for nothing. Because God's priorities are the opposite of the world's. Jesus modeled this attitude of putting God first and trusting him for everything. When Jesus died, he was a homeless man who didn't even have a shirt on his back. Nothing. When he made his choice between God and money, he went all the way.

People who think money and wealth will bring them happiness usually find that money and wealth bring only the desire for more money and wealth: "Those who love money will never have enough. How absurd to think that wealth brings true happiness" (Ecclesiastes 5:10).

We may not be as passionate in our pursuit of wealth as Darren was, but we buy into the same philosophy that led him down that path: money leads to happiness; wealth leads to contentment; if I want happiness, I must have money.

Contrast that with these words of Jesus: "A person is a fool to store up earthly wealth but not have a rich relationship with God" (Luke 12:21).

PUTTING MONEY IN ITS PLACE

God is all we need to be content. Security comes from his presence, not the presence of possessions. As the writer of Hebrews put it, "Keep your lives free from the love of money and be content with what you have, because God has said, 'Never will I leave you; never will I forsake you'" (Hebrews 13:5 NIV).

Rather than always striving for more, we should be content with enough. Through the strength Christ provides, we can find contentment in any circumstance, just as Paul did: "I have learned how to get along happily whether I have much or little. I know how to live on almost nothing or with everything. I have learned the secret of living in every situation, whether it is with a full stomach or empty, with plenty or little. For I can do everything with the help of Christ who gives me the strength I need" (Philippians 4:11–13).

When Paul said, "I can do everything," he wasn't saying he could turn into a superhero and leap over tall buildings with a single bound or bend steel bars with his bare hands. The context makes clear that Paul was saying he had learned that the secret to true contentment lies in the strength God provides. He was saying, "I've learned to live above my circumstances, whether they're good or bad, by relying on the help and strength of God rather than on myself. I can handle it because he can handle it."

The amount of wealth is of no consequence—whether much or little. It's our attitude about it that matters. Paul discovered a simple solution that gave him strength and comfort despite circumstances: faith. Confidence in Christ is the secret to contentment, not acquiring wealth or investing wisely.

We need to beware of what we pursue with our lives. The pursuit of wealth has many pitfalls; the pursuit of God has none. Our goal as believers should be simply to please God and let the chips fall where they may. Because "people who long to be rich fall into temptation and are trapped by many foolish and harmful desires that plunge them into ruin and destruction. For the love of money is at the root of all kinds of evil. And some people, craving money, have wandered from the faith and pierced themselves with many sorrows" (1 Timothy 6:9–10).

In that passage Paul painted a pretty graphic picture of the dangers of pursuing wealth. And look at the parallels between his warnings and Darren's life before that day in the prison cell: trapped by foolish and harmful desires . . . evil resulting from the love of money . . . plunging into ruin and destruction . . . craving money . . . wandering from the faith . . . piercing himself with many sorrows . . .

Not only can the pursuit of wealth distract us from God, so can the allure of stuff.

MINDING WHAT MATTERS

We're physical creatures, and we need stuff to survive. God made us this way. We need a place to sleep and live, tools and equipment to do our jobs, and clothes to cover our bodies. To live through the winters of life, we have to store food and supplies. (And remember, all of this physical work is done not outside of but within the spiritual realm. Working and living in a physical world is not somehow less spiritual than studying the Bible or contemplating God.)

Yet taken to an extreme, we can forget the spiritual and lose ourselves in

165

the physical. Enjoying food can lead to gluttony. Enjoying stuff can lead to extravagance. Enjoying enjoyment can lead to indulgence.

Stuff easily encumbers us. That's the problem. It holds us to a certain place and a specific endeavor. But the things that take our breath away and fill our hearts today are going to fill the garbage dump tomorrow. Denis Haack, in *The Rest of Success*, wrote: "I think all Christians should regularly visit the city dump. Have a quiet time there. Spend some time in the Scriptures and in prayer, preferably with your car window open. As you do so, remind yourself of what is around you. In huge rotting piles is the accumulated stuff which some have lived for, and perhaps even died for. By God's grace may we be saved from ash-heap lives."[1]

"IN HUGE ROTTING PILES IS THE ACCUMULATED STUFF WHICH SOME HAVE LIVED FOR, AND PERHAPS EVEN DIED FOR."

Preoccupation with stuff will always distract us from following God. Everything that invades our hearts becomes another brick in a towering wall that separates us from him. Brick by brick, it slowly blocks the view as we become entranced by staring at our stuff and admiring it. Until it finally imprisons us.

That's the nature of stuff. It entices, it lures, it entangles, and then it leaves us distracted and weary. The consumer gets consumed. The more stuff we cling to, the smaller and more shriveled our souls become.

Because the more stuff we get, the more time and energy we must give to it: acquiring the stuff (shopping, driving around town, surfing the Internet, paging through catalogs . . .), installing the stuff (carrying it home, rearranging to find space for it, reading the instructions, connecting the wires, calling the customer-service hotline . . .), maintaining the stuff (painting, storing, dusting, vacuuming, mending, washing, waxing, repairing, updating . . .), and then replacing the old stuff with newer stuff. And the cycle starts all over again.

Whew. It's wearisome to even think about. Everything we own in turn owns a portion of our time and our energy and our lives. Too much stuff means too little life left for the things that matter most.

So we walk the line between simplicity and necessity. And the moment we think we deserve more than we have or that our possessions can make us rich or that we deserve to be comfortable in this life, we've fallen to the side and forgotten that we're simply pilgrims on a swift and certain journey home.

LETTING GO OF THE WORLD

The importance of daily reliance on God (rather than on wealth) is woven throughout the Bible. In the Old Testament, the children of Israel had to trust God for daily bread (literally) while they wandered through the desert. In the New Testament, Jesus told his followers they should pray for daily bread too. He even emphasized the point by being redundant: "Give us *this day* our *daily* bread" (Matthew 6:11 NASB, emphasis added).

We should take each day as it comes, trusting that God will provide enough for us for right now, and stop worrying about tomorrow. And that means being wary of any schemes or investment strategies or retirement plans that promise a safe-and-secure future, guaranteeing us tomorrow's bread.

Security will never come from investments, only from the knowledge that an all-powerful God has promised that he'll take care of us when we make his kingdom our primary concern. Tomorrow is in God's hands, not the bank's.

God works on a day-to-day basis. And the more we have stored up for tomorrow, the less likely we'll be to rely on him today.

ONLY ONE MASTER

Holding on to Jesus means letting go of the world. When Jesus calls us to follow him, he calls us to a life of sacrifice and discipleship, not comfort and convenience: "No one can become my disciple without giving up everything for me" (Luke 14:33).

If we want to really follow Jesus, we need to give up our own dreams and ambitions, our own goals and philosophies, our own agendas and intentions, and embrace his instead. We need to wrap our hearts and lives and minds and time and resources around those things that matter most to Jesus. Christ's words in Matthew 16:26 really put things in perspective: "How do you benefit if you gain the whole world but lose your own soul in the process? Is anything worth more than your soul?"

Jesus told the rich young ruler to get rid of his wealth and then to follow him (see Mark 10:21). Before this man could follow Jesus, he needed to get rid of the thing that was separating him from being a true disciple: his stuff. "At this, the man's face fell, and he went sadly away because he had many possessions. Jesus looked around and said to his disciples, 'How hard it is for rich people to get into the Kingdom of God!'" (Mark 10:22–23).

As far as we know, that young man never found the kingdom of God. As far as we know, he never returned to Jesus.

We need to do the same two things Jesus told this man to do: (1) weed out the things in our lives that hold us back from total commitment, and then (2) follow Jesus wherever he leads.

We cannot serve both God and ourselves. In his classic book *Basic Christianity*, John R. W. Stott cautioned, "If you want to live a life of easy-going self-indulgence, whatever you do, do not become a Christian."[2]

We can't serve two masters. So if you've been seduced by the alluring whisperings of wealth, take time right now to tell God you've been walking the wrong road and pursuing the wrong things. Ask him to be your master and to lead you into the love, devotion, and service only he deserves.

It's a process. It doesn't happen all at once. It's not the last step in the journey to becoming real, but it is one of the most important. If we're that honest, our lives will be transformed. Just like Darren's was the day the door slammed shut, his facade fell away, and a new life opened wide before him.

Chapter 14

THE VISIBILITY SYNDROME

Redefining Success

Never let success hide its emptiness from you.
—DAG HAMMARSKJÖLD

The crawfish stream bubbled past our feet as we waited for the forest ranger to hand out nets to our children. My daughter was in first grade, and this was my first time chaperoning one of her field trips.

They called it a Brook Look, which I guess is a cool way of saying thirty little kids tromping up and down a creek for an hour, scooping up bugs and lizards in fishing nets.

I should tell you I don't mind speaking in front of a thousand people, but I've never been very comfortable in small group settings. I get shy. I never know what to say. So I was standing quietly near my daughter when a cluster of other chaperones (they were all moms) approached me.

They smiled politely and pointed out their children. Finally I said awkwardly, "I'm, um, Ariel's dad."

And then one of them said, "Are you the storyteller?"

They all stared at me expectantly.

"Well, I guess so," I stammered. "I'm *a* storyteller, I don't know if I'm *the* storyteller."

"From what I've heard, you're *the* storyteller," she gushed. "And a successful author?"

Oh, brother.

The other moms beamed at me while I turned beet red. "Um, well, I guess that depends on how you define success. I've had a few things published, yes." Just then the forest ranger rescued me by handing out the nets.

A few minutes later, as I trudged through the stream with my daughter, helping her look for minnows and salamanders, I began wondering—*was that woman right or wrong? Am I successful or not? What does it mean to be successful anyway? How do I define success? Is it the number of books I've written? The number of people I speak to each year? The amount of money I make? How many degrees appear after my name? The kind of car I drive?*

What really makes for a successful life?

DEFINING SUCCESS

After talking with Darren (see chapter 13), I knew money alone would never lead to success. But what does? It's an important question to ask because our views of success shape our attitudes, priorities, choices, and identities, as well as our views of how we fit into God's world and his plan. And pursuing success with the wrong definition will never lead us to become the people God wants us to be.

Whether we realize it or not, we each have a certain idea of success, just like that mom from my daughter's class. And we all want to be successful. Nobody sets out to become a failure. Nobody wakes up in the morning and says, "I hope everything I attempt today turns out to be a big, fat failure. I can't wait to get to work and mess everything up! Then I'll come home and do all I can to ruin my marriage, and maybe someday my kids can all grow up to become a burden on society!"

Of course not. Everyone wants to be successful, even though each of us has a slightly different idea about what that means. For some of us, success means lots of money in the bank. For others it's control or the ability to tell other people what to do and when to do it. Or it's the opportunity to travel when and where we please. Maybe it's a healthy family life or the financial freedom to finally buy that house we've always wanted. For some it's the image we portray or the clothes we wear or the big promotion we're trying to get, but whatever factors we slip into the equation, all of us want to be successful.

After interviewing people about their definitions of success, author and speaker Denis Haack wrote, "Most people I've asked seem to have little trouble identifying the predominant version [of success] in society: *Success means attaining some measure of money, fame, power and self-fulfillment—and then looking the part.*"[1]

I'd say that's a pretty accurate definition of our society's version of success. I mean, think about it. How much of our lives are spent in the pursuit of money or fame or power or self-fulfillment (however we define that) and then making sure people notice?

For instance, why are you wearing the clothes you have on? Or why do you drive the car you do? Why do you live in the house or the neighborhood you do?

"But Steve," you say, "I can't afford a nicer car or a better house."

That's right. But if you had the money, you'd buy it. If you had the opportunity to get a better car, or nicer clothes, or a bigger home, you'd get them, right?

Most of us would. Why? So people will notice and think we're successful. After all, in our society, how successful are we—really—if no one notices?

Once, when Socrates saw a woman all dressed up for a trip to the city, he remarked, "I suspect that your trip is not to see the city, but for the city to see you."[2]

It's sobering, I might even say heartbreaking, to realize how much of our lives we spend in this futile and frantic attempt to become and appear

WHAT DOES IT MEAN TO BE SUCCESSFUL ANYWAY?

more successful than the very people Jesus has called us to serve and to honor above ourselves. Solomon noticed the same thing three thousand years ago: "I observed that most people are motivated to success by their envy of their neighbors. But this, too, is meaningless, like chasing the wind" (Ecclesiastes 4:4).

So a person with lots of stuff might still be suffering from the greatest poverty of all. That's pretty heavy stuff. As I observed in my book *How to Smell Like God,* "Most people spend their life working in a job they don't like, for a boss they don't respect, with people they don't get along with, to make the money to buy stuff they don't even need. And if they endure this lifestyle long enough, we call them a success!"[3]

A success? What could be further from the truth?

Our culture has hypnotized us into being continually dissatisfied. Jesus warned, "Beware! Don't be greedy for what you don't have. Real life is not measured by how much we own" (Luke 12:15).

If real life isn't measured by how much we own (or by what people think we own), then what does real life consist of? If true success isn't measured by money, fame, power, self-fulfillment, and image, what is it measured by? What does make for a successful life?

Remember Jesus's words in Luke 12:21? "A person is a fool to store up earthly wealth but not have a rich relationship with God."

A rich relationship with God. That's what lies at the heart of real life. That's what defines a truly successful life.

GRASSHOPPERS FOR DESSERT

John the apostle wrote this about John the Baptist: "God sent John the Baptist to tell everyone about the light [Jesus] so that everyone might believe because of his testimony" (John 1:6–7).

Here's what we know about John the Baptist. He came to prepare people to meet the Messiah, the light of the world. He lived in the wilderness, wore clothes made of camel's hair, and ate grasshoppers and wild honey. (And this was way before reality TV.)

John preached a message of repentance, and the people responded. Eventually he was imprisoned for speaking out against the immoral lifestyle of the king. While in prison, he heard of Jesus's ministry of preaching and teaching in the towns of Galilee. John sent his followers to ask Jesus if he truly was the Messiah, and Jesus confirmed that he was. After John's followers left, Jesus turned to the crowd and said these words about John the Baptist:

> Who is this man in the wilderness that you went out to see? Did you find him weak as a reed, moved by every breath of wind? Or were you expecting to see a man dressed in expensive clothes? Those who dress like that live in palaces, not out in the wilderness. Were you looking for a prophet? Yes, and he is more than a prophet. John is the man to whom the Scriptures refer when they say, "Look, I am sending my messenger before you, and he will prepare your way before you." (Matthew 11:7–10)

So John broke the ice: he rolled out the red carpet and set the stage for Jesus's ministry. John was a man of conviction. He wasn't easily swayed. He swam against the tide. He wasn't a pampered, fashion-conscious fad watcher. He didn't strut. He was bold, fearless, passionate, and humble. He was "more than a prophet." He ate grasshoppers, and Jesus called him the greatest man to ever live.

That's right. In the next breath, Jesus said this: "I assure you, of all who have ever lived, none is greater than John the Baptist" (Matthew 11:11).

Pause for a moment and think about those words.

Imagine hearing Jesus say them about you. "Of all who have ever lived, none is greater than Joe the accountant . . . than Raja the professor . . . than Beth the stay-at-home mom . . . than Ricardo the plumber . . ."

Could there be any greater compliment in all the world than to have Jesus say those words about you?

True success—real success—doesn't come from impressing others but from nurturing a rich relationship with God. Like John the Baptist did.

If we examine the life of the person Jesus called the greatest man in history, we'll find three keys to pursuing this rich relationship with God. Three things we all can do.

1. Discover Your True Identity in Christ

Even before John became a prophet, he was a believer in the God of Abraham. The Bible says he was filled with the Holy Spirit even before his birth (see Luke 1:15). God was at the center of John's life; God was not an afterthought. John's entire identity was wrapped up in this God he lived to serve.

God's intention for you mirrors his intention for John the Baptist. God wants you to find your true identity through your faith in Jesus Christ—to become a believer, to be filled with his Spirit: "Let heaven fill your thoughts. Do not think only about things down here on earth. For you died when Christ died, and your real life is hidden with Christ in God. And when Christ, who is your real life, is revealed to the whole world, you will share in all his glory" (Colossians 3:2–4).

As a believer, your identity (your new identity, your true and complete identity) is wrapped up in Christ. So you live by trusting in him, as Paul did: "I myself no longer live, but Christ lives in me. So I live my life in this earthly body by trusting in the Son of God, who loved me and gave himself for me" (Galatians 2:20).

Faith—immersing ourselves in Christ—is the secret to living an authentic life. The clearer you understand your true identity, the more you will love God. And the less you'll be concerned about yourself and what other people think about you.

Through faith we become citizens of heaven and members of God's own family. That's the destiny, the identity, God has in mind for us. Just as with John the Baptist, God's will is that we find ourselves by finding ourselves in him.

Without God in the equation, our lives will never amount to success, no matter how many other variables are added in. Fame can evaporate in an instant, a fortune can disappear in a single business deal, reputation can be ruined by one mistake, integrity can be lost through a momentary indiscretion, possessions can go up in flames, even our health will one day disintegrate before our eyes. Only our relationship with God will last.

As Solomon summarized at the end of Ecclesiastes, "Now all has been heard, here is the conclusion of the matter: Fear God and keep his commandments, for this is the whole duty of man" (Ecclesiastes 12:13 NIV).

If finding, fearing, and following God is the whole duty of man (of woman, of all of our lives), a life devoid of God will end in failure, no matter which way we cut it. If that's what life is really all about and we're not on board, we've missed the boat and are heading in the exact opposite direction.

If God isn't at the center of our lives, we'll never attain true success. Whatever else we may weave into our definitions of success, discovering new life with God has to be the foundation.

2. Deepen Your Relationship with Christ

Toward the end of the movie *Indiana Jones and the Last Crusade*, there's a climactic scene where the adventurers find the Holy Grail.

Indiana Jones heals his father with water from the Grail, and then, as they're ready to leave the cave, they remember that if the Grail crosses a seal on the ground, the ceiling will fall in.

So of course, since this is Hollywood, they do cross the seal. Down come the boulders, the floor opens up—a big crack in the earth's crust—and the Holy Grail tips and falls onto a little ledge some ways down. Then the woman Indiana Jones likes, the scientist Elsa, slips as she's trying to reach for the Grail. Indiana grabs one of her hands, and with her other hand, she's reaching for the Grail.

"I can reach it! I can reach it!" she cries.

But she's slipping from his grip.

"Give me your other hand!" he yells. "Give me your other hand!"

And then we see her glove slowly peal off, and . . . "Ahhhhhhhhhhhh!" *Thud.*

She's gone. No sequel for her.

Then the ground caves away and Indiana Jones slips, and he's in the same position she'd been in. His father, played by Sean Connery, grabs Indiana's hand, just like Indiana had done for Elsa. Only now, Indiana Jones is reaching for the Holy Grail.

Sean Connery says, "Junior, give me your other hand. I can't hold on!"

The music fades down low, and Indiana Jones looks at the Grail. Then he looks at his dad, and his father says, "Indiana, let it go."

And he does. He takes hold of his father with both hands, his dad pulls him up, and they ride off into the sunset, happily ever after . . . until the next movie.

And so it is with us.

We hold on to our Father with one hand, and with the other hand, we have so many things we want to grab—our careers and our goals and our dreams.

And all the while, the Father is saying, "Let it go. Give me your other hand. I'll fill your life with all you need and more. Let it go."

Here's how Jesus put it: "Don't worry about having enough food or drink or clothing. Why be like the pagans who are so deeply concerned about these things? Your heavenly Father already knows all your needs, and he will give you all you need from day to day if you live for him and make the Kingdom of God your primary concern" (Matthew 6:31–33).

WITHOUT GOD IN THE EQUATION, OUR LIVES WILL **NEVER** AMOUNT TO SUCCESS.

Most Christians are pretty content to hold on to God with one hand, but with our other hand, we've got a whole armload of stuff. "God," we say, "I could hold so much more if you'd let me use that hand too. Then I could fill up my life with all these very important things."

Many of us never venture out into the depths of what it means to truly follow God because everything in our relationship with him is halfhearted and filled with excuses and hesitations and practical considerations.

Jesus called John the Baptist the greatest man who ever lived. What were John's priorities? What was his philosophy of life? It's recorded for us in the Bible. Here's the context: John was talking to his followers, who were upset that Jesus was baptizing people and folks were beginning to follow him. John told them, "He [Jesus] must become greater and greater, and I must become less and less" (John 3:30).

Do you think John the Baptist cared about seeing his name in lights? About the power to tell people what to do? About the size of his bank account? About his image? Are you kidding? This was a guy who wore a camel's hair sport coat to formal dinners! Did John the Baptist care about having this year's model donkey parked out front in the driveway?

No way.

All he cared about, all he was passionate about, was disappearing into Jesus so Jesus would become more and more visible and John would become less and less memorable. John wanted Jesus to take over more and more of his life. And Jesus called him the greatest man who ever lived.

John wanted to live with Jesus, in Jesus, for Jesus, by Jesus, and through Jesus. To him, life was all about Jesus.

The second step toward true success is to deepen our relationship with Christ. That means we stop filling our hearts with things other than Jesus and instead hold on to God with both hands. We need to let him become greater and greater to us as we disappear into his love, into his grace, and into his calling for our lives. True success can only be found by living for God wholeheartedly and making his kingdom our primary concern.

3. Unashamedly Embrace God's Calling for Your Life

Rabbi Zusya was an eighteenth-century Hasidic rabbi. The story is told that when he was old and near death, he awoke one morning pale and trembling.

"What's wrong?" asked his followers, who were sitting by his bed.

"I had a dream," he said. His voice was shaking. "And in my dream an angel asked me a question. After I heard the question, I awoke with my heart full of fear and regret."

None of his followers could understand what question could have caused him such fear. After all, he was a devout man. "But you're a holy man!" they stammered. "You study and follow God's law! What was the angel's question?"

The Rabbi replied, "The angel did not ask me, 'Zusya, why were you not a Moses, leading God's people out of slavery?' That was not the question the angel asked. The angel did not ask me, 'Zusya, why were you not a David, conquering kingdoms for my name?' That was not the question the angel asked."

"But what was the question?" his followers asked again.

He responded, "The angel asked me, 'Zusya, why were you not Zusya?'"

God is not going to say to me one day, "Steve, why were you not a Billy Graham, preaching to a hundred million people?" Or, "Steve, why were you not a Jerry B. Jenkins, writing a best-selling apocalyptic fiction series for adults?"

But I dread to think that one day, when I stand before him, I might hear God say, "Steve, why were you never Steve? Why, when I shaped you and I planned and I gifted you and I poured interests and abilities into you—why did you spend your whole life trying to be someone else? Always posturing and pretending and striving to be like those you admired and never becoming the person I prepared you to be? Why, Steve? Why were you not Steve?"

John the Baptist unashamedly embraced his calling. Or we might say his calling embraced him. He lived for the single purpose of pointing people to Jesus. He wanted people to see Jesus, not John. In fact, when people asked John the Baptist his name, he just called himself the "voice" (John 1:23). He told those who were sent by the Pharisees that he wasn't even worthy to untie Jesus's shoes (see John 1:24–27). Another time he called himself "the bridegroom's [Jesus's] friend" (John 3:29). He wasn't concerned about people remembering his name or his accomplishments.

Too often we want to make a name for ourselves. John was content to be anonymous. "I'm the voice," he said. "I'm the friend. That's all you need to know. That's the extent of who I am. Don't look at me, look at the One I speak about. Go to the Friend I serve."

His whole life was an arrow pointing to Jesus.

Did he have any ambitions? Just this: to prepare the way, step out of the way, and then point others to the Way. And that's strikingly close to the calling God has given to each of us.

CURRENTS OF SUCCESS

Even though it would make for a better story, I can't say that I found all of life's answers lurking in the stream that day with my daughter. I didn't flip over a rock and say, "Aha! A salamander! That's the meaning of life! Just as I've been looking in the wrong place for salamanders, so I've been looking in the wrong places for success. Eureka!"

No, nothing like that.

But I did have a lot of time to think about some important questions. And that's a good first step. As Ravi Zacharias points out, "If a company does not know why it exists, then it will never know if it is failing or succeeding. How indicting, then, it is to all of us who will labor for hours to establish a mission statement for a company to sell toothpicks or tombstones but never pause long enough to write one out for our individual lives."[4]

Do that now. Take out a sheet of paper and pencil and begin working on a mission statement for your life, a roadmap for being truly successful in God's eyes.

And no fair, writing, "To glorify God and to enjoy him forever." That one's been used already.

Maybe you look successful on the surface, but in your heart, you're lonely, hurting, desperate, and unfulfilled. Maybe you don't have a rich relationship with God; maybe you don't have any relationship with him at all. But finally, now, today, you're ready to embark on the greatest journey of all. The journey to Jesus.

Then start it.

Maybe you're stuck at stage two. You're a believer. You've met God. You've started the journey. But you haven't moved on from there. You've gotten distracted by the bright lights or the soft whisperings of the world. You're holding on to God with one hand, but with the other, you're reaching out for all the world has to offer. You've gotten bogged down or spiritually worn out. And you're ready today to hold on to God with both hands.

Reach out to him. Let go of everything else.

Or maybe you're ready to unashamedly pursue the life to which God has called you. If so, keep your pencil handy. We'll explore the idea of God's calling more in the next two chapters. It's a big topic, and we'll need a bit more space to tackle it.

What would make for a successful life?

That's a good question.

"Look, Daddy!" my daughter squealed that day at the stream. "Look!"

I saw a minnow skirt through the water. Then we found a baby crawfish, netted some water striders, and caught three tadpoles.

And I glimpsed something even more elusive that day as I tromped through the mud with my daughter: a brief look beneath the surface of my own life and into the ripples of true success.

Chapter 15

ANSWERING THE CALL

Beginning to Live for God

*I shrink to give up my life, and thus do not
plunge into the great waters of life.*
—RABINDRANATH TAGORE

When I first moved to Tennessee with my wife and daughters, I felt that God wanted me to write and speak full time. The only problem was, nobody was asking me to write or to speak. I sometimes tell people I started writing full time when I was twenty-seven years old and started getting paid full time when I turned thirty.

That first year I made less than four thousand dollars—and that was before taxes or tithes or nacho chips or anything. One day, early in the second year, I said to a friend of mine, "Joe, I ought to get a job working at a church or a college or something."

"Why would you want to do that?"

"Well, for a steady income."

"Steve, you don't want a steady income."

I was dumbfounded. "I don't?"

"No. You don't. If you know you've got a check coming every week, you won't have to trust God. If you have ten thousand dollars in the bank, you won't have to rely on God to provide. This way, you'll have to trust God every time you go to the post office."

"Yeah. No kidding," I said.

I thought for moment. "OK then, for job security."

Joe shook his head. "There's no such thing as job security. You work at a church, they get a new pastor, and you're gone in six months. You work for a college somewhere, you become a professor, and the next semester they have budget cuts and you're out of there. Ask anyone who's been around long enough, and he'll tell you the same thing—there's no such thing as job security."

"OK then," I said, "to provide for my family." I knew I had him this time. I even had a Bible verse on my side. (First Timothy 5:8 says that those who don't provide for their families have denied the faith and are worse than unbelievers.)

"Wait a minute. Who provides for your family?" Joe asked.

"I do!"

"Who does?"

I sighed. "OK, God does." (He had a Bible verse on his side too—1 Timothy 6:17 says that God provides us with all we need.) "But if I'm not supposed to get a job based on how much money I make or how much security there is or how many benefits there are, what am I supposed to do?"

ONE QUESTION

Joe leaned forward and said, "Steve, there's only one question you need to ask yourself: where does God want me to serve him right now?"

I knew the answer to that right away. "I think he wants me to write and speak."

"Then you write and you speak. And you trust."[1]

Well, I kept writing, and I kept an eye out for speaking engagements, and there were times when we had very little money—times when we had almost nothing.

But God always provided. Now I can look back and see countless moments of ministry throughout North America and around the world that never would have happened if my wife and I had gone the practical route.

Relying on God like that isn't easy. A lot of people will look at your life when you're living that way and offer practical, sensible advice that'll sound so, so reasonable: "Steve, you really ought to plan more for the future. Invest. Get a steady job. You don't even know if this book you've been working on for the last year is going to get picked up by a publisher."

That was the year a woman from our church said to my wife, "Your husband really ought to get a job." She thought I was unemployed just because I wasn't employed by anyone.

My wife said, "He has one. He just won't get paid for a couple of years."

(Yeah, guys. She's married to me. How did I ever get so lucky?)

I can identify at least a little bit with John the Baptist. It sure wasn't sensible to move out into the desert and start telling people what they didn't want to hear. But he did it. And God provided for him, just like God has provided for me.

At least I never had to eat grasshoppers.

Pursuing our calling won't always make sense. It won't always be easy or comfortable or popular. It wasn't for John the Baptist, and it won't be for us.

But it will be worth it. I can guarantee you that.

FINDING OUR TRUE CALLING

Joe's question was brilliant because it refocused me on the two aspects of serving God that are easily forgotten in our culture. A true calling is in tune with (1) God's will—rather than my own—and (2) God's timing—rather than my own.

Where does God want us to serve him right now?

A job is something we do to pay the bills; a calling is a lifestyle we pursue to fulfill the work of God in the world. Our calling is much more than our career. It's the life God has shaped us for, and it's time to embrace it, pursue it, and live it out.

A true calling doesn't mean we have to serve "in the ministry" but rather that we minister in whatever position God has placed us. Our work—whatever it is—matters to God.

How can we find our true calling?

Step 1: Live to Please God Rather Than Ourselves

The goal of our lives should be to please God. While it's certainly true that Jesus died so we could receive eternal life, it is not true that he died to make our lives easier or so we could reach all of our own career goals. On the contrary, "He died for everyone so that those who receive his new life will no longer live to please themselves. Instead, they will live to please Christ, who died and was raised for them" (2 Corinthians 5:15).

Jesus died so that we would no longer live for ourselves. He died so we might become totally, wholeheartedly his—not so we could continue to indulge ourselves.

People often ask me, where do you want to be in five years? Or, what do you want to be doing in ten years? And I never really knew what to say until I read that verse in 2 Corinthians. Now I think I finally know the right answer.

Where do I want to be in five years?

In the will of God.

What do I want to be doing in ten years? In twenty years? In ten minutes?

The will of God.

It's the only answer that really makes sense. As Henri J. M. Nouwen put it, "The question of where to live and what to do is really insignificant to the question of how to keep the eyes of my heart focused on God."[2]

It's sobering to look at our dreams, goals, intentions, and aspirations and honestly ask how many of them focus on pleasing ourselves, and how many actually focus on pleasing God.

If we're motivated solely by our next paycheck, our next sales incentive, or our next promotion, who are we really working for—God or ourselves?

Paul said our goal should be to please God, not to please ourselves. We can't be Jesus pleasers and people pleasers (or ego pleasers) at the same time. So the first step to finding our true calling is to discover and pursue the will of God.

Step 2: Live Lives Worthy of Children of God

At Pentecost, when Peter preached to the crowds, he told them they had to turn from their sins, turn to God, and be baptized. He concluded by saying, "Then you will receive the gift of the Holy Spirit. This promise is to you and to your children, and even to the Gentiles—all who have been called by the Lord our God" (Acts 2:38–39).

The Lord our God calls us to believe. That's our calling.

Once we begin to follow God, our lives should reflect his glory as we honor and obey him. In Ephesians 4:1 Paul gave this challenge: "I, a prisoner for serving the Lord, beg you to lead a life worthy of your calling, for you have been called by God."

In the next few verses, Paul told the Ephesians specifically what kind of life they were called to lead: "Be humble and gentle. Be patient with each

184

other, making allowance for each other's faults because of your love. Always keep yourselves united in the Holy Spirit, and bind yourselves together with peace" (Ephesians 4:2–3).

Humility. Gentleness. Patience. Understanding. Love. Unity. Peace. These are the marks of our calling. So whatever careers we pursue, they cannot be those that lead us along the opposite path toward pride, harshness, impatience, resentment, hatred, divisiveness, or bitterness. If our jobs drive us into habitual sin, we have the wrong jobs.

Sin never pleases God. He would never call us to a lifestyle that requires us to disobey him. For example, no one is called to be a drug dealer (for God takes care of, not advantage of, the needy) or a marketing director who slants the truth (for God is a God of truth, not of half-truths) or a lawyer who knowingly works to get the guilty acquitted (for God is a God of justice, not of impunity).

The principles are the same no matter what job we have, whether it's designing widgets or stapling papers or performing brain surgery or preaching to a congregation. Integrity, faithfulness, compassion, and a proper perspective should shape our lives and our careers.

Each of us needs to ask, "Does my work allow me to live a life worthy of my calling to be a child of God?" It's a good question.

To God, one job isn't any more glamorous than another. We can honor him just as much by being an accountant as by being a missionary or a real-estate agent or a day-care worker or the president of the United States. Power and prestige mean nothing to God. What matters to him is our genuine desire to glorify him with our lives and to offer our careers to him as gifts of love. We shouldn't feel guilty if we don't work for a "ministry"—or proud of ourselves if we do. Paul said: "You should continue on as you were when God called you. . . . So, dear brothers and sisters, whatever situation you were in when you became a believer, stay there in your new relationship with God" (1 Corinthians 7:20, 24).

What matters most is the life we lead, not the job title we have.

Step 3: Remember That We're Already Full-Time Ministers

We need to get rid of this idea of professional church workers as the only people involved in full-time ministry. Every follower of Jesus is called to full-time ministry, wherever that is—in a doctor's office, at a job site, or at home taking care of the kids. It doesn't have to be working at a church. "Whatever you do, work at it with all your heart, as working for the Lord, not for men, since you know that you will receive an inheritance from the Lord as a reward. It is the Lord Christ you are serving" (Colossians 3:23–24 NIV).

See that? Whatever we do, we need to remember that it's for the Lord. Apart from those things not in line with God's character, we can bring him whatever job we have as an offering. Ultimately, we're either serving God with our time, or we're serving ourselves. Sure, the boss may benefit from our work, but as this verse says, "it is the Lord Christ you are serving."

Our work can either promote God's kingdom or our own agendas. He leaves that choice up to us. Nothing is more inspiring than seeing someone offer her entire life to do God's service, wherever that might be. And nothing is sadder than seeing other people spend their whole lives pursuing things (like fame, fortune, glory, and prestige) that are worthless to God.

Step 4: Remember That We Are Shaped to Serve God

Whatever our interests, gifts, talents, and abilities, God gave them to us for a reason (see 1 Peter 4:10). We were born in the places we were, to the parents we were, at the times we were because God—knowing our inner identities—knew the most ideal place in history for us to find and honor him.[3]

If God cares enough about our individuality to make our fingerprints and retinas and the genetic makeup of our skin cells unique, wouldn't he take even more care to mold our personalities, our identities, the very "shape" of our souls?

He has designed each one of us for a purpose. Now we need to let him use us to carry out his plans.

Step 5: Evaluate Our Financial Responsibilities

God will provide for our needs, but not necessarily our greeds. Supplying food and clothing and shelter and protection for our families is a part of anyone's calling, but that's not what most of us work toward. Most Americans would rather go into debt, burying themselves in a self-indulgent lifestyle, than take one step toward pursuing the life for which God has created them.

When children are young, one of the first things they start doing is staking out their territory. They learn the word *mine* right away. So we teach them to share: share your toys, share your room, share your crayons. But when they grow up and become independent adults, just like us, what do they do? Stake out their territory all over again—just like us.

We buy our own houses, our own cars, our own tools, our own clothes, our own toys—boats and backpacks and self-grinding wheat mills and chainsaws. In fact, we borrow money from others so we can have these things for ourselves. We'd rather owe people money than share our stuff. We've become a nation of selfish, self-indulgent brats.

Mine! Mine! Mine!

Most of our decisions rest upon the two pillars of comfort and convenience. We long to be comfortable so all our needs are taken care of and we can live the way we please. And we long for convenience—a life in which our troubles are ironed out, our frustrations disappear, and all that surrounds us and all that happens to us and all that touches us doesn't disrupt our plans or put a crimp in our schedules. We want life to revolve around us.

> MOST OF OUR **DECISIONS** REST UPON THE TWO PILLARS OF COMFORT AND CONVENIENCE.

But the truth is, God doesn't orchestrate the universe to make us more comfortable, and he isn't a cosmic string-puller making certain we're never inconvenienced.

We seem to prefer the god of Comfort to the God of comfort. And in our desperate struggle to become comfortable, we lose perspective beneath a pile of misplaced priorities. We don't stop to ask, as Calvin Miller does, "Could it be that our wonderful, abundant culture is really the jackal that preys on our peace? Yes, because our love of convenience trains us to believe that we can have as much as we want, of whatever we want, whenever we want it. We are deceived into believing that material abundance grants us peace, not that it steals it. But steal it does."[4]

When anything disrupts our quest for comfort or convenience, we think life isn't fair—because we think we're entitled to a comfortable life, that we have a right to feel frustrated when circumstances don't go our way.

It's not necessarily wrong to get frustrated, but we may want to ask ourselves whether we're getting frustrated because God's will isn't being done or because the world isn't bending over backward to make our journey one without any potholes.

My guess is, if we're honest about it, we'll have to admit that most of our frustrations grow from our unmet desires for more comfort or more convenience.

Yet both of these pillars—both comfort and convenience—are firmly set in the foundation of self-love, and neither leads us closer to God. They lead to the illusion that we can become (or should even try to become) comfortable on this planet—when Jesus has said we should expect the exact opposite.

Strive to meet your financial responsibilities, but don't let keeping up with the Joneses become more important than keeping in step with the Spirit.

Step 6: Nurture Our Relationships

Family and interpersonal relationships are another important consideration. For those of us who are married, it's part of our calling to honor our spouses. If we have kids, it's part of our calling to nurture, care for, protect, provide for, and love them. It's part of our calling to respect our parents.

We're called to represent Jesus Christ in all of our relationships—with friends, relatives, coworkers, our entire sphere of influence: "Whatever you do or say, let it be as a representative of the Lord Jesus, all the while giving thanks through him to God the Father" (Colossians 3:17). Wherever we work, whatever we do, whatever we say, we are representatives of Jesus Christ.

It's no mistake that we're in the place we are or that we know the people we do. God wants us to begin serving him right now by living out a real life, expressing genuine love where we are and with those we already know.

ENJOYING THE JOURNEY

To summarize, our lives should be shaped by these four things:

- God's character—who he is, his attributes and his purity
- God's priorities—what pleases and displeases him, what matters to him

- Our abilities and interests—the gifts that we have to offer him, our life experiences and passions

- Our families and interpersonal responsibilities—nurturing our marriages, caring for our children, and honoring our relatives, associates, and friends

All jobs have some drudgery. But if we're just putting in our time at work, hoping to someday enjoy ourselves when we finally retire, we've got it backward. "To enjoy your work and accept your lot in life—that is indeed a gift from God" (Ecclesiastes 5:19). We should enjoy our work now. If we're miserable and just working to pay the bills, we at least need to change our attitudes, and perhaps even the trajectories of our entire career.

Sometimes, as we consider these big questions of calling and service, God sends our lives in an entirely new direction. It may be time to make a radical change and embrace God's calling.

You might be thinking, *But Steve, are you telling me to give up my career as a chief financial officer and become a missionary?* Yes, if that's where you can serve God best right now. Or give up your career as a missionary and work as a chief financial officer if that's where you can serve God best right now.

Sometimes God calls us to new careers, and sometimes he calls us anew to our present careers. Maybe God isn't telling you to leave your job, maybe he's telling you to bring it to him. Perhaps he's saying, "I want you to keep your job, but I don't want you to keep thinking of it as a job, because for the last fifteen years, all you've been doing is putting in your time and making a living when I've given you the chance to bring me the offering of your life."

ANSWERING THE CALL

How can we know what our calling is? As much as I've read and thought about and studied this topic of God's calling, I'm not sure we ever know, at least not in the same sense that we know two plus five equals seven.

Knowing your calling is more like knowing you're in love or knowing you're hungry or knowing you're not content. It's not something you can logically prove. You just sense it. It has something to do with your faith and your convictions and your desires all coming together, and God's Spirit confirming to your soul, "Yes, yes. This is where I want you and what I want you to do at this point in your life."

It has less to do with figuring out what God wants you to do with your life and more to do with following what he wants you to do this moment. Because in truth, that's all he has given you. This moment is your life.

Here is our duty, our business: to love and honor God right now. Wherever we are. Whatever we do.

Obedience to God is a moment-by-moment decision. Don't fret about obeying God tomorrow or pursuing your calling someday. Just do it now. This instant. And if you've drifted into an attitude or action that's displeasing to him, admit it. Tell him you need him to forgive you, and then move on to the next moment with him, dwelling in the depths of his love.

That's all he asks of you. So rather than wonder what God's will for your life is, ask him what his will for this moment is. And then do that. And then the next thing. And before you know it, you'll be living out your calling, moment by moment, by depending on his grace and leading.

When we unashamedly pursue God's calling, we move one step closer to being real because we stop doing what the world expects and begin letting God shape us—our careers, our lives, and our relationships. That's when we finally become available for God's hand to begin using our lives to write his story on the pages of the world.

THE PLAN

Too many people go through life trying to make a living rather than pursuing the life for which God has shaped them. Others sit around waiting for God to unveil his master plan, hoping he'll send them someplace exotic.

The entire idea of stepping out and pursuing the life God has prepared us for is frightening and paralyzing. We want guarantees. We want it all spelled out. But God doesn't work that way. He requires us to trust him each step of the journey and to rely on him more than on our sensible-sounding plans.

I can just picture John the Baptist approaching his mom one day: "Hey, Ma, guess what? I'm gonna move to the desert, dress like a camel, eat grasshoppers, and become a Baptist preacher."

"Why would you want to do that? It doesn't sound very practical."

"Who said anything about being practical? It's what God has called me to do."

Or God calling Jeremiah to preach: "Jeremiah, I want you to become a preacher."

"I'm too young for that stuff."

"Don't worry about that, I'll be with you."

"OK."

"I want you to preach repentance."

"Sure thing."

"By the way, in all the decades of your ministry, not a single person will repent, not a single person will believe, and not a single person will listen to anything you have to say."[5]

"When can I get started?"

At the end of his life, we might have said, "Look at Jeremiah. He didn't have a single convert. What a failure." But God says, "Oh yes, Jeremiah—you were one of my greatest success stories."

Because when God looks at our lives, he doesn't ask how much we've earned. He asks how faithful we've been. God isn't at all concerned with how much we acquire, but he cares deeply about what we do with what we've been given. "Much is required from those to whom much is given, and much more is required from those to whom much more is given" (Luke 12:48).

I have a feeling that many of the people we think of as successful now are going to be speechless the day Jesus returns, as they whip out their Day-Timers to show God how much they did for him.

Because when they open them up, they're going to be empty.

"How did that happen?" they'll cry. "I worked hard my whole life!"

And God will say, "Oh, maybe you forgot. Only the things you did for me are permanently recorded there. The ink from everything else just fades away."

ONE MORE SUCCESS STORY

When our lives are finally over and we stand before God, he isn't going to ask how many trophies we've won, how many promotions we've received, how many cars we've owned, or how much we can bench press. He isn't going to look at our resumes or our letter jackets or our diplomas or our bank accounts or our wardrobes. God isn't going to say, "OK, let's see that financial portfolio. Let's see how well you made out in life."

There's only one thing God looks at, one thing he cares about: our hearts. What he'll evaluate is our lives, to see whether we lived for him or for ourselves.

If we're faithful to him, even though we may have lived in obscurity or poverty or anonymity on this planet, there will be no greater joy than to see him smile and lean over and say, "Ah, yes—well done. You are one of my greatest success stories. Come and share in your master's happiness."

Chapter 16

WELCOME SIGNS

Reprioritizing Family Relationships

Making the decision to have a child—it's momentous. It is to decide forever to have your heart go walking around outside your body.

—ELIZABETH STONE

Glancing at the sky, I noticed the clouds beginning to gather over the ocean. I was at a church fellowship dinner in Gulf Breeze, Florida. We'd all been nibbling our food and acting polite and interested, nodding and smiling and making small talk until none of us seemed to have anything else small to say.

Someone told me storms were common there because it rained all the time, and someone else brought up how much he liked the weather in Florida, and then somebody mentioned baseball.

That's when one of the gentlemen from the congregation, a pathologist, leaned forward and told this story:

One of the other doctors at the hospital was at his son's Little League game just last week. His son's team was behind and wasn't playing too well. The ninth inning rolled around, and just as his son was walking up to bat, this doctor was paged. Someone needed him at the hospital. Again.

Now this wasn't a life-or-death page, but it was important. He probably thought, *My kid isn't very good; he needs to hit a home run to win this game, and he's never done that before. Since the game is almost over, I'll slip out and answer the page.*

So he walked to the parking lot and hopped into his car. As he was pulling around the back of the bleachers, he heard the crowd erupt in applause. But he didn't think much of it; he just continued to the hospital.

When he got home later that night, his wife told him his son had hit the game-winning home run. But that's not all. As his son rounded the bases and turned toward home plate, the crowd was going wild, and this kid glanced up in the stands to the place where his father had been sitting.

And the seat was empty.

As soon as the kid saw that, he dropped his head. He was staring at the ground as he crossed home plate.

The pathologist finished by saying, "No one should be staring at the ground when he crosses home plate."

We sat there without saying a word. The evening seemed much colder and darker than it had a few moments earlier.

Then the pathologist looked up at us and said, "You don't get many second chances."

Someone said something about how hard it is to say no when we're paged but how easy it is to say no to our kids. Another person said he wondered if he would have answered that page too.

As the storm clouds mounted in the distance, I slid the cold potato salad around on my plate and asked myself the same question: Why is it so easy to let my work take precedence over my family?

KIDS VERSUS CAREERS

Families matter to God.

If God chooses to entrust children to our care, he has determined that a central part of our life's calling is to raise those children. And just as he would equip us to perform any duty he calls us to do, he'll equip us to raise our children with love, patience, and compassion.

But the choice of how to raise them and how to look at them (as a blessing from God or as a roadblock to our careers) remains with us. Jesus's warning to his followers still applies to us today: "See that you do not look down on one of these little ones. For I tell you that their angels in heaven always see the face of my Father in heaven" (Matthew 18:10 NIV).

A few years ago, as I was leaving a conference, a fellow attendee asked if he could ride along with me to the eastern part of Tennessee, near where I live. It's a five-hour drive, so I was glad to have the company.

As we traveled he told me a little about his life. He lived in Florida and was working part time at a church in the children's ministry department. He wanted to go to eastern Tennessee to visit his two-year-old daughter, who lived with his ex-wife. He hadn't seen his daughter in about a year. Then he said, "Yeah, I'm praying about whether God wants me to work full time in the children's ministry at my church."

Now I've never been accused of being too tactful. In fact, one of the pastors at my church once told me, "Steve, I think you have the gift of getting in people's faces."

So I said to this man, "You don't have to pray about it."

"I don't?"

"No. I can already tell you what God wants you to do."

"What's that?"

"Quit your job in Florida, move to Tennessee, and become involved in the life of your daughter."

I don't think he was too happy that we still had three hours together in the car.

If our jobs are more important to us than our children, our marriages, or our families, then our jobs are too important to us. And we can't use ministry as an excuse. God will never call us to a ministry that destroys a marriage. He will never call us to a career that destroys a family.

THE CALLING OF A PARENT

Every year I meet men who are working hard to get ahead in their jobs, while at home, in the hearts of their kids, they're falling further and further behind. They've bought into the lie that success is measured by the number of people we manage or how many promotions we receive or how much stuff we can accumulate over the years.

Yet it is a great and noble calling from God to be a father.

Of all the ways God could have chosen to describe his relationship to us, he chose to call himself our Father. He's referred to as Father nearly two hundred times in the Gospels.

Now for some people, that isn't too exciting. They remember how their own fathers weren't there for them, didn't express love to them, or walked out on them. Some people have never even met their fathers, and that resentment carries over to God.

None of this surprises God. He knew all along that some of us would be disappointed in our dads. Yet he still chose the term *Father*. Why?

A faithful father has a fierce love for his children. He's willing to do anything to protect them, even if it means sacrificing his own life. He provides for them and defends them. He disciplines them when they stray into dangerous territory because he cares about them. He's dependable and tender yet tough and strong. He has a warrior's heart and a gentle hand. You can rely on him. You can trust him. He won't let you down. He has an intense, unflinching, unfailing love.

When King David reflected on God's character, he summed it up like this: "The LORD is like a father to his children, tender and compassionate to those who fear him" (Psalm 103:13).

See? We all know what we want in a dad. And God delivers. He always responds to us like the ideal father would. And it's the job of all earthly fathers to become more like that. More like him.

Every year I meet women who feel like failures and second-class citizens because they're not working at a job outside the home. They've chosen to stay home and raise their kids. And they've become collateral damage from the destructive lie (so prevalent in North America) that it's more respectable and honorable to carry around a briefcase than it is to carry around a baby. They forget the incredible blessing they are to their children and husbands (see Proverbs 31:27–28), and they get discouraged.

Yet it's a great and noble calling from God to be a mother.

If God chooses to honor you and your spouse with children, it's a central part of your life's mission to care for, love, respect, honor, and raise those children.

Sometimes I talk with moms who say they've had to "put their lives on hold" while they raise their children. Now answer me honestly: would you want that to have been true of your mother? Would you have wanted someone to raise you who was thinking the whole time, *I'll put up with this duty as long as I have to, and then I'll get on with the really meaningful pursuits of my life*?

Wherever we work—at home, at a job site, an office, a garage, wherever—we need to make sure the pressures of our culture don't strangle the lives of our families.

Mothers are called to mother.

Fathers are called to father.

What could be more tragic in the life of a child than to get the message that she is a roadblock to her father's dreams? Or that she is less important to her mom than a client, a patient, a phone call, or a pile of dirty laundry?

Love is not a duty, it's an offering. And parents who don't offer their time to their children as a gift but rather put up with them as a temporary inconvenience until they can get on with their careers are to be pitied even more than the children they raise.

We are called to welcome children into our hearts, into this world, into our churches, and into our homes. They are so precious to God that in a mysterious way, when we welcome children in his name, we're actually welcoming him: "Anyone who welcomes a little child like this on my behalf welcomes me, and anyone who welcomes me welcomes my Father who sent me" (Mark 9:37).

SOMEONE CLOSE TO MY HEART

I was moved to tears when I first read this letter written by then fifth-grader Susan Olive. It still touches my heart every time I read it. I share it with you here with her permission.

Someone Close to My Heart

I would like to share from my heart about a topic that is very personal and dear to me, it has to do with being adopted. One of my dreams is to meet my natural mother one day. I am so glad that God placed me in the family which I am living now, but I know that it was a very hard decision for my natural mother to make and this is why she is someone close to my heart.

First, I think making the decision to carry a baby for nine months and then deciding to place me for adoption, showed that my mother was not selfish. I am happy that she chose not to kill me through something like abortion but loved me enough to let me live a fun and joyful life.

Sometimes I wonder if this tough decision lives with her every single day. Does my mother think of me on Mother's Day and on my birthday? I also go over in my mind if I have the same musical talents as she did. And what does she look like, does she have blond hair and baby blue eyes like me? Is she easily angered like me, is she very sensitive? These are all special things about me that I can thank my mother for.

I pray that my natural mother is a Christian, and if she already is, I hope that she will grow closer to God and be able to witness to other people about His love and care. It is also my hope that she can use my adoption and all she must have gone through to God's glory. I do not want her to be sad, but I want her to be proud of making the right decision.

One day I would love to meet my natural mother. I want to tell her that I love her. I want her to see how God has taken care of me and allowed me to grow. I want to thank her for choosing life, not death, for me. I want to pray with her in praise and thanksgiving to God for being there for both of us. She is really someone close to my heart, and I don't even know her . . . yet.[1]

That girl has things in the right perspective.

We've got to value our children, not look down on them. We need to respect them, make time for them, and let them know how much they matter to us and how much they matter to God.

It will make all the difference in the world.

OUT OF THE MOUTHS OF BABES

In the kingdom of God, things are reversed. The last are first, the first are last, and children are the greatest teachers of all.

Kids cry when they're hurt. They whine when they're tired, they giggle when they're happy, and they tell us when they need a hug. Kids live life with refreshing (and sometimes brutal) honesty.

But as we get older, we begin to wonder what other people think of us. We worry more and more about our images, where we fit in, and our identities. And we start searching for belonging, acceptance, and success in the eyes of others.

We mess things up as bad as the disciples did.

They thought kids needed to become more grown-up and "spiritual" before Jesus would be interested in spending time with them. But Jesus welcomed the kids with open arms and rebuked his disciples. He told them they had it all backward—the kids didn't need to become more grown-up; the grownups needed to become more like kids. "Jesus called a small child over to him and put the child among them. Then he said, 'I assure you, unless you turn from your sins and become as little children, you will never get into the Kingdom of Heaven. Therefore, anyone who becomes as humble as this little child is the greatest in the Kingdom of Heaven'" (Matthew 18:2–4).

All kids are believers. Not in a specific religious or theological sense—no one is born a Christian. But children are born full of faith. We trusted completely in our parents and caregivers and teachers. We believed in fairy tales and monsters and Santa Claus. We only learned to question things later. And still later, to doubt. Kids don't rationalize away their faith. They only learn how to reason their way out of it when they grow up. No one is born a skeptic.

Most of us adults are so concerned about acting our ages and being mature and making sure people respect us that we forget we're supposed to have childlike humility and childlike faith—that we're supposed to view life and God through the eyes of a child. Unashamed. Receptive. Genuine. And humble.

All of us can learn from kids. Let's start letting our children know how important they are to us—and how important they are to Jesus.

BEING REAL AT HOME

Usually it's not too tough being real around the people we live with. Because when we live with someone long enough, reality moves in as well. What's often harder than being real with our relatives is simply being kind to them. Paul knew that when he wrote, "Now a word to you fathers. Don't make your children angry by the way you treat them. Rather, bring them up with the discipline and instruction approved by the Lord" (Ephesians 6:4).

Make the extra effort to be patient with children, tender with them, and careful with how you treat them. If we step on a child's heart, it may stay bruised for a lifetime. So be gentle. Value and respect children. Schedule time with them. Admit when you mess up, and ask them to forgive you. They will. Few people are quicker to forgive than children. They're some of the only people who actually want to forgive and love others.

Sacrificing our dreams and our time to nurture our families may not help us advance in our careers, but it will help us to fulfill our life's calling.

■

Months after that fellowship dinner in Florida, as I sit typing this, my wife calls down the stairs to me that it's time to tuck our girls in bed, and will I be coming up or should she do it? And I'm ready to tell her to go ahead because I want to finish this chapter. But then I remember that kid crossing home plate, and I catch myself.

"Yeah," I call upstairs. "I'll be right there."

Chapter 17

THE ROAD TO REAL

Becoming Transparent with Others

*If you let yourself be absorbed completely,
if you surrender completely to the moments
as they pass, you live more richly those
moments.*

—ANNE MORROW LINDBERGH

I was at Target to buy coasters. That was all. For my office. The woman in front of me in the checkout line had a cart piled full of towels, dresses, and children's puzzles. The checkout woman glanced up at her for a fraction of a second. "So, how are you," she said.

It wasn't really a question.

Without looking up, the woman said, "Fine."

And it wasn't really an answer.

Then she unloaded her items one by one so the clerk could scan them. And without another word, she walked away. Their eyes never met. It was my turn.

"So, how are you," the checkout woman said, staring at the cash register.

"Actually, I'm tired."

She looked at me for the first time. Our eyes met. "I'm tired too," she said. "I've been working since seven o'clock."

It was 5:30 p.m.

I nodded. "That's a long day. It's been a long day for me too. I just want to get home and spend some time with my kids. Do you have any kids?"

I handed her my coasters and my credit card.

"No, just a couple of cats." There was a long pause. "But I hope to . . .

someday." Then she looked at me oddly and said, "Most people just say, 'I'm fine' or, 'Good.'"

We talked about kids and cats and going home at the end of the day. I told her about my three daughters and how she should have kids sometime, then she was done taking care of me and it was the next person's turn, so I grabbed my coasters and headed for the sliding doors.

I hadn't made it ten feet before I heard her say to the next person, "So, how are you."

And from behind me I heard another nameless someone say, "Fine."

I couldn't help but smile. I turned and glanced back at the clerk. She had turned, too, and was looking at me. Smiling.

EYE CONTACT, HEART CONTACT

That brief encounter in the checkout line resonates in my mind. We shared a moment, that was all. So simple. So human. So true. So rare. Because people don't share moments much anymore. We're busy and lonely and lost to each other.

Most of our relationships are superficial. We talk in catch phrases and clichés and go through our lines and then nod our heads and walk away without ever making eye contact.

Without ever making heart contact.

We spend our lives skimming along the surface of our relationships. Somewhere along the line we've forgotten that each and every encounter with another individual is a chance to love (or to overlook) a person who matters to God. A chance to connect with (or isolate ourselves from) those God has asked us to serve.

Becoming real is a process that grounds us in the moment and frees us to begin loving other people more than our agendas.

We have places to go and people to see, so we rush past opportunities to express God's love and live out his grace. And we forget to be here. In this place. Right now. And we don't see the person beside us. Right here.

I met a man whom I'll call Tim. Whenever I talked to Tim, he would look me in the eye and nod and listen. Really listen. As though there were nothing he'd rather be doing than talking with me. When I asked him about it one day, he said, "Well, there isn't anything I'd rather be doing."

That's how real our relationships need to become. People are not a means to an end.

Kierkegaard wrote, "We shrink from being revealed. Therefore we live, if not in utter darkness then in the twilight, in hoaxes, in the impersonal. But Christianity, which knows the truth, knows that life means: revelation."[1] Let's take a look at some specific ways we can become more transparent with others as we let our selfish agendas vanish into genuine relationships.

REAL RELATIONSHIPS

Most of the time, when we relate to other people, we try to impress, manipulate, coerce, and control them. We impress through flattery, manipulate through subtlety, coerce through intimidation, and control through deception. We're quick to meddle, criticize, and give advice, but we're slow to really listen, like Tim did.

The sad truth is that most of us are phonies. We deceive others about our true intentions. We cover up our objectives so we can keep up appearances. Or massage our reputations. Or win friends and influence people.

Too many of our motives are soaked in selfishness. We become real only when we abandon all these games and accept people as they are without trying to do anything more than simply love them.

"But if people really knew me," you ask, "if they knew some of the things I've done—if they could see into my heart and search my motives and sift through my mistakes—what would they think of me?"

My guess is they'd think you're human, just like them. That you make mistakes, just like they do, and that you're brave enough to admit it—just like they wish they were.

I'm always more at ease with people who know they're not perfect. I'll bet you are too. The people who turn me off and annoy me the most are the ones who think they're perfect and spend all their time trying to get me to agree with them.

WHAT TRANSPARENCY IS NOT

When I talk about being real and transparent, I don't mean recounting all our deepest secrets, unloading all our inner struggles, or confessing all our personal problems to everyone we meet.

I don't mean that every encounter turns into a group therapy session.

"Hi, I'm Steve. I have a hard time being transparent with other people."

And everyone nods and says, "Hi, Steve."

Eek.

That's not the kind of life I'd want or how I'd want other people to treat me. That kind of emotional regurgitation might help us get stuff off our chest, but it won't help us take any real strides toward being more authentic.

Honesty is not the same as openness.

Honesty is always appropriate, but the amount of openness we have with others depends on the circumstances and the relationship we have with each person. It's naive and foolhardy to think we should act the same way with everybody. The way we talk with our spouse will be different from the way we talk to the taxicab driver or our fifteen-year-old son. It'd better be!

THERE'S A TIME TO SPEAK AND A TIME TO BE SILENT.

But underlying the words we use in all situations should be a carpet of compassion, honesty, respect, and authenticity. The level of openness should be different, but the level of honesty should remain the same.

We have to be wise when we open up to people, because the more vulnerable we are with someone, the more intimate that relationship will become. Openness is a powerful thing. A lot of affairs start with men sharing secrets with women who are not their wives. Why? Because openness breeds intimacy.

Jesus was never concerned about making a good impression. He just wanted to make an accurate one. He never had to let his guard down, because he never had it up. And his outright honesty was disarming to his enemies and refreshing to his friends.

Simply put, Jesus was real with people. (In fact, in John 18:37 he said the purpose of his life was to come and testify to the truth.) But he wasn't always open about his mission or intentions; he didn't always clarify his stories; he talked in riddles and metaphors. It wasn't until his last night on earth that the disciples finally understood what Jesus was even talking about (see John 16:29–30). No, Jesus wasn't deceptive. He didn't manipulate people. He wasn't always forthcoming with information people didn't need to know, but he was always honest.

We should strive to be real in all situations, as Jesus was. But we also need to recognize that sometimes its best not to say everything that's on our minds. There's a time to speak and a time to be silent. There's a time and a place to be vulnerable. We need to use tact, sensitivity, and common sense as we open the door to transparency and the gateway to our hearts.

BECOMING REAL

So being transparent means being honest. But it doesn't mean being rude, tactless, insensitive, and uncaring. It doesn't mean being harsh, coercive, or inconsiderate.

Becoming transparent doesn't mean becoming a nuisance.

Our goal isn't to air our dirty laundry, but it's not to appear squeaky clean either.

It's just to be real.

We need to say what we mean—request what we want rather than hint and manipulate and beat around the bush. We should do it with love, gentleness, and respect. But we should do it.

Not distort, deflect, blur, beguile, and withhold information. Not search for loopholes. Just be real.

We need to saturate our lives with the three ingredients of authenticity: honesty (telling it like it is), sincerity (meaning what we say), and vulnerability (admitting when we're wrong). It's time to peel off the platitudes, lose the religious jargon, stop playing games, and be real.

Being transparent means living with no hidden agendas and no ulterior motives. It means living with our guard down because we have nothing to hide. This kind of living may make others wary at first, because it's so rare. They may wonder if even our honesty with them is just another clever disguise.

Why is she being so nice? they might think. *What does she want from me?*

Yet when people realize we don't want anything from them—that we're not trying to impress, manipulate, coerce, or control them, that we're shooting straight from the hip and don't have a hidden agenda, that we're not being kind as a means to an end but because we genuinely care about them and respect them as individuals—it'll shake them up. It'll show them real love. And it'll show them a glimpse of Jesus. "Wherever we go he [Jesus] uses us to tell others about the Lord and to spread the Good News like a sweet perfume. Our lives are a fragrance presented by Christ to God" (2 Corinthians 2:14–15).

We smell like Jesus to the world. We share his fragrance by the way we live our lives. And the more we step out of the way, the more we'll begin to smell like him.

THE ROAD TO REAL

Let me give you three words of caution as you walk the road to becoming real: don't be too quick to judge others, don't let your agenda interfere with compassion, and don't be too curious about another person's relationship with God.

The Judgment Trap

Most of us go about life backward. We're quick to criticize others and slow to find fault with ourselves. Jesus said we should first deal with our own relationship with God, and only then will we see clearly to point others in the right direction (see Luke 6:41–42). It takes a lot of courage to say, "I'm the one who needs to change. I'm the one who must sort out my life, not you."

Judging others will distract us from our own pursuit of transparency. Instead we should strive to accept others as God has accepted us.

The Agenda Trap

To Jesus, people were always more important than the lesson plan. People were more important than any ministry agenda. People were even more important than religious rules, regulations, and rituals (see Mark 2:28; 3:4).

People who are controlled by an agenda always act as if they're accountable to a list rather than to other people. But agendas are here to serve us, not the other way around.

As you walk through your day, always be ready to show compassion, even if it wasn't in the original game plan. Our plans should always be drawn in sand so they can be rewritten on the spur of the moment by the wind of the Spirit.

The Curiosity Trap

A few years ago, I was on a retreat in Kentucky when I went for a walk along one of the site's many nature trails. Sunlight was filtering through the mesh of autumn leaves when I came to a wooden cross about four feet high, propped upright in a rock garden. Nestled between two of the rocks was a piece of paper.

Someone had written a note and stuck it there. It was weather-beaten, and some of the ink was bleeding through. It had obviously been there for some time.

I wonder what it says? I wonder what someone placed at this cross?

I looked around to make sure I was alone; then I picked up the water-stained and wrinkled paper.

I knew I shouldn't be reading the note. I knew I should have left it there and walked away. But it was too tempting.

I unfolded it and began to read. The note began with these words: "For Jesus."

Even though it had been written for Jesus alone to read, I read the note. The whole thing. I eavesdropped on a woman's prayer.

And after I'd read it, I knew without a doubt that I shouldn't have. I knew I was peeking at her private conversation with God. I had intruded. My curiosity had led me to go where I wasn't supposed to go. I'd trespassed through someone's prayer.

I folded the paper back up and put it back by the cross.

"Forgive me," I whispered. And then I walked away to have my own much-needed private talk with Jesus.

We shouldn't be too quick to peek under the surface of other people's lives. Let's leave their level of transparency up to them and focus on our own.

REAL INTEGRITY

Often we hesitate to be real because we fear rejection, embarrassment, and suffering. We fear others' opinions. We don't want to offend them or hurt their feelings. But as long as we wonder what people will think, we'll always beat around the bush, walk on eggshells, and then hide our indirectness behind a guise of concern.

But when our only concern is what God will think, it puts things in an entirely different light.

Put yourself in Daniel's shoes for a moment.

As a young man, you were captured during a military campaign. Despite pressure to conform to the godless culture in which you live, you unashamedly pursue your relationship with God. You advance steadily through the ranks until you become one of the most trusted advisors to the king. Then one day the king announces that because of your exceptional work, he's going to promote you to the highest office in the land.

Daniel was truly a success: "Daniel soon proved himself more capable than all the other administrators and princes. Because of his great ability, the king made plans to place him over the entire empire. Then the other administrators and princes began searching for some fault in the way Daniel was handling his affairs, but they couldn't find anything to criticize. He was faithful and honest and always responsible" (Daniel 6:3–4).

Without wasting any time, your coworkers embark on a smear campaign. They figure if they can unearth a few shady deals, uncover some white lies, or dredge up some past mistakes, they can ruin your career.

Think about going through that kind of probe. All of your public and private affairs picked over and sorted through. Most of us would dread that kind of inquiry.

But despite the best efforts of these political opportunists, they couldn't dig up any dirt on Daniel. Finally they had no choice but to give up.

Daniel had nothing to hide.

He didn't complain about people prying into his private life, because he lived with integrity. And integrity has no private life. Something with integrity is sound and complete. It's whole and uncorrupted.

A life of integrity is totally transparent. It's the kind of life that's focused on God and unashamed to make choices that honor him. It's free from the fear of what people might discover, free from corruption and negligence, free from shame and regret.

That's a refreshing kind of freedom. That's the kind of freedom we find when we follow God wholeheartedly, like Daniel did. And that's the kind of freedom our coworkers will notice and want for themselves.

But no one's perfect, right? Everyone makes mistakes. We're only human. We can't do the right thing all the time, can we?

Of course we can't.

But living with integrity means spending our time and energy doing the right thing rather than covering our tracks, cooking the books, or hiding our mistakes. Something with integrity is the same inside and out. It's solid through and through. What you see is what you get.

Where did Daniel get the resolve to live a life with that kind of integrity year after year?

The secret is found in his passionate pursuit of intimacy with God. Even when it meant being thrown into the lion's den, he wouldn't alter his prayer life or give up the thing that was most important to him: spending time worshiping God. Daniel's work ethic didn't spring from ambition, selfishness, or egoism. It came from his passionate desire to put God first in everything he did, despite the cost.

Integrity means doing our best, even when no one will notice; giving it our all, as if God had hired us; and making choices we can live with, even if they become public. That's real transparency.

PRACTICAL TRANSPARENCY

Jesus talked about praying in secret so others won't notice our times of devotion (see Matthew 6:5–6), but then he also said that we should let our lights shine (Matthew 5:16). How does that work? Doesn't one contradict the other?

Here are the two principles underlying these commands: (1) we should never make a show out of our spiritual practices, and (2) we must never be ashamed or afraid to live out our faith and the convictions that accompany it.

Either way, we should be real. We shouldn't spend our days hiding who we are and what we believe in, nor should we spend our days showing off or drawing attention to ourselves. Paul put it like this: "You must never be ashamed to tell others about our Lord" (2 Timothy 1:8). Jesus put it like this: "If a person is ashamed of me and my message, I, the Son of Man, will be ashamed of that person when I return in my glory and in the glory of the Father and the holy angels" (Luke 9:26).

If we're ashamed of Jesus, he'll be ashamed of us. Because it shows that we're still more ashamed of needing a savior than of admitting our sin.

And that means we're still putting ourselves first.

So when we're at a restaurant with our unbelieving friends, should we bow our heads to pray or not?

We can do either, as we're led by God. But if we pray publicly, it must not be for show, so people will notice. And if we don't pray publicly, it must not be for fear of the same. No showing off. And no wimping out.

Paul dealt with these kinds of issues in the early Christian church. He concluded that we are free in Christ but that our freedom should not be an excuse to sin or to go around offending people. What we do doesn't matter as much as why we do it. So we should always try to choose what's beneficial or helpful in leading others closer to Christ.

Paul warned that even though we may be free to do something, it might be best to avoid it if that will help lead folks closer to God: "I don't just do what I like or what is best for me, but what is best for them so they may be saved" (1 Corinthians 10:33).

We're free. Now we must be wise.

We might also want to limit our freedom in certain areas so we don't end up being controlled by our choices. Even freedom can have its addictions: "You may say, 'I am allowed to do anything.' But I reply, 'Not everything is good for you.' And even though 'I am allowed to do anything,' I must not become a slave to anything" (1 Corinthians 6:12).

Our choices shouldn't be dictated by pride or selfishness or fear or addictive behaviors. We're free, so let's live like it and be led by our love for God and by a heartfelt desire to lead others closer to him. In situations where there's no clear right or wrong choice, listen for the gentle whisper of God's Spirit and then follow where he leads.

MY LIFE AS AN AMBASSADOR

One day two elders from the Church of Jesus Christ of Latter Day Saints came to my door. It was lunchtime, so after my wife made them some roast turkey sandwiches and beef stew, the older of the two (though neither of them looked old enough to be out of college—doesn't *elder* mean old?) began telling me about Joseph Smith and The Book of Mormon, and I interrupted. "I'm glad to talk with you about God as long as we're honest with each other, and you tell me what you believe rather than just what you've been told to say."

There was an awkward silence, as if no one had ever asked them to be honest before. Finally the young man told me there were certain things they were supposed to say.

"Let's just pretend we're a bunch of guys looking for the truth," I said. "Let's see where that takes us."

But they didn't want to go down that road, so they hopped onto their mountain bikes and rode off to their next appointment. Because they had a speech to give and a quota to fill. Just like someone selling used cars or vacuum cleaners. They were salesmen.

And I've been just like them.

When we witness to people, the conversation must never be a hoax. A trap. A set-up. A spiel. A speech.

Yet, unfortunately, too often it is. We even refer to sharing the Good News as "giving a gospel presentation." To us it's a presentation. To an unbeliever it's a sales pitch.

If our friendliness is just a means to an end, we're not being transparent. We're not being real. Remember, we're not trying to close the deal—we're supposed to be sharing good news on behalf of the King. After all, we are representatives of Jesus Christ: "We are Christ's ambassadors, and God is using us to speak to you. We urge you, as though Christ himself were here pleading with you, 'Be reconciled to God!'" (2 Corinthians 5:20).

No one has ever been converted by cleverness or fancy preaching or manipulative tactics. No one has ever been coerced into God's kingdom. Gimmicks might get people to church, but they'll never bring them to Christ. Only through the work of the Spirit can new life be received. And the Spirit works through the embodiment of the gospel on the tongues and in the lives of believers. What brings people to Christ is sincerity, compassion, and the genuine devotion of people living real lives before God. Not manipulation and sales pitches. When our lives are transformed by God, we won't have to rely on coercive strategies to share our faith; it'll happen naturally, in God's timing and in God's way.

When you tell others about the Christian life, don't make it sound like a beach party. Talk about the tough times and the struggles and show them what Jesus means to you. Just tell them the truth and watch what happens. They may reject it or they may accept it, but the truth will never leave them disillusioned with God—which is what happens every time we sugarcoat the gospel.

The apostles Peter and John spoke the truth clearly, boldly, and persuasively. And their lifestyle matched their words: "The members of the council were amazed when they saw the boldness of Peter and John, for they could see that they were ordinary men who had had no special training. They also recognized them as men who had been with Jesus" (Acts 4:13).

The council members saw ordinary people who'd been with Jesus, and they were amazed. Wouldn't it be great if people saw us like that too?

COMFORTABLE UNTIL I DIE?

Being a follower of Jesus is not always easy or comfortable or popular.

In Luke 14:25–35 Jesus made it plain—if we want a life of comfort and convenience, we may as well not even get started following him, because this disciple life is full of crosses, not comforts. Carrying a cross is not comfortable. Giving up everything for Christ is not convenient. Jesus actually guaranteed that his followers would have a tough life on this planet. In John 15:18–21 he promised his followers that they would be hated and persecuted.

As Peter Kreeft points out, "Love makes more waves than hate. Wicked men will hate and fear you more for loving them than for hating them. They will quickly forgive you for being wrong, but they will never forgive you for being right. . . . If nobody wants to crucify you, you're not doing your job. Or else your job isn't *his* work."[2]

Most of us are more concerned with how we appear to others than how we appear to God. The point is not to hide ourselves, or our mission, from anyone—neither God nor other people. Jesus loved people enough to tell them the truth. Usually we love our reputations so much that we're afraid to tell people the truth.

Christians are called to be people of great confidence, boldness, humility, and transparency. But none of that comes from ourselves (2 Corinthians 3:4–5). Speak the truth in love. Nurture real relationships with others. And as you do, you'll spread the fragrance of Christ throughout the world.

WHAT ARE THE CHRISTIANS GONNA DO?

Showing Genuine Compassion

Stagnant faith stinks, like stagnant water.
And the world has sensitive nostrils.
—PETER KREEFT, *BACK TO VIRTUE*

Right away I knew what the guy wanted. Grime streaked his face. He wore no gloves despite the bitter cold. A thin coat draped his shoulders. Greasy, tangled hair fell around his eyes and down past his neck. His tennis shoes were the kind you buy for a dollar at Goodwill stores.

So as he shuffled toward my car, I knew what he wanted. He produced an ID card to make his request sound more legitimate. I tried not to notice him. I didn't roll down my window. Maybe if I ignored him, he wouldn't bother me. Maybe he would just walk away and leave me alone.

For a moment he stood outside my window, then he rapped on the glass. Finally, I sighed and rolled it down. "Yeah?"

"I'm a homeless American vet. Could you spare a few dollars for me to buy food?" He shoved the ID card toward me.

"Um, yeah. Here." I pulled out my wallet and handed him a couple of bucks.

I was in no mood to talk with homeless beggars. I'd had a long day and still had a long night in front of me. It was New Year's Eve, and I was scheduled to perform a storytelling concert at a community-wide event an hour from home.

Not only that, it was freezing outside. A biting wind had dragged the temperature way below zero—pretty arctic for Tennessee. I hated having to open my window. It was so toasty warm in my car.

"Thank you, sir," he said, stuffing the bills into his pocket.

But he didn't leave.

Feeling a little guilty by then, I decided to make small talk. "Um, are you gonna be at the festivities tonight?"

"What festivities?"

"There's this big alcohol-free community celebration."

Then he said it: "What are the Christians gonna do? I'm a Christian."

Huh. What a weird question. The words slid off me without making much of an impact. But they didn't go away.

"I don't know. The same as everyone else, I guess . . . Here." I handed him my backstage pass. "This'll get you into any of the events. There are, um, hospitality tables with free food and stuff." He thanked me and disappeared down the street. But I knew he wouldn't use the pass.

IT SURE IS COLD

For a while I sat there in the car collecting my thoughts, trying to decide which stories to tell. But I couldn't concentrate. I'd met homeless people before, but this guy stuck with me. His question echoed in my mind.

"What are the Christians gonna do?"

I need to grab some supper for myself . . . maybe . . .

I caught up with him two blocks away asking some stagehands for money. "Want some supper?" I asked.

He narrowed his eyes at me, scanning me closely, then he nodded.

"I'm Steve. What was your name again?" I thrust out my hand. His fingers were so cold it felt like I was shaking hands with a corpse. I wondered how long it'd been since this guy had been warm.

"I never told you my name," he said and handed me the card again.

Next to a picture, which looked only slightly like the man walking next to me, was the name M. Sherwood Little. I doubted it was his card or his name, but I played along.

"So, Sherwood, have you been in the area long?"

"For a while."

We both fell silent as we walked toward the restaurant. Then Sherwood sighed. "In order to keep the conversation going, I'll tell you more about myself. I think . . . I like you. When we get to the restaurant, I'll tell you about my job."

"Are you looking for work?"

"Well, now, what can I say. The things I do and the work I'm qualified for, it's . . . it's tough for me to make contacts and get back into it."

I figured it was construction or something. Most of the homeless people I meet tell me they work construction.

As we crossed the parking lot near the restaurant, I muttered, "Sure is cold out."

"I'm used to it," said Sherwood.

I DON'T KNOW WHAT HAPPENED

We slipped into a little pizza place and shook off the cold. I was ready to order when Sherwood told me he didn't want any food. "I haven't eaten in I don't know how long. I tried eating something this morning, and I threw it up. But you go ahead."

How could I eat with him watching me?

I ordered two coffees and we sat down. I didn't know what to say.

Sherwood looked across the table at me. "Let me tell you my story. I'm a Native American. A Sioux. I raised two boys. Their mom lives on a Cherokee reservation in North Carolina. That's what brought me down south from the Midwest—South Dakota—where I was born. I went to four years of college, pursued a law degree for a while, and then attended medical school—eventually got a degree in library science. I worked for a while in a library. Also served in the navy . . . had a scholarship to Penn State in track."

Law degree? Medical school? Library science? Track scholarship? Not this man. Not this homeless bum!

I decided to test him a little—see if he was lying to me.

"What did you run in track?"

"The mile."

"How fast? What was your time?" I used to run the mile. I was checking his facts.

"My best was four thirty-eight—that's pretty fast."

I paused in my interrogation; 4:38 was fast. And it was about the right time for a track scholarship fifteen to twenty years ago. I decided he was telling me the truth.

Now I really didn't know what to say.

By then he'd finished half of his coffee. He turned away and stopped looking me in the eye. Facing the wall, he whispered, "And then one day, I don't know what happened. I became a drunk."

MAYBE HE JUST WANTED SOMEONE TO HEAR HIS STORY.

He didn't talk like a drunk. His sentences were clear and well constructed. He chose his words carefully. He was articulate, although it was evident that it took effort. It was as if he was trying to remember a part of himself he'd lost. Or abandoned. A part he hadn't told anybody about in a long time. Maybe it wasn't food he was hungry for. Maybe he just wanted someone to hear his story.

It was only then that I noticed how sunken his eyes were, how his breath reeked of alcohol, how his hands trembled as he picked up his coffee, and how yellow his teeth were.

"What are the Christians gonna do?"

We talked for a long time. He showed me the New Testament he carried in his pocket. I offered him a place to stay at my apartment, but he refused.

"I can't come to your apartment tonight," he said. "I need to drink or else the d.t.'s will come back. And you don't even know what that's like. I remember a spider this big, the size of my hand, came down like this . . . it laid its babies on my face, and they crawled all over me. You don't know what it's like."

"Do you want to quit?" I asked.

"Yeah. I wanna stop. But I'm gonna be honest with you. I'm gonna drink tonight. That's why I'm out there panhandling. I panhandled you! I don't even know what day it is . . . what day is it?"

"It's New Year's Eve."

"No, the day of the week."

"It's Wednesday."

"Wednesday . . . Wednesday . . ." He repeated it slowly, as if he were looking over a puzzle to which he'd just been given a long-lost piece.

Finally he drifted back to our conversation. "I wanna stop, but I can't."

PRAY FOR ME

I tried telling him Jesus could help, that God was more powerful than his problem. And I think he believed it. He said he did. But then he drained the last sip of coffee from his cup and started looking around nervously.

"I'm getting uncomfortable. I need to get out of here. I need something to drink."

I felt helpless. I wanted to do so much more. He was standing up.

"If you don't stop, you're gonna kill yourself!" I blurted.

"I know that," he said slowly.

I was like a desperate man trying to force him into a corner, to obligate him to accept my help. "You need to make a decision. Right now! I can help if you'll let me!"

Sherwood paused. A storm played across his face. His eyes blazed with remembrance and then clouded with tears. He quivered slightly, like a hopeless man. Like a criminal watching the cell door slam shut. "I've made my choice," he said finally.

Then he looked me in the eye. "Steve, God bless you."

Words were screaming in my head. *No! No, don't walk away! Not now, not after all we've talked about. Let me help you! There's gotta be something I can do. I want to help. I do!*

"God bless you, too, Sherwood," I sputtered.

Then he reached for my hand. His dirty fingers, still cold after all that time, curled around my clean, warm ones. "Pray for me tonight. I could really use it."

"I will," I stammered.

Then Sherwood walked out the door. I stared in silence as it closed behind him. Wind whipped snow across the pavement. There was nothing else I could do, so I finished my coffee and left.

As I stepped outside, I gazed toward the parking lot. Maybe I was hoping Sherwood would reappear and beg for my help.

But he didn't.

I glanced at my watch and hurried over to the main stage to take my place in the "celebrity parade." That night I met the mayor, a congressman, newscasters, reporters, and wealthy business executives.

I've forgotten all of their names.

But I haven't forgotten Sherwood.

WHAT ARE THE CHRISTIANS GONNA DO?

I can't get Sherwood's question out of my head. I can't shake those words. Because now one of the nameless millions of homeless people has become real to me. I know what it feels like to smell his breath, touch his hand, and look into his eyes.

What are the Christians going to do about people like Sherwood?

I know one thing. The correct answer is not "The same as everyone else, I guess."

How do I know that? Because "religion that God our Father accepts as pure and faultless is this: to look after orphans and widows in their distress and to keep oneself from being polluted by the world" (James 1:27 NIV).

How did James define God-pleasing religion? Praying five times a day? No. Going to church three times a week? No. Saying the rosary? Going to confession? Getting baptized? No, no, no.

He said true religion expresses itself by showing genuine compassion (by looking after orphans and widows) and pursuing purity in life (living in the world but not letting ourselves get corrupted by it). And God tells believers to live holy lives: "Be holy because I am holy" (1 Peter 1:16). The word *holy* means "set apart." So we set our lives apart from the corruption of the world and show unconditional love to those who can't repay us. That's the kind of religion God is looking for. The only kind that matters.

That's real faith made visible to the world. And to God.

Living a life of genuine compassion means having sensitivity to and awareness of what people are experiencing. That takes time. And energy. It means going below the surface in our relationships with others.

Our faith is useless unless it changes the way we live and the way we look at the world. If we don't put our faith into practice, it's as good as dead (see James 2:26).

Without love at the center, service becomes a chore, obedience a ritual, and belief a mere intellectual exercise. Without love at the core of our relationship with God, our religion becomes a sham. And without love at the core of our relationships with others, we don't have the kind of religion that pleases God our Father.

Therefore, true religion that pleases God is revealed when we live out our faith by living lives of unreserved compassion and unashamed holiness.

According to James 1:27, that's what real religion looks like. That's the way Jesus was religious. He let compassion guide his life. He entered into the world, he didn't retreat from it. Yet he didn't become corrupted by his immersion into the culture of his day.

A FUNNY THING HAPPENED TO ME ON THE WAY TO CHURCH

God is more interested in seeing us live out what we confess than he is in seeing us back at church next week. Jesus said, "If you are standing before the altar in the Temple, offering a sacrifice to God, and you suddenly remember that someone has something against you, leave your sacrifice there beside the altar. Go and be reconciled to that person. Then come and offer your sacrifice to God" (Matthew 5:23–24).

Jesus would rather we spend time being reconciled with each other than time going to church. Basically, he said, drop whatever you're doing, even if you're in the middle of a church service, and make peace with others.

Why would Jesus say this? Because if our relationship with God means anything at all, it must change the way we relate to other people (see James 2:14–17).

Love is practical, and it meets people in their moment of need. Our lives are the primary way God has chosen to remind the world that he's still alive. And he does that through the love we extend to hurting people.

How does that love express itself?

Well, in big ways and small.

1. Stop Viewing People as Mere People

When I first met Sherwood, I immediately looked down on him. I saw only a grimy, homeless panhandler. I was judging him by what he looked like on the outside, not on the inside. Yet God loved that homeless drunk enough to die for him.

I'd messed up and done just the opposite of what Paul said believers do when they meet people: "From now on we regard no one from a worldly point of view" (2 Corinthians 5:16 NIV).

Ouch. That's a big shift. No longer evaluating people by what the world thinks of them. To stop viewing people as mere people. C. S. Lewis touched on this:

> It is a serious thing to live in a society of possible gods and goddesses, to remember that the dullest and most uninteresting person you talk to may one day be a creature which, if you saw it now, you would be strongly tempted to worship, or else a horror and corruption such as you now meet, if at all, only in a nightmare. All day long we are, in some degree, helping each other to one or other of these destinations. It is in the light of these overwhelming possibilities, it is with the awe and circumspection proper to them, that we should conduct all our dealings with one another, all friendships, all loves, all play, all politics. There are no ordinary people.[1]

The more we become like Jesus, the more we'll start seeing people from his point of view. And God doesn't look down on anyone. He loves us all the same.

When we begin our relationship with God, we begin to see everything differently. We see him differently, ourselves differently, and other people differently. Instead of looking at people as obstacles or stepping stones, we start seeing them as dearly loved children of God. We realize that we love God by loving people. We don't look down on them, we value them and accept them as they are.

Authentic living means letting our faith seep into our relationships with others. It's a complete shift in perspective. Instead of seeing ourselves at the center of the universe, we see God seated on the throne of our hearts. Instead of seeing other people as getting in the way of our success, we see them as worth more than life itself. We see people through the eyes of Jesus.

That's real love.

2. Put Love into Action

To love means to give—not just money or words but a piece of ourselves. John put it this way: "Dear children, let us stop just saying we love each other; let us really show it by our actions" (1 John 3:18).

Here it is in a nutshell: To desire and acquire is hunger, not love. To adore and sacrifice is love, not hunger.

True love—self-sacrificing love—doesn't make much practical sense. It doesn't fit in well with the prevailing winds of our culture because it seeks the good of others at the expense of self. It's tough to get a grip on.

Yet we're all drawn to true love on the deepest level. Selfless love is what our poets and prophets and preachers have pointed to throughout the ages as the greatest ideal, the pinnacle of perfection, and the most magnificent act of all.

Real love is at one and the same time the greatest evidence of God in the world, and the greatest evidence of Jesus in our hearts.

Jesus made that clear when he pointed out that his followers would be recognized not by their faith or their obedience or their doctrinal statements or their political affiliation but by their love: "A new command I give you: Love one another. As I have loved you, so you must love one another. By this all men will know that you are my disciples, if you love one another" (John 13:34–35 NIV).

And love is never just talk. It's action.

Look someone in the eye and tell him, "I love you." Fly a kite with your son. Stop talking about going camping with your kids and do it. Listen to your daughter's poem. Stop and talk to a homeless person and listen to her story. And be willing to go the next step and help her.

We must not confuse feeling sorry for people with loving them. Real love meets people where they are. It can be a dirty business. It can be costly. Jesus proved that.

But real love doesn't mind. Because it's love.

The defining characteristic of a Christian disciple is love. Not just any kind of love, but the kind of love Jesus had. Jesus-love. A love that offers all to the beloved. Even life itself.

3. Learn to Be a Lens

Jesus is indeed the Light this dark world needs to see, but how does he choose to shine? Through us: "Let your good deeds shine out for all to see, so that everyone will praise your heavenly Father" (Matthew 5:16).

Let your light shine. Don't muddy it up. Don't hide the difference God has made in your life. And don't take credit for the changes in your life either. The point of letting our lives shine isn't so people will compliment the lens through which Jesus shines, but so they can praise the power source himself.

In Matthew 25:31–46 Jesus told a story about the final judgment: On that day the true believers will be amazed that they ever served God at all. They'll be shocked to discover all the times they ministered to others while they were on this earth. They'll be surprised to find that they ever walked within the will of God at all. You see, love doesn't keep track of itself. It gives and then forgets the gift.

The most compassionate and loving people don't give their time and their lives for the spotlight or the photo op. They'd be the last ones to brag, because they barely even notice the love they extend.

Compassion doesn't have to be elaborate. As Jesus pointed out in his story, it can be expressed by simply meeting real needs. Buy someone a cheeseburger. Share a cup of coffee. Visit an inmate. Welcome a stranger. Go shopping for a new set of clothes for someone who can't afford them. Sit by someone's side in the hospital. These are the kinds of practical things Jesus was talking about.

And in a mysterious way, all of those compassionate acts serve the King of heaven himself: "The King will tell them, 'I assure you, when you did it to one of the least of these my brothers and sisters, you were doing it to me!'" (Mathew 25:40).

I didn't just meet Sherwood that day. I shook hands with Jesus.

WHAT ARE YOU GONNA DO?

So I guess we have a choice.

We can keep our windows rolled up and our doors closed. We can ignore the faces outside the glass and hope the problem will go away. We can hand out a couple of dollars so we don't feel guilty anymore and then roll up the window again.

Or we can buy someone coffee on a cold day. We can listen to his story. We can open up our lives enough to discover real people behind the statistics— people like Sherwood with real names, real families, real tears. People who need real love.

Sponsor a child. Help build a church. Take a homeless person out for lunch. Bake cookies. Garden with your neighbor.

And even if someone won't let you do anything else for her, pray for her like you mean it.

The answers aren't easy, but the solution is always the same—compassion. God's kind of compassion lived out in our lives every day. The more real God's love becomes in our lives, the more real our lives will become. That's what changes hearts. That's what changes nations. That's what changes the world.

What are the Christians gonna do?

What are you gonna do, today?

QUESTIONS
For Discussion and Life Application

Chapter 1: MIRROR, MIRROR ON THE WALL

1. When people talk about finding themselves, what do you think they mean? How is this different from knowing ourselves? Explain.

2. What are some ways people hide from the truth? Why does it often hurt to hear the truth? What insight does that give you into human nature and motivation?

3. Read John 3:19–21. Why do you think it's hard for us to examine our thoughts and motives? With what do these verses compare conversion? How does this relate to what Jesus said about spiritual birth? (see John 3:3).

4. What criteria should we use to discern right from wrong and truth from lies in our lives? Why don't we?

5. Read Hebrews 4:12–13. What is the purpose of God's Word as described in verse 12? How much of your life is visible to God according to verse 13? How does that make you feel? Why?

6. In Psalm 38 David explored some painful inner experiences in detail. What were some of the issues causing pain in David's life? Where did he turn for help?

7. List several ways you typically try to deaden or distract yourself from pain in your life. Are these healthy or unhealthy methods? What might God prefer you do instead?

8. How many of the twelve attitudes listed in the chapter could you relate to? What does that tell you about yourself and about human nature in general?

9. What attitudes are getting in the way of your transparency? What are you going to do about it?

Chapter 2: THE GAME YOU CANNOT WIN

1. Share about a time when you played the comparison game and lost. How did it feel? Why? Why do you think we constantly compare ourselves with others?

2. Does anyone ever win the comparison game? Explain your answer.

3. Do you agree with the author's statement "Humility before God is the key to spiritual intimacy with God"? Why or why not? What life-changing implications does this statement contain?

4. Read Luke 18:9–14. Draw a line down the center of a sheet of paper. On one side write *Pharisee* and on the other side write *Tax Collector*. List as many attributes about each of those people as you can on the appropriate side of the page. Which side better describes your life?

5. Note in verse 9 who was Jesus's audience for the story. After reading the story and thinking about humility, would you say you're included in that group? Why or why not? If you are, what are you going to do about it?

6. List five specific ways pride rears its head in your life.

7. How does pride affect your prayers? How does it affect the way you look at other people?

8. All of us take care of our bodies and avoid deadly situations when we can. At what point does self-interest become selfishness? How should a follower of Christ view his or her self-esteem? How much (if any) is healthy?

9. Romans 12:9–16 describes specific guidelines for expressing love. How many times does Paul emphasize humility in these verses? (see especially verses 10, 14–16). Why is there such a close connection between humility and love?

10. Read Philippians 2:3–8. What does Jesus's humility teach you about the true essence of humility? What does it teach you about yourself? How will it change the way you live your life?

Chapter 3: THE JOURNEY OF NO RETURN

1. Name five industries that profit from promoting the illusion of eternal youth.

2. Read Ecclesiastes 7:2, 4. Why would Solomon write that wise people think much about death? Why are we hesitant to talk about death in our culture? In light of Solomon's observation, what do his words imply about our culture?

3. Have you known someone who died in the midst of something? What was it? How much impact did that have on your life? Why?

4. In light of the brevity of life (see James 4:14), how much should we plan for the future (as opposed to embracing and experiencing today)? Why do we often do precisely the opposite?

5. Try to imagine life on this planet with you gone. (It's not easy to do.) Why is it so hard? What does that reveal to you about yourself?

6. Looking at the brevity of our lives helps us see life through a new set of eyes. How is Paul's attitude (see Philippians 1:20–24) honest about both life and death? Do you share his perspective on life and death? Do you think it's healthy? Why or why not?

7. Read Matthew 6:19–21. List three earthly treasures people typically have in our culture. List three heavenly treasures you think Jesus is talking about in this verse.

8. How will you put Jesus's words into practice today and stop storing up earthly treasures? What will you get rid of in light of this verse?

9. What two things would you do today if you *knew* you were going to die tomorrow?

10. What two things would you do today if you *believed* you might die to-morrow? Will you do them?

Chapter 4: NO CARICATURES IN HEAVEN

1. Describe three characteristics of popular culture's view of Christianity. Are they accurate? Explain.

2. Why do you think people have misconceptions about God and about Christianity? Why is the truth hard to accept?

3. Do you agree or disagree that it's "nice" to be a Christian? Explain.

4. Do you think most people in North America consider themselves Christians? In view of the information in this chapter, would you say they're probably right or probably mistaken?

5. Read Luke 19:10. What was Jesus's mission on earth all about? Whom did Jesus come to seek? Whom does that include?

6. What are the implications of failing to believe the testimony God has given regarding his Son? (see 1 John 5:10–11).

7. Explain how Christianity is a religion. Explain how it is a relationship.

8. What baggage goes along with the term *religion*? Which do you think people would be more interested in: a religion about God or a relationship with God? Explain.

9. Write a paragraph summarizing the main message of the Christian faith. Compare your summary to the apostle Paul's in Romans 4:25–5:2.

10. How will the information in this chapter affect your relationship with God and others?

Chapter 5: PSST . . . I'VE GOT A SECRET

1. Think of a time when you tried to cover up a wrong. Did it work? Did it catch up with you in the long run? Explain.

2. Discuss a current news story about a corporate cover-up, sex scandal, or murder investigation. What secrets are at stake? What consequences might result?

3. Why do we try so hard to keep our secrets hidden from people? Do we really think we're the only ones with these problems? Explain.

4. Review Matthew 23:25–28. Does it seem Jesus was overly harsh? Considering the fact that Jesus is God and God is love, how do these words constitute love? In other words, why was it loving of Jesus to expose those people's secret sins?

5. How many of the sins listed in Mark 7:21–23 are visible? How many are invisible?

6. In the list of The Top 10 Invisible Sins, which ones seem most common in your community? Among your friends? Which are most common in your own life?

7. Were there any sins in this list that surprised you? If so, identify them and explain why you didn't expect to seem them listed.

8. This chapter ends with a call to confession and an assurance of God's forgiveness. What other practical ways can you think of to apply the truths taught in this chapter?

Chapter 6: LETTING GO OF THE BOAT

1. Contrast faith and sight. Explain how they differ and give a practical example of each. Which is easier? Why?

2. Typically people want proof before they'll believe. But according to

Hebrews 11:1, does proof lead to faith, or does faith lead to proof? How do you explain this?

3. Read 2 Corinthians 4:16–18. Paul contrasted our bodies and our spirits, our present troubles and our future blessings, and the attention we pay to them, respectively. Identify his main points. What conclusion did he reach about the focus of our lives?

4. How do the truths in verses 16–17 lead to the conclusion in verse 18? How does faith help you deal with the everyday problems of life? (Hint: see verse 18.)

5. Read Matthew 6:24–34. Explain how verse 24 relates to verse 25.

6. Based on what Jesus said in this section of Scripture, is it wrong to worry? What truths did Jesus emphasize to help us overcome worry in our lives?

7. How does worry relate to faith? Can they exist at the same time in the same person? Explain.

8. Look up Psalm 20:7. What did David say people in his time trusted? If you were to rewrite this verse about our nation, what would you include instead? What if you were rewriting it about your church? Your family? Yourself?

9. Read Matthew 25:14–30 to understand Jesus's references to the faithful and unfaithful servants. What aspect of faith is highlighted in this story? What changes would this story bring to your life if you were to apply its teachings? Are you willing to make them?

10. How can you consciously live more by faith? What changes do you need to make in the way you view life, handle money, think about the future, and plan for the unexpected to live more by faith and less by sight?

Chapter 7: WORSHIPING GOD BY DOING THE DISHES

1. When you think of worshiping God, what do you typically think of? What unique aspects of worship did this chapter bring to light for you?

2. Did Jesus ever stop worshiping God, for even a moment of his life? Explain.

3. Since Jesus dwells in the hearts and lives of all believers, what does this say about the potential in your life for constantly worshiping God?

4. How does realizing God is less interested in spiritual activity than he is in spiritual union change the way you look at life's daily duties? How does it change your view of worship?

5. What does it mean to "pray without ceasing"? (1 Thessalonians 5:17 NASB). Could it really mean what it says? How would that change the way you pray and relate to God on a daily basis?

6. According to the author, real worship is self-forgetting. How can you forget yourself in worshiping God? Do you ever need to worry about what other people will think of you? Why or why not?

7. Compare John 5:43 and 2 Samuel 6:16, 22. In one case, fear of others' opinions kept people from God. In the other case, total disregard for others' opinions led David to be misunderstood. Is there a happy medium we should shoot for, or should we learn to worship God without reservation as David did? How would that affect the way you worship when you gather with other believers?

8. Read Romans 8:26–27. What insights into prayer do these two verses offer? How do they free you to pray from the heart?

9. How will this chapter change the way you pray to and worship God?

Chapter 8: IN SYNC WITH THE SPIRIT

1. How well have you been walking in step with the Spirit? How can you tell when your life is out of step with the Spirit? What clues are there?

2. First John 5:2–6 reveals a close connection between love and obedience. How does it say we express our love for God? Why is this the only method we have for showing God our love?

3. When you consider that all God asks of us in this moment is our obedience for this moment, does it seem all that tough? Why or why not?

4. Read Galatians 5:16–18. Contrast the new life in the Spirit with the old life of the sinful nature. Why are they in opposition to each other? Will you ever be free from this inner struggle? Why or why not?

5. According to Galatians 5:19–23, what are the consequences of walking out of step with the Spirit? What are the results of staying in sync with God's will? How will knowing the difference change your life?

6. Read 1 John 3:2–3. What knowledge motivates us to pursue purity?

7. Read Hebrews 12:1–2 in several different Bible translations. What unique perspectives do the various translations bring out? What are some of the other things you sometimes look to rather than Jesus?

8. What changes do you need to make in your life to begin experiencing more of the presence and peace of God?

Chapter 9: TOO BUSY FOR YOUR OWN GOD?

1. How do you respond when people ask you if you're keeping busy? Generally, do you look at busyness as a good thing or a bad thing?

2. Review the account of Mary and Martha in Luke 10:38–42. Is the main difference between Mary and Martha what they were doing or how they were doing it (i.e., their activity or their attention)? How does that difference affect your view of busyness?

3. Was Martha wrong to be concerned about fixing the meal for Jesus? Explain. Could she have done both—found the one thing Mary had found while still staying focused on the task at hand? Explain.

4. How do commitments, obligations, and responsibilities interfere with your pursuit of an authentic spiritual life? How do they help?

5. Why do we sometimes spend the most time and energy on things we don't really care about? Why have insignificant things taken on so much significance in our lives? How can we realistically reclaim control of our schedules to value God and our families as we should?

6. Where did we get the idea that faithfulness equals productivity? When did our definition of a saint change from someone marked by genuine devotion and compassion to someone who can check more things off his to-do list than the rest of us? What can be done about this?

7. In John 14:27 Jesus mentioned that the peace he gives isn't like the peace of the world. What's the difference? Which type of peace do we typically pursue? Why?

8. What are some practical steps you can take when you notice you've become more like Martha than like Mary? What changes do you need to make in your schedule or priority list today?

9. In the chapter, stillness and reflection are emphasized. How can times of contemplation help you refocus your life on God and pursue the priorities that are important to him? When will you "cease striving" and meditate on him?

10. What are three practical ways to stay focused on God amid the duties of your everyday life?

Chapter 10: AT THE FEET OF JESUS

1. Read Luke 7:36–50. When Jesus arrived at Simon's home for the meal, Simon gave him a rude welcome (vv. 44–46). What three differences did Jesus point out between Simon's greeting and the woman's? What does this tell you about Simon?

2. Both Jesus's story of the forgiven debts and the account of the prostitute at the dinner have three main characters. Who are they? Which story characters relate to which real-life characters?

3. What does the monetary debt in the story represent in real life?

4. Do you find anything surprising about Jesus's question in verse 42? What would you have expected Jesus to ask instead? Why do you think the Pharisee said, "I suppose" in response to Jesus's question?

5. When Simon looked at the prostitute, he saw her great sin (v. 39). When Jesus looked at her, he saw her great love (v. 47). What else did Jesus see? (Hint: see verse 50). What does this reveal about how God views you?

6. The woman's actions were prompted by her great love. What does this imply about the amount of love in the Pharisee's heart?

7. Who would you say had a higher self-esteem in the story: the Pharisee or the prostitute? In God's eyes, which one had a healthier self-esteem? Explain.

8. Based on what Jesus said in verse 42, did Simon have any right to feel good about himself? Why or why not? Do we have any right to feel good about ourselves? Why or why not?

9. Most of us try to minimize or excuse our sins and failures. Based on what Jesus said in this section (vv. 42, 47), how will doing that affect your love for God? According to Jesus, what is the secret to loving God much?

10. In what other practical ways does this story apply to your life today?

Chapter 11: FLIRTING WITH THE FORBIDDEN

1. Think of a time in your life when you peered into forbidden territory. What were you thinking at the time? What were you not thinking? What was so alluring about that specific temptation?

2. Review Genesis 39:1–20. What aspects of the story are surprising when you look at it carefully? Why do you think Joseph, who was muscular and well built, couldn't pull away from Potiphar's wife without leaving his shirt behind? Do you think he hesitated? Explain.

3. How might Joseph have avoided that situation?

4. Why are subtle temptations often the most effective?

5. What aspects of temptation surprise you? Does it seem odd that each of us keeps falling into the same patterns and temptations? Why is that? What can be done about it?

6. In 1 Corinthians 10:12–13, Paul gave both a caution and an assurance. Identify them. How do these verses change the way you look at temptation?

7. Will the stories from this chapter change the way you deal with temptation? Explain.

8. In Matthew 5:29–30, what specific steps did Jesus list for overcoming temptation? What do you think he meant by his comments? How do you need to apply his advice in your life today?

Chapter 12: SLAYING THE MONSTER

1. Hebrews 10:17 describes how God deals with the sins of believers (see also Isaiah 43:25). What does it say he does with them?

2. How does knowing this help you understand why, in Hebrews 11 where heroes of the faith are listed, none of their sins or failures are listed?

3. What assurance does this give you? Does it motivate you to forgive others? Why?

4. Read Colossians 3:13 (see also Matthew 6:14–15). According to this verse, is forgiveness optional for believers? Why should we forgive others?

5. Contrast Jesus's response to injustice (Luke 23:34) with Samson's response (Judges 15:3, 7, 11). What can you learn from these two accounts?

6. Explain the difference between excusing behavior and forgiving it.

7. Review the three characteristics of true forgiveness. Which part is most difficult for you? Why?

8. Why is it hard to truly forgive and to admit that we need to be forgiven? What usually happens instead?

9. How can we tell when we've genuinely forgiven someone? Is there someone you need to forgive? Will you do it?

Chapter 13: THE MILLION-DOLLAR MAN

1. In what ways is your life similar to Darren's? In what ways is it different? Have you ever had a "moment of clarity" like Darren did? Explain.

2. Proverbs 28:11 says, "Rich people picture themselves as wise but their real poverty is evident to the poor." Explain how a rich person can still be poor. List three ways people can be poor. Then list three ways they can be truly rich (see also Matthew 6:19–21).

3. With this in mind, examine how truly rich or poor your life is. Why do we spend so much of our lives pursuing riches that don't make us rich at all? What practical steps can we take to pursue true wealth?

4. How does materialism distract us from the things in life that matter most? Share an example of a time in your life when you've seen this happen.

5. How comfortable should a child of God be in this world? Explain.

6. Read Matthew 6:19–21. How do these words of Jesus contrast with the advice of Christian investment strategists to get out of debt and then invest wisely? Are the two approaches to money management compatible? Explain.

7. According to those verses, what are the only kinds of wise (or lasting) investments? Explain what you mean and how that applies to your life.

8. Read 1 Timothy 6:17–19. What practical advice did Paul give for managing wealth? List four commands he gave. How can you be always ready to share when you're in debt?

9. How should a believer respond to a society in which the economic structure is based on personal consumption, greed, waste, and acquisition? How can we be "in but not of" our economic system? Should we just accept it? If not, how should we work to change it?

10. How will this chapter change the way you strive to live as an authentic child of God in an affluent society?

Chapter 14: THE VISIBILITY SYNDROME

1. How does our definition of (and pursuit of) success shape our lives? How does it affect the process of becoming real with ourselves, with others, and with God?

2. How do you define success? What three things mark a truly successful life? Why are they hard to pursue? In light of what true success is, how can we better train our children to be successful?

3. Can anyone be truly successful when he or she lacks inner peace? If not, why don't we structure our lives according to a God-centered definition of success?

4. How do we differentiate between wants and needs? When God says he will provide for our needs (see 2 Corinthians 9:7–9), what does he have in mind? How does God's definition of needs differ from ours? Why is that?

5. What role does "stuff" really play in the life of a disciple of Christ? (Hint: contrast 1 John 2:15 with Luke 16:9 to get a balanced perspective.)

6. Read Philippians 3:18–19. What three characteristics are attributed to those who are enemies of Christ? (Hint: one is what they desire, one is what they brag about, and one is what they think about.)

7. How do the things you desire, brag about, and think about compare with the ones listed in verse 19?

8. How will this verse shape and change your attitudes and priorities?

9. Write a mission statement for your life, as suggested in the chapter. Share it with someone and begin taking steps to implement it today.

Chapter 15: ANSWERING THE CALL

1. When you think of pursuing a calling versus pursuing a career, what differences come to mind?

2. List several misconceptions about God's calling. What do you think God's calling entails—a lifestyle or a job title? What difference does that make for your life today?

3. What insights can we draw from Ecclesiastes 5:19 and 8:15 concerning career choices? Is it possible to truly enjoy your current career? If not, what are you going to do about that?

4. What are three practical ways you can minister within your current job or life situation? What limitations exist?

5. Is your standard of living determined more by your current level of income and opportunity, or by your biblical convictions and priorities? In other words, do your choices about how much you spend depend on how much you make, or on how much you think God wants you to spend? What's the difference?

6. Is your standard of living determined more by how much you can buy (because you have the means) or on how much you should buy (because you're putting God's kingdom and priorities above your own kingdom and priorities)? How do these choices reflect your priorities? What changes might you need to make?

7. If you were totally free of financial obligations and could pursue your gifts and calling without restraint, would you? How can you get to that point? (Or don't you need to? Explain.)

8. Are most of your career choices dictated by the desire to be more comfortable or to be more faithful? What's the difference?

9. How much of your life do you end up devoting to the pursuit of comfort and convenience? Why? What would God have you devote yourself to instead? Will you begin making the changes necessary in your life to do that?

Chapter 16: WELCOME SIGNS

1. Tell about a time in your life when you let a job or a responsibility come between you and your family.

2. More than 50 percent of all North American marriages fail. What factors do you think contribute to this?

3. Even though this chapter focused more on parent-child relationships, our spouses are vitally important as well. What does Malachi 2:16 say God's attitude toward divorce is? How does that affect your perspective?

4. Ultimately, who (besides God) decides how much time you spend with your family—you or your boss? Explain.

5. How can career choices and priorities undermine family life? What will you do to make sure they don't undermine yours?

6. How are your attitudes toward children the same as the apostles'? How are they different?

7. Explain what you believe the difference is between a childlike faith and a childish faith.

8. In what ways do you need to become more childlike?

9. List four specific steps you will take this week to let your family members know how much you love and appreciate them. Then put the ideas into practice.

Chapter 17: THE ROAD TO REAL

1. Think of a brief encounter, like the one in the Target store, in which you made a connection with someone. What happened (or didn't happen) to make it memorable?

2. Describe the concept of transparent living as you understand it. Why is

it so rare? Why do you think we have such shallow communication and surface relationships these days?

3. Read Ephesians 4:15 and 1 Peter 3:15. What three characteristics of transparent communication do these verses emphasize?

4. Compare your church with the early Christian church described in Acts 2:42–47. What similarities are there? What differences? How are these differences related to questions 2 and 3?

5. How does Ecclesiastes 3:7 help us understand the difference between openness and honesty?

6. What were some of Jesus's motives in being kind to people? (see Luke 19:11; John 18:37; John 10:10). What should our motives be?

7 Read 2 Corinthians 2:14–17. How do our lives share the fragrance of Christ? Why do you think Paul said we smell like death to those who are perishing?

8. How does integrity relate to truth and openness? What changes would you make in your life if you knew everything you did would appear the next day on CNN? Everything we do will eventually be made known (1 Corinthians 4:5). How will knowing this change your life?

9. Read 2 Corinthians 5:20–21. How does it make you feel to be called an ambassador of Christ? Does it relieve or add pressure? Explain.

10. Have there been times when you were ashamed to talk about or identify yourself with Jesus? How important is it that you get over this feeling? (see Luke 9:26). What will you do to change?

Chapter 18: WHAT ARE THE CHRISTIANS GONNA DO?

1. When you meet people like Sherwood, how do you feel? What do you typically do? What do you think Jesus would do?

2. Review Matthew 5:23–24. What matters to God more than your church attendance? Why?

3. How can we be authentic, spiritually focused, life-affirming believers without (1) being subtly influenced by our godless culture or (2) retreating from it completely?

4. How do we account for the vast difference between the early church's concept of Christian community and our individualistic approach to community today? Is it simply cultural, or have we missed something

intrinsic to what it means to follow Christ? Explain your answer. What Scripture verses support your claim?

5. In John 13:34–35 Jesus said to love others as he has loved us. What specifically does he mean by that? How can you begin doing that today?

6. Explore James 1:27. How well are you doing at applying the two marks of acceptable religion? Explain.

7. For the purposes of discussion, let's define affluence as the ability to make choices about what we consume, purchase, and pursue. Most of the people in the world wear what they do, eat what they do, and live where they do because they can't afford to do differently. Yet most people who bought this book probably live in an affluent society. How should a devoted follower of Jesus live in such a society? How does the way you spend your time and your money reveal what's important in your life?

8. John wrote, "If anyone has material possessions and sees his brother in need but has no pity on him, how can the love of God be in him?" (1 John 3:17 NIV). Who do you think he means by "brother in need"? Orphans? Starving children? Persecuted believers in other countries? Or just people we meet on the street? In other words, how far should we go in applying this verse to our lives?

9. In light of the needs and suffering in the world, how can we justify lifestyles defined by consumerism? Explain.

10. How will this chapter change your life and your priorities?

NOTES

THE DAY YOU BECAME REAL

Epigraph. William Shakespeare, "All the World's a Stage," *As You Like It*, Act 2, Scene 7.

Chapter 1: MIRROR, MIRROR ON THE WALL

Epigraph. As quoted in Thomas Cleary, trans., *Living a Good Life: Advice on Virtue, Love, and Action from the Ancient Greek Masters* (Boston: Shambhala Publications, Inc. 1997), 10.

1. As quoted in Cleary, *Living a Good Life*, 57.
2. Peter Kreeft, ed., *Christianity for Modern Pagans: Pascal's Pensées* (San Francisco: Ignatius Press, 1993), 48.
3. See World AIDS Day Resource 1998, http://cob868.dn.net/stats.html.
4. See http://www.aegis.com/topics/test/.
5. Dag Hammarskjöld, *Markings* (New York: Alfred A. Knopf, 1991), 66.
6. Francois de Fénelon, *The Seeking Heart* (Jacksonville, Fla.: Christian Books Publishing House, 1992), 180.
7. As quoted in Robert Maynard Hutchins, ed., *Great Books of the Western World*, vol. 33, *Pascal*. (Chicago: William Benton, Encyclopedia Britannica, Inc., 1952), 191–92.
8. Aleksandr Solzhenitsyn, *The Gulag Archipelago*, cited in Terry W. Glaspey, *Great Books of the Christian Tradition* (Eugene, Ore.: Harvest House, 1996), 105.
9. As quoted in Charles E. Moore, comp., ed., *Provocations: Spiritual Writings of Kierkegaard* (Farmington, Penn.: Plough Publishing, 1999), xxvii, 221.

Chapter 2: THE GAME YOU CANNOT WIN

Epigraph. Arthur Bennett, ed., *The Valley of Vision: A Collection of Puritan Prayers and Devotions* (Edinburgh, U.K.: The Banner of Truth Trust, 1999), 6.

1. See Luke 9:23, Luke 9:24, and John 12:25, respectively.
2. Andrew Murray, *Humility: The Journey toward Holiness* (Minneapolis: Bethany House Publishers, 2001), 63.

3. Ibid., 17.

Chapter 3: THE JOURNEY OF NO RETURN

Epigraph. Rabindranath Tagore, *Gitanjali* (New York: Scribner Poetry, 1997), 58.

1. As quoted in Kreeft, *Christianity for Modern Pagans*, 144.

2. Coleman Barks, trans., *The Soul of Rumi: A New Collection of Ecstatic Poems* (New York: HarperCollins, 2001), 240.

3. C. S. Lewis, *The Weight of Glory* (New York: HarperCollins, 1976), 26.

Chapter 4: NO CARICATURES IN HEAVEN

Epigraph. St. Augustine, "Prayer of Conversion," *Soliloquies*, as quoted in http://conservation.catholic.org/prayers.htm.

1. This book was released in 2001 by Standard Publishing, Cincinnati. It is currently out of print.

2. In Mark 14:7 Jesus mentioned that there would always be poor people on this planet. In John 16:33 he told his followers they'd have trouble in this world. In Luke 21:17 he said the world would hate them.

3. I found this comment in my sermon notes from a message given by my pastor, Tom Oyler. He told me later that it's a common quote, but I found it uncommonly insightful. My thanks go out to him for sharing it.

4. Moore, *Provocations,* 171.

5. The phrase "kill us to life" comes from Siegbert W. Becker, *The Foolishness of God* (Milwaukee: Northwestern Publishing House, 1982), 140.

6. Eberhard Arnold, as quoted in *Seeking Peace,* by Johann Christoph Arnold (Farmington, Penn.: The Plough Publishing House, 1998), 188.

7. Thurman, *The Lies We Believe,* 69. Thurman credits this quote to Tim Hansel in *When I Relax I Feel Guilty* (Elgin, Ill.: Cook, 1979).

8. John R. W. Stott, *Basic Christianity* (Downers Grove, Ill.: InterVarsity Press, 1971), 17.

9. Some of the material in this chapter first appeared in *Living with Teenagers,* January 2000. © Copyright 1999 LifeWay Christian Resources of the Southern Baptist Convention. All rights reserved. Used by permission.

10. Hutchins, *Great Books of the Western World,* 245.

11. Although I cannot find any specific references to the material in this paragraph, I was greatly influenced by the writings of Peter Kreeft and Blaise Pascal when writing it. Many of the ideas in this section grew from their strands of thought. My thanks goes out to both of them.

12. Battistina Capalbo, comp., and Paula Clifford, trans., *Praying with Saint*

Teresa (Grand Rapids: Wm. B. Eerdmans Publishing Co., 1997), 17.

13. Bennett, *The Valley of Vision*, 62.

Chapter 5: PSST . . . I'VE GOT A SECRET

Epigraph. Arthur Waley, trans., *The Analects of Confucius* (New York: Random House, Inc., 1989), 114.

1. William Backus and Marie Chapian, *Telling Yourself the Truth* (Minneapolis: Bethany Fellowship, Inc., 1980), 55–56.

2. Bennett, *The Valley of Vision*, 58.

Chapter 6: LETTING GO OF THE BOAT

Epigraph. As quoted in http://thevirtues.org/site/01-Faith.html.

1. For more information about the wreck of the *Priscilla* and the life-saving efforts of Rasmus Midgett, see Dennis L. Noble's intriguing book, *That Others Might Live: The U.S. Life-Saving Service, 1878–1915* (Annapolis, Md.: Naval Institute Press, 1994), 133–35.

2. Helmut Thielicke, *The Silence of God* (Grand Rapids: Wm. B. Eerdmans Publishing Company, 1962), 30.

3. For a more complete version of this folk tale, see *The Fire on the Mountain, and Other Stories from Ethiopia and Eritrea* by Harold Courlander and Wolf Leslau (New York: Henry Holt and Company, Inc., 1950), 8–14.

Chapter 7: WORSHIPING GOD BY DOING THE DISHES

Epigraph. Frank Laubach and Brother Lawrence, *Practicing His Presence* (Sargent, Ga.: The SeedSowers, 1973), 56.

1. Fénelon, *The Seeking Heart*, 15.

2. Thomas R. Kelly, *A Testament to Devotion*, as quoted in J. Manning Potts, *Listening to the Saints: A Collection of Meditations from the Devotional Masters* (Nashville: The Upper Room, 1962), 62.

3. Capalbo and Clifford, *Praying with Saint Teresa*, 8.

Chapter 8: IN SYNC WITH THE SPIRIT

Epigraph. As quoted in Angela Ashwin, ed., *The Book of a Thousand Prayers* (Grand Rapids: Zondervan, 2002).

1. Jean-Pierre De Caussade, *Abandonment to Divine Providence* (New York: Doubleday, 1975), 48, 53.

2. F. E. Marsh, *Five Hundred Bible Readings: Or Light from the Lamp of Truth* (Grand Rapids: Baker Book House, 1963), 324.

3. See 1 John 5:3–5.

Chapter 9: TOO BUSY FOR YOUR OWN GOD?

1. Laubach and Lawrence, *Practicing His Presence*, 3–4.

2. Kreeft, *Christianity for Modern Pagans*, 168.

3. See Doug Sherman and William Hendricks, *Your Work Matters to God* (Colorado Springs: NavPress, 1990), 201.

4. Tom credits this quote to Larry Moyer in his evangelism training material *You Can Tell It.*

Chapter 10: AT THE FEET OF JESUS

Epigraph. Thomas à Kempis, *The Imitation of Christ* (Grand Rapids: Zondervan Publishing House, 1983), 143.

1. April Oursler Armstrong brings out this point in her insightful book *The Tales Christ Told* (Garden City, N.Y.: Doubleday & Company, Inc., 1959), 145.

2. See Jeremiah 31:3, Psalm 13:5, Psalm 89:24, John 3:16, and Psalm 106:1, respectively.

Chapter 11: FLIRTING WITH THE FORBIDDEN

Epigraph. From his book *On the Government of God.*

Chapter 12: SLAYING THE MONSTER

1. Arthur Pierson, *The New Acts of the Apostles* (New York: Baker and Taylor, 1894), 266.

2. Thomas Ken and Genevan Psalter, "Doxology," from *Songs of Faith and Praise* (West Monroe, La.: Howard Publishing, 1994) 66.

3. Pierson, *The New Acts of the Apostles*, 266.

PART 3: EMERGING

1. Watchman Nee, *Spiritual Knowledge* (New York: Christian Fellowship Publishers, Inc., 1973), 53.

2. Peter Kreeft, *Back to Virtue* (San Francisco. Ignatius Press, 1986), 100.

Chapter 13: THE MILLION-DOLLAR MAN

Epigraph. Boethius, *The Consolation of Philosophy* (Baltimore: Penguin Books Ltd., 1969), 58.

1. Denis Haack, *The Rest of Success* (Downers Grove, Ill.: InterVarsity Press, 1989), 59. Denis credits this idea to "Ash Heap Lives," a sermon by Francis Schaeffer

published in *No Little People* (Downers Grove, Ill.: InterVarsity Press, 1974).

2. Stott, *Basic Christianity*, 119.

Chapter 14: THE VISIBILITY SYNDROME

Epigraph. Hammarskjöld, *Markings*, 55.

1. Haack, *The Rest of Success*, 40.

2. As quoted in Cleary, *Living a Good Life*, 18.

3. Steven James, *How to Smell Like God* (Cincinnati: Standard Publishing, 2002), 138.

4. Ravi Zacharias, *Jesus Among Other Gods* (Nashville: W Publishing Group, 2000), 12.

Chapter 15: ANSWERING THE CALL

Epigraph. Tagore, *Gitanjali*, 95.

1. In my book *More Worship Sketches 2 Perform* (Colorado Springs: Meriwether Publishing, Ltd., 2002), I fictionalized this conversation for the purposes of presenting it within a dramatic format (see "The Calling" on pages 108–13). Some conversations come almost ready-made for the stage, but they're still true!

2. As quoted in Arnold, *Seeking Peace*, 144.

3. See Acts 17:26–27.

4. Calvin Miller, *The Unchained Soul* (Minneapolis: Bethany House Publishers, 1998), xvii.

5. See Jeremiah 7:27.

Chapter 16: WELCOME SIGNS

Epigraph. As quoted from http://www.wisdomquotes.com/001739.html.

1. "Someone Close To My Heart" by Susan Olive. Copyright 1998. All rights reserved. Used by permission.

Chapter 17: THE ROAD TO REAL

Epigraph. As quoted from http://www.storycircle.org/quotes/alpha/l.html.

1. As quoted in Moore, *Provocations*, 316.

2. Peter Kreeft, *How to Win the Culture War: A Christian Battle Plan for a Society in Crisis* (Downers Grove, Ill.: InterVarsity Press, 2002), 54.

Chapter 18: WHAT ARE THE CHRISTIANS GONNA DO?

Epigraph. Kreeft, *Back to Virtue*, 68.

1. Lewis, *The Weight of Glory*, 45–46.